I0123674

GENDER VARIANCES AND SEXUAL DIVERSITY IN THE CARIBBEAN

GENDER VARIANCES
AND SEXUAL DIVERSITY
IN THE CARIBBEAN

PERSPECTIVES, HISTORIES, EXPERIENCES

EDITED BY
MARJAN DE BRUIN
AND
R. ANTHONY LEWIS

The University of the West Indies Press
Jamaica • Barbados • Trinidad and Tobago

The University of the West Indies Press
7A Gibraltar Hall Road, Mona
Kingston 7, Jamaica
www.uwipress.com

© 2020 by Marjan de Bruin and R. Anthony Lewis

All rights reserved. Published 2020

A catalogue record of this book is available from the National Library of Jamaica.

ISBN 978-976-640-741-4 (print)
978-976-640-742-2 (Kindle)
978-976-640-743-8 (ePub)

Cover illustration: Steve Johnson on www.unsplash.com (https://unsplash.com/@steve_j). Untitled; described by the artist as a simple celebration of inclusivity.

Cover design by Robert Harris

The University of the West Indies Press has no responsibility for the persistence or accuracy of URLs for external or third-party Internet websites referred to in this publication and does not guarantee that any content on such websites is, or will remain, accurate or appropriate.

Printed in the United States of America

Contents

Introduction

MARJAN DE BRUIN AND R. ANTHONY LEWIS

Over the last two decades, the question of lesbian, gay, bisexual and transgender (LGBT) identities and the politics associated with them have advanced significantly on the global stage. The protection of the human rights of LGBT citizens has become common cause across multiple national, regional and international organizations, among them, the Inter-American Court of Human Rights. The Caribbean – including the Commonwealth Caribbean, marked as it is by colonial-era legislation and attitudes that proscribe same-sex activities and nonnormative gender expression – has joined this emerging rights discourse. In fact, many Commonwealth Caribbean countries have in recent times become home to organizations focusing on LGBT issues. On 10 December 2018, for instance, Jamaica's J-FLAG, the country's best-known LGBT rights organization, celebrated its twentieth anniversary, while Guyana's Society against Sexuality Orientation Discrimination marked its fifteenth anniversary a week later. In the last five years or so, too, LGBT pride events across the region have increased – again, most remarkably for the Commonwealth Caribbean – with many taking on a semipublic nature, and laws criminalizing same-sex intimacy have been challenged in Belize and Trinidad and Tobago; in Guyana, the law against cross-dressing has been declared unconstitutional.

Notwithstanding progress on these multiple fronts, much of the Commonwealth Caribbean has remained relatively unwavering in its resistance to attempts to create a more visible space for LGBT citizens and residents. The churches of that part of the region, coalescing mainly under umbrella parachurch organizations, such as Jamaica Churches Action Uniting Society for Emancipation (Jamaica CAUSE), Belize Action/Family Forum, and TT CAUSE, have staged mass rallies against what has been dubbed the "gay agenda" – from Belize to Jamaica to Barbados and Trinidad and Tobago. And while there have been noticeable and meaningful steps towards openness and tolerance, including a significant decline in the output of anti-gay Jamaican dancehall music, some Caribbean spaces remain especially difficult to navigate for LGBT citizens, many of whom swell the ranks of diaspora groups in Canada, the United Kingdom, the United States and, increasingly, the Netherlands, through semi-voluntary or forced migration. The existence of LGBT citizens and residents of the region thus remains marked by the struggle for place and voice in an improving but relatively hostile environment. Furthermore, their lived experiences remain understudied and inadequately documented by the academy. In this regard, Kempadoo (2009) observes:

> Despite the mountain of grey documents that include some mention of sexual praxis (reports, conference papers, theses, and policy briefings) and the growing number of more accessible documents (published journal articles, electronic articles, chapters in books, media reports and books), there is little consistency in existing studies, thus little basis for comparison cross-ethnically, cross-nationally, or regionally. Repetition of ideas through multiple reviews of studies and several small-scale qualitative research efforts that are not replicable is also apparent. (p. 2).

A decade since Kempadoo's publication, little has changed.

The goal of this book is to update some of the existing work and work in progress on minority genders and sexualities in the Caribbean – particularly Jamaica – as well as to examine new insights on the fundamental questions of how sexual orientation and gender identities and performance in the region can be understood and differentiated. In this way, the book seeks to deepen the understanding of the lives, challenges and opportunities for those in the region who do not fall into the traditional binaries of heterosexual males or females – living in spaces where they are often treated as "socially excluded family outcasts" (Carr, 2009, p. 74).

Multidisciplinary Perspectives

The book, which approaches the issues of sexuality and gender through a multi-disciplinary lens, opens with various perspectives – from the historiographical and sociocultural to the biological and the religious – starting with Marjan de Bruin's exploration of the ways in which Commonwealth Caribbean scholars have used the term "gender" in their writings. Interrogating what was included in/excluded from their conceptualization, De Bruin brings into focus a number of blind spots in conventional Caribbean scholarly narratives on gender. She also highlights the role and influence of other fields of inquiry in framing discourse on gender in the region. She notes that growing HIV prevalence rates and the main mode of HIV transmission in the Caribbean – unprotected sexual intercourse – have forced governments in the region to understand the sexual behaviour of their citizens in ways they had never done before. She avers that the need to include the most vulnerable citizens in HIV prevention interventions has served as a catalyst for a new kind of discussion on gender and sexuality in the region, in a manner similar to that in which the question of rights for women in the domestic and social spheres prompted scholarship on women. De Bruin's interrogation suggests a need to go beyond dichotomous and oppositional thinking about masculinity and femininity, and to avoid stepping into another set of binaries based on homo- and heterosexuality.

Likewise, in her chapter, Rhoda Reddock critiques conventional thinking that establishes hard binaries such as "male and female", "masculine and feminine", "heterosexual and homosexual", and argues for greater acceptance of the variability in human sexual and gender behaviour. She also cautions against monolithic responses to homophobia in the developing world that mimic those in the West, such as the transformation of sexuality from a term that delineated behaviour and practice into one that establishes and essentializes individual and personal identities. Referencing non-identity-based constructions of gender and sexuality in precolonial societies such as those in Africa and India, Reddock asserts the contingency of assumed demarcations that establish a polarity between masculine and feminine, hetero- and homosexual and their relationship to male and female. She points to alternative distinctions, such as "fertility" and "sexuality" in which sex for reproduction and sex for pleasure are not treated in the same way. Reddock concludes by calling for "a new framework for understanding the complexity of sex/gender" that goes beyond the existing binaries and dichotomous systems of thought and allows for the emergence of an understanding of sex/gender diversity that "opens up possibilities for liberating humanity from many of its social constraints".

In line with the multidisciplinary approach of this book, Ronald Young, in the third chapter, outlines the biological foundations of sex and gender distinction. He argues that irrespective of how the terms "sex" and "gender" are defined, it is important to understand the complex ways in which genes and the physical and sociocultural environments interact to determine sexual form and function – whether in an individual or in a population across generations. He contends that in this interaction resides a long-term biological imperative that is evolutionary in nature. Noting that this perspective allows for a broader appreciation of biological forces in discussions on variations in sexual orientation, he concludes with an important framework for evaluating variations in gender identity and sexual orientation and the social implications that derive from these.

The contribution from Anna Kasafi Perkins in the fourth chapter closes the range of multidisciplinary perspectives. Through an analysis of newspaper content that addresses Christian perspectives on LGBT issues, Perkins argues for a reinterpretation of traditional Christian views on sexuality and gender nonconformity. In her exploring the landscape of Christian proscriptions against minority sexuality and gender expression, she asks what space may be available within the Christian tradition to contest the normalizing and often discriminatory visions of same-sex intimacy and gender identity and practice. Perkins's intention is to identify resources within the various Christian traditions that can be marshalled to begin a new discussion about gender and sexual minorities in the Jamaican church. To this end, she calls for a more democratic national conversation in which the church is not the dominant party that crowds out other voices. She enjoins the Jamaican (and wider Caribbean) church "to embark upon a more honest and critical (re)reading of Scripture" that questions the ways in which it has been used to "deny the dignity and value of the human person".

Socializing Forces

The chapters that follow focus on the socializing forces that buttress and/or challenge conventional conceptions of gender and sexuality, demonstrating the power of social exclusion and discrimination. Writing from a broader Caribbean perspective, David Plummer, in chapter 5, reports on the emergence of what he calls "hard masculinity", and the impact it has on outcomes such as sexual behaviour and education in the Caribbean. The findings come from the *Caribbean Masculinities Project*, which sought to document the experiences of Caribbean adolescents growing into manhood in a variety of settings. Based on 138 detailed interviews in seven Caribbean countries and one dependent territory, using purposive sampling, the chapter provides analysis through grounded theory of the social and cultural constructions of gender in the region. In seeking to account for the relatively high levels of misogyny and homophobia in the Caribbean, Plummer dismisses as facile the conventional explanation that this resulted from "heterosexism". By contrast, he identifies dominant, hard masculinity as the primary driver of both phenomena. Central to this form of masculinity, he posits, are the taboo against softness and the idea of masculine obligation to be a "real man". He notes that the "combination of taboos on softness and the obligations of manhood drives a vicious cycle of pressure on boys to act out their masculinity in hyper-masculine ways".

In chapter 6, Moji Anderson performs a sociocultural analysis of how a given group of gay men navigate life in Jamaica, using Ervin Goffman's theorization on stigma and impression management. The narratives of these men, garnered through participation in focus group interviews, reveal a complex pattern of motivations and behaviours – strategies for coping with life in Jamaica. Anderson identifies three typical coping mechanisms: performance of heterosexuality, overt rejection of this performance, and a strategy between these two poles. In deploying these strategies, the men use the meanings associated with specific social markers such as dress and behaviour to mask or reveal their sexuality. However, their appearance and acting "have serious implications not just for their well-being, but for the place of homosexuality in Jamaica, the development of Jamaican heterosexual masculinity and even for scholarly analysis of Jamaican homophobia". Anderson meticulously delves into the concept of "passing", dissecting the range of behaviours and performance associated with it.

"Gemma D.", in chapter 7, challenges the way in which the struggle of sexual minorities in Jamaica has been defined primarily by the violence meted out to gay men, and by legal proscriptions against same-sex intimacy between them. She notes that proscriptions against same-sex intimacy between men "is but one facet of a larger system of heterosexism at work in Jamaica" and that "a more integrated vision of the complex ways in which that system operates" will provide better options for confronting it. Pointing to contextual challenges like the occlusion of practices such as the "corrective rape" of lesbians, she enjoins gay men to interrogate their assumptions in regard to the supposed "free pass" that lesbians get in Jamaican society and recognizes the ways in which queer women are also victims of Jamaican homophobia. She calls on gay men to examine how lesbians share in the struggle for acceptance and equality in the country, and how their collective victimization requires that both gays and lesbians act in solidarity and appreciate that they "are mutually imbricated in each other's struggles".

Popular Culture

One of the forces generally believed to be influential in shaping normative conceptions of gender and sexuality is popular culture. Donna P. Hope, in chapter 8 on the impact of Jamaican popular culture on normative and nonnormative formations of gender and sexuality, acknowledges that it is indeed "difficult to pinpoint impact without conducting scientific, longitudinal studies". But, she explains, interrogating Jamaican popular culture, social activity and gendered cues can be done in a variety of ways. In her chapter, she outlines the traditional, normative standards of gender and sexuality that have historically provided the foundation for popular cultural themes, and current trends driving their formation. Going back to the 1980s and 1990s, and into the first decade of the twenty-first century, she follows the path of major dancehall artists and their representation of the "natural" heterosexual in their lyrics versus the "feminized, passive, homosexual male" and analyses the seemingly contradictory changes that occur in some of the artists' bodily articulations. Hope uses examples from dancehall, roots theatre as well as slang to map a thematic structure of popular cultural output and its construction and dissemination of normalizing cues that have an impact on conceptions of gender and sexuality. In this regard, her chapter points to a perceptible shift in the construction and performance of gender and sexuality stereotypes, thus clarifying the range of expressions that is now given space within popular cultural arenas.

In the final chapter, R. Anthony Lewis explores how local and international LGBT activists worked collaboratively to modulate the violent tenor of anti-gay Jamaican popular music. He assesses how the discourse on LGBT rights that emerged post the HIV and AIDS panic in the United States formed the backdrop of a resistive anti-(neo)colonial rhetoric among Jamaican popular entertainers. He argues that by formulating their resistance in anti-gay narratives while depending on markets in the global North for sustenance, these entertainers laid the foundation of their own social and political undoing. Tracing dancehall's evolution as a popular Jamaican art form, he posits that language linked to an incipient vernacular nationalism was a critical vehicle for disseminating, consolidating and masking its anti-gay discourse. When, through processes of global networks and exchanges, the language was translated to reveal the violent nature of its anti-gay content, barriers to its international transmission were established and reinforced. Because of how deeply enmeshed dancehall had become in global capitalist networks, Lewis contends, it was inevitable that purveyors of anti-gay music would be forced to resile from their entrenched positions given that "their lyrics and craft were components of global ideological narratives over which they had only apparent control".

Synthesis

The issues explored in this volume are timely, given that they continue to dominate global civil and political discourse. In the Caribbean, exclusion, stigmatization, discrimination and violent responses to constructed "outgroups", of which the LGBT community is only one of the most obvious, continue. Yet what might seem to be slow progress is reflective of the region's democratic evolution over last forty years. Caribbean societies have in fact shown their willingness to follow new directions in regard to addressing the concerns of their LGBT populations. At the local level, some businesses and some of the larger tertiary educational institutions across the region have begun to embrace the principles of equity, diversity and inclusion. Caribbean media, over the last five or so years, have also been engaging in frank and open discussions on gender and sexualities, giving space to all beliefs, perspectives and world views; and certain churches have demonstrated an explicit interest in reconciling the principles of their religion with those of social justice or in re-evaluating them in the light of new insights.

If there is one concern about the discourse on rights for LGBT people in the region, it is the way in which it has been significantly coloured by the preoccupation with laws that proscribe same-sex intimacy, with public and political debates on LGBT issues often placing anti-buggery laws at their centre. Notwithstanding, several Commonwealth Caribbean governments (e.g. the Bahamas, Belize, Guyana, Jamaica) are signatories to the International Covenant on Economic, Social and Cultural Rights. This treaty covers essential – but for LGBT persons often neglected and violated – rights to living in dignity. The convention references the right to fair and just conditions of work; to social security; and to an adequate standard of living, including adequate food, clothing, housing, health and education. Increasingly, discussions on rights are being nudged in the direction of these concerns.

It is hoped that the perspectives and insights shared in this book can contribute to the Caribbean's evolution towards nationalisms that are more relevant and meaningful for the new century and beyond, and that ultimately these nationalisms may reflect and will be emblematic of the desires of societies seeking decisively to turn their backs on a past defined by marginalization, exclusion and the subjection of persons deemed to be "other" to actual or discursive violence.

References

Carr, R. (2009). Social exclusion, citizenship and rights. In C. Barrow, M. de Bruin, & R. Carr (Eds.), *Sexuality, social exclusion and human rights: Vulnerability in the Caribbean context of HIV* (pp. 71–92). Kingston, Jamaica: Ian Randle.

Kempadoo, K. (2009). Caribbean sexuality: Mapping the field. *Caribbean Review of Gender Studies*, 3, 1–24. https://www.researchgate.net/publication/242247250 _Caribbean_Sexuality_Mapping_the_Field

1.

"Gender" in Caribbean Discourse
Ruptures, Revisions, Reconstructions

MARJAN DE BRUIN

Over the last couple of decades, the term "gender" has come into common use in anglophone Caribbean discourse not only in academic circles but also among the general public. The rising popularity of the term may be attributed to varying social, cultural, economic and political factors. A main driving force seems to have been a configuration of power dynamics within the networks of development partners, influencing change at the local and regional levels. Civil society organizations (CSOs), for instance, have been among the main diffusers of the term, frequently deploying it over the years in their interaction with government bodies and national stakeholders. Major contributors to the popularity of the term, however, have been at least two fields of activism and knowledge production – with different perspectives, priorities and histories. One is the Caribbean women's movement, revitalized in the 1960s and 1970s, and focused on eradicating the subordination of and discrimination against women. The other is the Caribbean response to the HIV and AIDS pandemic, which had manifested itself in the early 1980s. Within years, the Caribbean region had to address a persistently high HIV prevalence rate – the second highest after sub-Saharan Africa – especially among "vulnerable groups". In the field of HIV and AIDS, the concept of gender was strongly associated with addressing "social (in)justice". However, what exactly "gender" stood for was not always apparent. To better understand its meaning, this chapter will examine anglophone Caribbean scholarly literature as an important source of developing this concept.

Focus of This Chapter

This chapter has three broad goals. First, using the lens of gender studies in the Caribbean, it will explore the main meanings given to the concept of "gender". In this regard, the chapter will examine the parameters of the term, assessing what it includes and, equally important, what it excludes, focusing primarily on the writings of Caribbean leaders in the field of gender who have inspired discussions on the subject and shared their insights through major publications between 1970 and 2015. This approach implies that some works in this field of inquiry will not be covered in the chapter if the authors' texts, directly or indirectly, did not include a conceptual discussion on gender. Second, the chapter will review how the meanings assigned to the term have been influenced by thinking in the field of HIV and AIDS. Lastly, the chapter will seek to identify current conceptual challenges relating to gender as well as some of the questions that have remained unanswered in debates about it.

"Gender" in Caribbean Discourse

Prior to Independence in the Caribbean Region: Addressing "Women's Issues"

Women in the Caribbean, especially middle-class women, had established and participated in "social welfare" and charitable organizations from as early as the 1920s and 1930s (Ramkeesoon, 1988). These organizations played a crucial role in various areas of Caribbean life, such as religion, the labour movement and the political arena. During the 1940s and 1950s, many of these associations formed national umbrella organizations, which decades later – when the second wave of feminism emerged in the Caribbean – laid the foundation for strengthening regional connections (Reddock, 1988). Women had been active for decades and even centuries, as Massiah pointed out (1986b), "whether they [had] been resisters of the pernicious system of slavery (Mathurin Mair, 1975), controllers of the internal marketing system (Mintz, 1955), modern day international commercial traders (Le Franc et al., 1985), or mothers rearing their families single-handedly (Edith Clarke, 1957)" (p. 164). The common phrase used in reference to the struggle for women's equal rights was "women's issues". Gender as a concept in Caribbean "gender literature" only surfaced after "women and development" literature had emerged in the region in the late 1960s and 1970s.

The 1960s was a tumultuous period in the Commonwealth Caribbean. Several countries, led by Jamaica and Trinidad and Tobago, had gained independence. Caribbean citizens were challenging colonial frames of mind, questioning old paradigms and establishing new frameworks for advancing their young societies. Against this backdrop, in 1962, the University College of the West Indies – established in Jamaica in 1948 and operating under the aegis of the University of London – gave way to the University of the West Indies (UWI), the first independent degree-granting institution in the anglophone Caribbean. This was a major step forward in the process of indigenous knowledge production.

In this period of change, the re-emergence of the international women's movement "ushered in a new era in Caribbean women's struggle" (Reddock, 1998, p. 57). Addressing women's issues was strongly connected with the social, economic and political needs of the entire population – a focus that set the Caribbean women's movement apart from women's movements in other parts of the world, such as the United States and Europe.

The 1970s: Global Support for Women's Rights

In the 1970s, women's rights became a strong, globally supported United Nations (UN) cause, with a dedicated, carefully designed timeline of five-yearly International World Conferences on Women – the first of which took place in Mexico in 1975. This support, Massiah (2016) observed, meant that "at the highest level, the status of women was now being seen as a human rights issue". Alongside this international support came "the active involvement of national governments" – a major step-up from "the isolated efforts of women's organizations" (p. 4). Women in the Caribbean would benefit from this global development for decades to come.

Demonstrating its commitment to the region, the young UWI took on board two regional initiatives, offering academics and women activists the opportunity to work together: the Women and Development Unit (WAND) and the Women in the Caribbean Project (WICP). Women activists had understood well "the necessity of linking women's NGOs with universities and the major political and economic structures of the region" (Massiah, 1998, p. 10). WAND and WICP became the engines for innovative research, new approaches and steady knowledge production on the social position of women, their roles and rights, as well as opportunities for positively changing these. They constituted the first intellectual efforts to break the general pattern of conventional male-dominated research in the Caribbean. In the new initiatives, women – not men – designed, conducted and interpreted research, and implemented interventions (Massiah, 1986a). This was groundbreaking, considering that up till then, few women – notably Edith Clarke and Elsa Goveia – participated in academic research. The new studies on women in the Caribbean were led by women who lived in the region, knew the region, and loved the region; not by researchers who mostly resided outside of it. In the mid-1980s, a new autonomous regional organization – the Caribbean Association for Feminist Research and Action (CAFRA) – was established and this strengthened regional connections.

WICP focused on producing "engendered indigenous knowledge" to build a "truly indigenous understanding" of women's lives (Barrow, 1998a, p. xix), which could serve policy-oriented research to inform planning decisions (Massiah, 1986a); WAND collected rich data through programmatic interventions in diverse fields. Both projects aimed at altering social inequalities and deliberately extended their coverage "to accommodate variations in ethnicity, race and class" (Massiah, 1986a, p. 12). Their feminist participatory qualitative research was more than another new technique. It reflected a readiness to supplant conventional forms of knowledge if the evidence justified it. In this way, their principals sought "not only to extend knowledge, but in the process, to reconstruct it" (Mathurin Mair, 1988b, p. 8). Research included drawing actionable recommendations and proposing new policies. WICP turned away from the "artificial distinction" between qualitative and quantitative research and favoured a method that blended the two (Massiah, 1986a) – in current-day jargon, mixed methods. It was in search of a theoretical paradigm to analyse Caribbean realities that did not indiscriminately transport "class formulations, appropriate to western European-type style societies, to a region which is so culturally differentiated" (p. 11). While shifting research approaches was a strong priority at the time, conceptual definition was not.

The 1980s: Pushing the Theoretical Analysis Further

In the early 1980s, the Caribbean had its first cases of the human immuno-deficiency virus (HIV). The main mode of transmission of the virus in the region was unprotected sex. What started as a small outbreak among a few patients in Jamaica soon manifested as a serious health disaster for the entire region. Although gender was a major factor in the transmission of the virus, only much later did concerns relating to it come to feature in discussions about HIV. When, in the early 1980s, gay men in the United States were the main group dying from acquired immune deficiency syndrome (AIDS), the end stage of HIV infection, in the Caribbean "many responded that AIDS was God's punishment for those men's 'unnatural' behaviour" (de Bruin & Carr, 2007, p. 7). Similar reactions were portrayed by Caribbean media practitioners, who, in the late 1980s and early 1990s, depicted HIV infection as a problem affecting "the outcast and minorities . . . prostitutes, homosexuals, migrant farm workers, and inmates of penal institutions" (de Bruin, 1994, p. 26). As the HIV and AIDS crises worsened, however, Commonwealth Caribbean governments were forced to discuss the sexual behaviour of their citizens in ways that they had never before needed to.

HIV had only just shown up on the public radar when WICP, between 1979 and 1982, conducted most of its studies on women's issues, producing a "large volume of documented evidence" (Barrow, 1998a, p. xviii), a fair amount of "accurate and reliable" information that could "have an indirect influence on policy outcomes" (Massiah, 1986b, pp. 176–177). This certainly gave gender relations in the region the attention that had been lacking, and the evidence that had been missing, up to that point in time. It also brought researchers face-to-face with a complexity that, although challenging to analyse and comprehend, at the same time had the potential to lead to innovative insights and to "reconstruct knowledge". Exploration of the ways "in which cultural concepts of gender guide social relations in the Caribbean" (Anderson, 1986, p. 320) was high on WICP's research priority agenda. The need to deepen the theoretical analysis was recognized as one of the more critical hurdles to be overcome in order to develop a more finely tuned understanding of the dynamics of gender ideology (Anderson, 1986).

A great public opportunity to carry forward this analysis was offered by UWI's regional seminar, in 1986, aimed at testing the waters for a new teaching programme by UWI's Women's Studies Group. Outside of the region, such programmes had been perceived as not only controversial but also subversive. New insights would challenge the traditional knowledge base – "knowledge being conventionally the preserve of masculine elites, mainly Western" (Mathurin Mair, 1988b, p. 8) – and threaten the status quo. The seminar was described as "only the beginnings of a collective exploration of the diverse conceptual and empirical issues involved" (Mathurin Mair, 1988a, p. xi). Its presentations – published in *Gender in Caribbean Development* (Mohammed & Shepherd, 1988); the first book in Caribbean gender literature that carried the word "gender" in its title – tended towards exploring empirical issues rather than attending to conceptual challenges. Most authors concentrated on women's issues and feminist theory (Chhachhi, 1988; Reddock, 1988), or women and development theories (Antrobus, 1988; Bolles, 1988; Girvan, 1988; Henry, 1988). Only a few such as Young (1988) set out to interrogate the notion of gender. Young posited that gender was "a shorthand term" which encoded "that our basic social identities as men and as women are socially constructed rather than based on fixed biological characteristics". She argued that what was perceived as typically inherent to masculinity or femininity had in fact been assigned through a structured set of behaviours, enacted between men and women ("two genders"). Through these behaviours, the "social relations of gender" were established (p. 100). These gender relations were "guided by norms and values, underpinned by ideology [and] sanctioned by a range of mechanisms" (p. 101). Several issues that required urgent attention, such as the, "gendering processes", "gender identities", "gender ambiguity", and the question on whether feminists were right "to discount so completely possible effects of biological difference" in the conceptualization of gender (Young, pp. 104–105). These were provocative and even contradictory questions, which, until recently, remained largely unanswered in Caribbean gender literature.

It was not only authors on women's issues who failed to provide clear definitions of gender. Miller (1986), for instance, in his *Marginalization of the Black Male,* used the term without providing any further definition or annotation. A revised, more grounded, but not drastically changed, version of his marginalization hypothesis, including Miller's perspective on gender, was presented in his *Men at Risk* (1991). His work received mixed reviews; "most academics rejected the marginalisation of the Caribbean male" (Barriteau, 2000, p. 3).

The 1990s: Multiple Fields in Action

Understanding the dynamics of sexual behaviour in the Caribbean, where HIV prevalence rates in the 1990s were still the second highest in the world, had become a survival imperative. Most HIV prevention in the 1980s and 1990s in the Caribbean, but also worldwide, focused on the risks of unprotected sex and emphasized the need to "Abstain, Be Faithful and use Condoms" – the so-called ABC approach, assuming that high-risk sexual behaviour could be changed into safe sexual behaviour simply by encouraging protected sex or abstinence (de Bruin, 2002). Insufficient knowledge and lack of rational decision-making were believed to be the drivers of unsafe sexual practices. Yet the concerns in public health that arose from the increasing HIV prevalence rates placed the notion of "a direct and rational link between beliefs and behaviour" (Ingham, Woodcock & Stenner, 1992, p. 164) under serious pressure. Similarly, at the international level, the belief was growing that individual-focused prevention work, in the absence of efforts to address structural determinants of vulnerability to HIV, would not alter the course of the pandemic "in any serious manner" (Mann, Tarantola & Netter, 1992, p. 1). Time and again in subsequent years, the decontextualized prevention approach would be critiqued by scholars in the field (Shannon, Goldenberg, Deering & Strathdee, 2014). However, without strategic conceptual alternatives, it would take a while before the influence of social variables – such as culture and gender relationships – gained recognition in Caribbean HIV prevention discourse.

This kind of focus was what women and development studies had been struggling with for years: the need to examine the structural dimensions of gender. Academics in this field had started to question and critique the ideological forces that fed individual and collective beliefs about the "natural" superiority of men and the inherent inferiority of women – perspectives that drove "perceptions about how gender [was] to be performed" (Barriteau, 1998, p. 192). Yet each of the fields – women and development as well as HIV and AIDS – worked mostly with its own network of experts and advocates, had its relationships with particular academic institutions, and related to different governmental agencies and departments. For both fields, understanding the concept of gender, its influence on relations, and the societal expectations relating to what the term entailed were pivotal. But there was little exchange of ideas and experiences between the two fields, certainly not institutionally. The few connections that were made between them were through initiatives from funding agencies, which commissioned researchers from one field to conduct research in the other.

During the 1990s, women and development studies continued to produce a steady stream of scholarly output in which "gender" appeared regularly. The constructionist paradigm that guided the thinking on the term seemed to have oriented discussions towards "the production of reconstructed understandings of the social world" (Lincoln & Guba, 2000, p. 158). Referring to a "social constructionist" approach, however, did not necessarily imply the presence of a unified perspective. Even at this stage, defining the concept was still not easy (Cole, 1997). A range of disciplines, with varying approaches, had embraced social constructivism, which had become "multifarious" (Brickell, 2006, p. 87). Scholars such as Barriteau (1998) noted the "confusion about the meaning of gender in the Anglophone Caribbean", which led to it being "misused daily" (p. 188). This frequent misuse may have been symptomatic of the absence of a conceptual framework within which to locate the term. This framework Barriteau (1998) provided when she, relying on earlier work, defined gender as involving "complex systems of personal and social relations through which women and men are socially created and maintained and through which they gain access to, or are allocated, status, power and material resources within society" (p. 188). Her definition took account of both an ideological dimension and a material dimension of the concept. At the ideological level, the term involved the social constructions relating to women and men. The material dimension took account of those elements of the discourse on gender that have typically been undervalued, such as how women and men gain access to or are accorded power, status and material resources within society. Barriteau contended critically that at all levels these two dimensions of gender relations reinforced each other. Barriteau's framework went beyond the traditional constructivist perspective, acknowledging the powerful ideological forces of individual and collective beliefs that drove the imbalance between male and female roles.

The social framing of femininity and masculinity, through the personal construction of gender identities as well as the social expectations relating to such identities, was seen as a major force establishing "the sexually differentiated socially constructed boundaries for males and females" (Barriteau, 1998, p. 191). Transgressions of these boundaries could produce "a shift in gendered relations of power", often followed by penalties (p. 192). Barriteau's examples of crossing boundaries referenced women taking on masculine responsibili- ties. Another example might have been the transgression of heteronormative boundaries in Caribbean societies, the penalties for which were – and are – well known. For years, diverging from heteronormativity would often lead to social exclusion, intimidation or even annihilation. In the gender literature of the 1990s, however, no examples of boundary crossings outside of the hetero- sexual realm were cited.

The thinking in the women and development field showed, towards the end of the 1990s, a strong interest in, and concentration on, gender ideologies and identities. Barrow (1998c) provided many cases and rich empirical data directly or indirectly connected to gender ideologies and identities. Only a few scholars, however, made the effort to define or operationalize these central concepts. One such was Leo-Rhynie, who described gender identity as "a personal recog- nition and general acknowledgment of oneself as part of a socially defined group – male or female, which may or may not be derived from the basic sex difference from which the group originated" (1998, p. 234). What her treatment did not address, however, was any explicit consideration of the complexity of the concept. Perhaps the time was not ripe for that kind of discussion, although Hall and du Gay had published their *Questions of Cultural Identity* a few years earlier, in 1996. It was only in the 2000s that interrogating and analysing social identities across disciplines became commonplace (Capozza & Brown, 2000; Mokros, 2002; Simon, 2004).

Although "the popular as well as intellectual interpretation of 'gender' at the time was still more or less synonymous with 'woman'" (Mohammed & Shepherd, 1999, p. xiii), men's issues did begin to enter the debate – initially more as deriva- tives of women's issues rather than in their own right. Men had been "dismissed as 'marginal' . . . sensationalized as 'at risk' and 'in crisis' as they are presumed to be overtaken by girls and women at school and at work" (Barrow, 1998a, p. xii). Taking a different perspective, Leo-Rhynie (1992) questioned: "Can we . . . as Caribbean feminists, ignore the increasing underachievement of boys and men in our schools, colleges and the university; and social repercussions of this situ- ation?" (cited by Massiah, 1998, p. 16). These questions and their social implica- tions could not be ignored for long.

By the 1990s, women had been outperforming men in significant areas of social endeavour: in the job market they occupied territory previously domi- nated by men. In professions such as teaching that men had fled, women took over and were dominating (Figueroa, 2004). By contrast, men were under- achieving at all levels of the educational system (Parry, 2000; Miller, 1991), and their enrolment in tertiary institutions significantly declined (Figueroa, 2004). It was therefore a matter of time before men's full inclusion in the gender debates would be realized. Publications during the 1990s showed more and more of men's perspectives (Besson, 1998), with analyses of Caribbean masculinity (Barrow, 1998b), attention to male socialization (Peacocke, 1998), men-women talk (Collins, 1998), and reviews of socialization and gender identity formation, including both male and female perspectives (Leo-Rhynie, 1998). By the end of the 1990s, "concerns with masculinity had emerged with full force, giving rise to a men's movement with various tendencies" (Mohammed & Shepherd, 1999, xiii). The region then counted several initiatives focused on creating men's organizations, at least two dozen, according to Prendergast and Hylton (2006). Several of these organizations, it seemed, focused specifically on fatherhood and/or religion. Yet it appeared the men's movement lacked support in general from men as they feared that participation in it could lead to them being labelled as gay (Prendergast & Hylton, 2006).

In the women/gender and development literature, recurring questions during this decade focused on how to better understand the power of ideologies: "who are Caribbean women and who are Caribbean men; how do gender ideologies and stereotypes define them and how, in turn, do they respond?" (Barrow, 1998a, xii); what does it mean to be "'male', 'masculine' and 'man' in Caribbean societies", and "how to discover and interpret gender beyond interpersonal relationships?" (Barriteau, 1998, p. 205). By this time, the concept of gender had been fully inserted into public and academic discourse, even if it lacked shared conceptualizations or interpretations (Barriteau, 2003, p. 30).

From the field of HIV and AIDS a set of new insights provided the catalyst for producing a more comprehensive understanding of the concept of gender. In the 1990s, HIV and AIDS scholars and activists shifted their focus from biomedical issues and individual behaviour change to a full recognition of the power of structural and distributional factors (Barnett & Whiteside, 2002). Risk for infection was no longer perceived as equally shared but as an outcome of varying types of susceptibility. This new perspective led to greater attention to human rights and acknowledgement of the existence of "marginalized" – later called "key" – populations such as those who identified as gay, bisexual or transgender. "Sexual orientation" had become a central phrase in the field of HIV and AIDS.

Between 2000 and 2010: A More Inclusive Perspective

Although in the 1990s some "mapping of the terrain" had taken place relating to men and masculinity, no systematic in-depth theoretical discussion on how masculinity was constructed, and its relationship with other social categories and relevant concepts, had taken place. In the first decade of the new century, men became active participants in the gender discussions on issues that concerned them, beginning "to think through what it [meant] to be a man in the Caribbean and to map the terrain of masculinity in contemporary societies" (Lewis, 2002, p. 529). They were acknowledged as important actors, instead of mainly as dominating perpetrators of gender oppression (Reddock, 2003). As the decade progressed, further inclusion of men in the gender discussions occurred with two seminal publications in 2004. One was Reddock's (2004b) edited volume *Interrogating Caribbean Masculinity*. This work signalled that although still "in its infancy" and affected by "the parameters of patriarchal rule" (Lewis, 2004, p. 238), Caribbean masculinity studies existed "as a critical area of enquiry in the field of gender and cultural studies" (Nurse, 2004, p. 4). The second publication was the edited collection *Gender in the 21st Century: Caribbean Perspectives, Visions and Possibilities* by Bailey and Leo-Rhynie (2004). The fruit of a 2003 academic conference by the same name, the 733-page volume comprised thirty-one chapters from scholars, policy developers and activists from across the region. Five of those chapters specifically related to masculinity(ies)/maleness/fatherhood (Miller; Figueroa; W. Bailey et al.; Reddock; Lewis). Framed against the backdrop of "the dynamic context within which gender was addressed internationally", the publication presented "a wide range of issues associated with the scholarship and activism of feminism, particularly in the Caribbean" (Bailey & Leo-Rhynie, 2004, p. xii).

Reddock's (2004b) anthology included a special section on theorizing Caribbean masculinities, with contributions by Nurse, Mohammed and De Moya. Nurse provided conceptual clarification by emphasizing that identifiers such as sex, class, race, ethnicity, age, sexuality and nationality always interplay with and influence how masculinity is deployed. In recognition of this intersectionality, he proposed that the plural term "masculinities" be used instead of the singular. The concept "masculinities" draws attention to the complex processes and dynamics of power differentials among and between men from different backgrounds. This leads to a differentiation between the hegemonic/dominant and subordinated/marginalized masculine (Nurse, 2004). In other words, the term allows for the consideration of ways in which the hegemonic masculine has an interest in, or need to, distance itself from the subordinated masculine. This distancing could result in the construction of the latter as "effeminate and infantile" (p. 7) – creating a behavioural remoteness that could function as a protective shield for the hegemonic masculine. In exploring further the ways in which hegemonic masculinities work individually and collectively, Nurse pointed to the levels of angst and anxiety that were frequently at play when these masculinities felt threatened from shifts in the gender order that challenged "traditional male power and privilege". Such shifts could be triggered by "the rise of feminism; the gay rights movements and resistance to racialised masculinities" (Nurse, 2004, p. 28).

Mohammed, too, focused on theoretical issues relating to the processes of masculinity construction and its relation to femininity. From a historicist perspective, the region was faced with a specific challenge: How to "examine Caribbean masculinity in relation to Caribbean femininity without replicating the stereotyped notions" (2004, p. 43) from a colonial past? Referring to the old essentialism versus constructivism debates, Mohammed questioned what biological differences between males and females meant for the construction of manhood and womanhood. She wondered how theorists could acknowledge the differences between masculinity and femininity without "returning to a pure essentialism of the body as male and female" (p. 48). In other words: "How do we employ the theoretical frames of essentialism and constructivism without creating other binary oppositions in thought?" (p. 49). Mohammed signalled the dangers of classificatory schemes based on dichotomous thinking and urged scholars and activists to avoid them and to work towards diversity. She contended that traditional stereotypes associated with masculinity should be unmasked even as scholars sought to deconstruct patriarchy. Her interrogations and provocative questioning, however, did not touch on how to problematize the binary of two sexes. This was also raised by De Moya, who questioned "the masculinity-femininity polarity" that seemed to be "paradoxically reluctant to dissolve" (2004, p. 100). Emphasizing the need to provide new evidence rather than developing theoretical frameworks, De Moya's research provided for a panoply of masculinities, mostly based on perceptions of sexual orientation (p. 80). It could perhaps be argued that the concept of gender was beginning to become more inclusive with the articulation of these new perspectives. However, how gender would relate to the other important social category – sex – did not feature in discussions, at least not in any profound way. Mohammed (2002a) touched on the variability of gender when she stated that "the biological and social possibilities of gender and sexuality are perhaps not limitless, but certainly changeable and variable across, and within, space and time", suggesting the recognition of greater complexity, one that "we are least able to fully grasp" (p. xiv). Other authors seemed to have sought to broaden their points of view too, adding more variation to previous perspectives. Where social constructivism, as a paradigm in the past, had been presented as being mutually exclusive of essentialism, Wieringa (2002) argued that it did "not convince as the all-encompassing paradigm some of its adherents claim it to be" (p. 17). Perhaps it was time for "rapprochement and new interdisciplinary research between social scientists and biologists . . . about issues related to sexuality, the body and behaviour" (p. 19).

Although the concept of gender itself remained unclear, "opaque" as Mohammed stated, and used "widely, popularly, very loosely sometimes" (2003, p. 109), its complexity had begun to be accepted more in Caribbean gender literature. Lewis, for instance, observed the void in Caribbean gender discourse and gender theory on issues of sexual orientation. In fact, scholars in the Caribbean have tended to shy away from this issue (Lewis, 2002). One notable exception was Chevannes, who, writing from an anthropological perspective about gender and adult sexuality, included "homosexuality" in his analyses of the persisting heteronormativity in the Caribbean (2002). "Sexuality", however, had become "completely invisible"; it was "reduced to heterosexual intercourse" . . . "absorbed into the gendered dichotomy" and becoming "an expression of seemingly natural biologically-driven relations between men and women" (Kempadoo, 2003, p. 60).

Reflections on other concepts such as gender identity evolved into a more sophisticated discourse that took into account its fluidity and malleability, recognizing it as a dynamic process (Mohammed, 2002a, p. xvi). Kempadoo's analysis of gender in the Caribbean context brought to the fore the critical variables that needed to be considered: "Gender, it has been established, is discursively and materially produced, is thoroughly indigenized, located socially, politically and theoretically as a pillar of Caribbean identity, and is an organizing principle of the society, the economy, oppositional consciousness and political struggle" (2003, p. 59).

Publications in the field of HIV and AIDS during this decade emphasized "sexual orientation" and its context of human rights, as an important factor when addressing gender issues in relation to HIV (Barrow, de Bruin & Carr, 2009). Notwithstanding, in the wider Caribbean literature on gender, this concept had generally not entered the debate yet. This led Gosine to posit that Caribbean scholarship needed "a broad and sustained discussion about sexualities, sexual rights and their relationship to local and global political transformations" (2009). The connection between the HIV and AIDS field and gender and development issues became now visibly closer with several comprehensive publications, commissioned by ECLAC and UNIFEM, focused on gender in HIV and AIDS programming (Pargass, 2005) as well as the implications of the relationship between gender and sex for HIV and AIDS in the Caribbean (Kempadoo & Taitt, 2006).

Between 2010 and 2015

In this period, Caribbean gender literature began to open up even more than in previous years – thematically as well as conceptually. A special issue of *Social and Economic Studies* (2011) on sexualities in the Caribbean presented a set of shared social beliefs, in which not only gender but also sex and sexuality played an important role. Never before had sex, gender and sexualities been presented as visibly and explicitly in Caribbean academic literature: transgender (James & De La Haye); the multiplicity of female same-sex relations, women who have sex with women, men who have sex with men; gay men; lesbians; bisexual persons (Carpenter & McKenzie); representations of homosexuality in Jamaica (Charles); exploring erotic desires in the Caribbean (Marshall) – a diversity of persons and sexual orientations that had been ignored and missing from Caribbean gender studies were now present in their own right in Caribbean academic discourse.

The latest homegrown Caribbean gender publication reflecting conceptual thinking – Barriteau's *Love and Power* – continued the new frankness through inclusion of work on desire, attraction, power, lust, loving, intimacy, sexuality and more. "What have we avoided in not theorizing love, lust and desire?" Barriteau asked (2012, p. 5). "How comfortable are we, within scholarship and society, with same-sex and heterosexual loving?" (p. 4). "Are there observable patterns of exploitation and the exclusion of women and *other marginalized* groups?" (emphasis added). Barriteau's questions represent a clear departure from the heteronormative thinking that had been so dominant in most of Caribbean gender literature.

In *Love and Power*, previous conceptual boundaries were crossed and new territories explored, including shifting and varying sexual identities – "continuing to disrupt and destabilise embedded and resilient patriarchal knowledge claims" (Barriteau, 2012, p. 4). In a mix of empirical discourse and conceptual explorations, Barriteau's publication focused on love and power, with love as the pivot to which desires, lusts and passions were connected. In her publication, the past is available for "re-examination" (p. 7) in what appeared to be the beginnings of a search for new meanings and new epistemological frames through which to examine gender in the Caribbean. A similar openness can be found in the online *Caribbean Review of Gender Studies*, established by UWI's Institute of Gender and Development Studies, which not only follows with the inclusion of men (Thompson, 2015) but also publishes discussions about queer, "hidden" populations (referring to lesbians and gays), and gender nonconforming performances, signalling a widening of interest.

Reflections and Conclusions

What does this analysis on the use of "gender" – its meaning and interpretations – in Caribbean gender literature over the last forty-five years show us? What did "gender" stand for; which parameters were set and for what reasons? The production of academic literature in the field of gender and development, over the last decades, has not only been motivated by the urge to understand the world in which we live; it was also driven by a passionate determination to use new insights towards greater justice and equity between women and men. Gender relations, however, were set in a universe of women and men, with an implicit assumption of heteronormativity. Other modes of relations were not explicitly rejected, but simply did not appear in the discussions – excluded – and constituted a blind spot for gender scholars.

For decades, the debates in the field of gender and development carried a binary perspective. Differentiations among women and between women and men were acknowledged but only according to variations such as race, ethnicity and class – sexual orientation was not one of those categories. The often implicit reference was to one locus of sexuality: heterosexuality. This binary perspective was combined with a linear "constructed" connection between sex and gender, in which "sex" was seen as "the relatively minimal raw material on which is then based the social construction of gender" (Sedgwick, 2008, p. 27).

The need to avoid dichotomous and oppositional thinking (Mohammed, 2004; Nurse, 2004; Lewis, 2004), and to question the masculinity-femininity polarity in Caribbean gender literature was signalled but not further elaborated. Recently, gender discussions in the gender and development field in the Caribbean began paying attention to its former blind spot. A new and frank point of view, referring to heterosexuals and homosexuals (gays or lesbians), developed. This new exploration of sexualities has only started, and will run full force into several other conceptual challenges. As Sedgwick (2008) proffered: "The dividing up of all sexual acts – indeed all persons – under the 'opposite' categories of 'homo' and 'hetero,' is not a natural given but a historical process, still incomplete today and ultimately impossible but characterized by potent contradictions and explosive effects" (p. xvi). This historical process that Sedgwick refers to is also emphasized by Appiah (2018), who warns that identities should not be taken for granted but problematized by exploring "the manifestations, the mechanisms and the motives of the multiple systems of classification human beings employ" (p. xiv). These interrogations can lead to contradictions and exclusion. In the Caribbean region, for instance, where the churches are powerful institutions and religion is an omnipresent social agent (see also Perkins in this book), diverting from majority perspectives can lead to "explosive effects" with cultural clashes contesting "who we are". However, to refer to *"pre-given* ethnic or cultural traits set in the fixed tablet of tradition" (Bhabha, 1994, p. 2) – that's how we are" – excludes and rejects other *existing* (my emphasis) identities.

Conceptual discussions about diverse sexualities and identities will unavoidably touch on perspectives on how we view the world and the people who live on it. The greatest challenge we will face will be whether we will be able to accept that "the right to 'signify' from the periphery of authorized power and privilege does not depend on the persistence of tradition" (Bhabha, 1994, p. 2).

References

Anderson, P. (1986). Conclusion: Women in the Caribbean. *Social and Economic Studies. Women in the Caribbean (Part I)*, 35(3), 291–323.

Antrobus, P. (1988). Women in development programmes: The Caribbean experience (1975–1985). In P. Mohammed & C. Shepherd (Eds.), *Gender in Caribbean development* (pp. 36–53). St Augustine, Trinidad: University of the West Indies, Women and Development Studies Project.

Appiah, K.A. (2018). *The lies that bind – Rethinking identity. Creed, country, colour, class, culture*. London, UK: Profile Books.

Bailey, B., & Leo-Rhynie, E. (Eds.). (2004). *Gender in the 21st century. Caribbean perspectives, visions and possibilities*. Kingston, Jamaica: Ian Randle.

Bailey, W., Branche, C., Jackson, J., & Lee, A. (2004). Fatherhood in risk environments. In B. Bailey & E. Leo-Rhynie (Eds.), *Gender in the 21st century. Caribbean Perspectives, visions and possibilities* (pp. 162–175). Kingston, Jamaica: Ian Randle.

Barnett, T., & Whiteside, A. (2002). *AIDS in the twenty-first century: Disease and globalization*. London, UK: Palgrave Macmillan.

Barriteau, E. (1998). Theorizing gender systems and the project of modernity in the twentieth-century Caribbean. *Feminist Review*, 59 (Summer),186–210.

Barriteau, V.E. (2000). *Re-examining issues of "male" marginalisation and "masculinity" in the Caribbean: The need for a new policy approach*. Working Paper 4, September 2000. Cave Hill, Barbados: University of the West Indies, Centre for Gender and Development Studies.

Barriteau, E. (2003). Theorizing the shift from "woman" to "gender" in Caribbean feminist discourse: The power relations of creating knowledge. In E. Barriteau (Ed.), *Confronting power, theorizing gender: Interdisciplinary perspectives in the Caribbean* (pp. 27–45). Kingston, Jamaica: University of the West Indies Press.

Barriteau, V.E. (2012). Disruptions and dangers: Destabilizing Caribbean discourses on gender, love and power. In V. E. Barriteau (Ed.), *Love and power: Caribbean discourses on gender* (pp. 3–37). Kingston, Jamaica: University of the West Indies Press/Institute for Gender and Development Studies, Nita Barrow Unit.

Barrow, C. (1998a). Introduction and overview: Caribbean ideologies. In C. Barrow (Ed.), *Caribbean portraits: Essays on gender ideologies and identities* (pp. xi–xxxviii). Kingston, Jamaica: Ian Randle.

Barrow, C. (1998b). Caribbean masculinity and family: Revisiting "marginality" and "reputation". In C. Barrow (Ed.), *Caribbean portraits: Essays on gender ideologies and identities* (pp. 339–358). Kingston, Jamaica: Ian Randle.

Barrow, C. (Ed.) (1998c). *Caribbean portraits: Essays on gender ideologies and identities*. Kingston, Jamaica: Ian Randle.

Barrow, C., de Bruin, M., & Carr, R. (Eds.). (2009). *Sexuality, social exclusion & human rights: Vulnerability in the Caribbean context of HIV*. Kingston, Jamaica: Ian Randle.

Besson, J. (1998). Changing perspectives of gender in the Caribbean region: The case of the Jamaican peasantry. In C. Barrow (Ed.), *Caribbean portraits: Essays on gender ideologies and identities* (pp. 133-155). Kingston, Jamaica: Ian Randle.

Bhabha, H. (1994). *The location of culture.* London, UK: Routledge.

Bolles, A.L. (1988). Theories of women in development in the Caribbean: The ongoing debate. In P. Mohammed & C. Shepherd (Eds.), *Gender in Caribbean development* (pp. 22-35). St Augustine, Trinidad: University of the West Indies, Women and Development Studies Project.

Brickell, C. (2006). The sociological construction of sex and gender. *The Sociological Review.* Blackwell, 87-111.

Capozza, D., & Brown, R. (Eds.). (2000). *Social identity processes: Trends in theory and research.* London, UK: Sage.

Carpenter, K., & McKenzie, M. (2011) Love on a continuum. *Social and Economic Studies, 60*(1), 111-136.

Charles, C. (2011). Homosexuality in Jamaica. *Social and Economic Studies, 60*(1), 3-29.

Chevannes, B. (2002). Gender and adult sexuality. In P. Mohammed (Ed.), *Gendered realities: Essays in Caribbean feminist thought* (pp. 486-494). Kingston, Jamaica: University of the West Indies Press/Centre for Gender and Development Studies.

Chhachhi, A. (1988). Concepts in feminist theory: Consensus and controversy. In P. Mohammed & C. Shepherd (Eds.), *Gender in Caribbean development* (pp. 78-98). St Augustine, Trinidad: University of the West Indies, Women and Development Studies Project.

Clarke, E. (1957). *My mother who fathered me.* London, UK: Allen & Unwin.

Cole, J. (1997). Gender, culture and Caribbean development. In E. Leo-Rhynie, B. Bailey, & C. Barrow (Eds.), *Gender: A Caribbean multi-disciplinary perspective* (pp. 4-13). Kingston, Jamaica: Ian Randle in association with the Centre for Gender and Development Studies and the Commonwealth of Learning.

Collins, M. (1998). Sometimes you have to drink vinegar and pretend it is honey: Race, class and man-woman talk. In C. Barrow (Ed.), *Caribbean portraits: Essays on gender ideologies and identities* (pp. 377-390). Kingston, Jamaica: Ian Randle.

de Bruin, M. (1994). *HIV/AIDS and responsible reporting: A content analysis in three Caribbean countries, Part 1.* Paper presented at the 11th Annual Intercultural and International Communications Conference, University of Miami, 1994, February 3-5.

de Bruin, M. (2002). *Teenagers at risk: High-risk behavior of Jamaican adolescents in the context of reproductive health – Observations and impressions.* Kingston, Jamaica: Youth.now and the US Agency for International Development (USAID).

de Bruin, M., & Carr, R. (2007). *Gender sensitivity in National Strategic Plans: An analysis of gender mainstreaming in HIV/AIDS plans in Barbados, Guyana, Jamaica, Saint Lucia and Trinidad and Tobago.* Bridgetown, Barbados: UNIFEM.

De Moya, E.A. (2004). Power games and totalitarian masculinity in the Dominican Republic. In R.E. Reddock (Ed.), *Interrogating Caribbean masculinities: Theoretical and empirical analyses* (pp. 68-102). Kingston, Jamaica: University of the West Indies Press.

Figueroa, M. (2004). Old (female) glass ceiling and new (male) looking glasses: Challenging gender privileging in the Caribbean. In B. Bailey & E. Leo-Rhynie (Eds.), *Gender in the 21st century. Caribbean perspectives, visions and possibilities* (pp. 134–161). Kingston, Jamaica: Ian Randle.

Girvan, N. (1988). Notes on the meaning and significance of development. In P. Mohammed & C. Shepherd (Eds.), *Gender in Caribbean development* (pp. 11–21). St Augustine, Trinidad: University of the West Indies, Women and Development Studies Project.

Gosine, A. (2009). Sexual desires, rights and regulations. *Caribbean Review of Gender Studies. A Journal on Caribbean Perspectives on Gender and Feminism, 3*, 1–4.

Hall, S., & du Gay, P. (Eds.). (1996). *Questions of cultural identity.* London, UK: Sage.

Henry, R. (1988). Jobs, gender and development strategy in the Commonwealth Caribbean. In P. Mohammed & C. Shepherd (Eds.), *Gender in Caribbean Development* (pp. 185–207). St Augustine, Trinidad: University of the West Indies, Women and Development Studies Project.

Ingham, R., Woodcock, A., & Stenner, K. (1992). The limitations of rational decision-making models as applied to young people's sexual behaviour. In P. Aggleton, P. Davies, & G. Hart (Eds.), *AIDS: Rights, risk and reason* (pp. 163–173). London, UK: Falmer Press.

James, C., & De La Haye, W. (2011). Challenges and treatment of a transsexual in Jamaica. *Social and Economic Studies, 60*(1), 137–151.

Kempadoo, K. (2003). Sexuality in the Caribbean: Theory and research (with an emphasis on the anglophone Caribbean). *Social and Economic Studies, 52*(3), 59–88.

Kempadoo, K., & Taitt, A. (2006). *Gender, sexuality and implications for HIV/AIDS in the Caribbean. A review of literature and programmes.* UNIFEM, Caribbean Office; the Barbados National HIV/AIDS Commission and the International Development Research Centre.

Le Franc, E., McFarlane, D., & Taylor, A. (1985). *Study of the informal distribution network in the Kingston Metropolitan Region.* Unpublished report. Kingston, Jamaica: Institute of Social and Economic Research, University of the West Indies.

Leo-Rhynie, E.A. (1992). *Women and development studies: Moving from the periphery?* Lecture presented at the Women and Development Studies Tenth Anniversary Symposium, University of the West Indies, Mona, Jamaica, December 8–10.

Leo-Rhynie, E.A. (1998). Socialisation and the development of gender identity: Theoretical formulations and Caribbean research. In C. Barrow (Ed.), *Caribbean Portraits: Essays on gender ideologies and identities* (pp. 234–252). Kingston, Jamaica: Ian Randle.

Lewis, L. (2002). Envisioning a politics of change within Caribbean gender relations. In P. Mohammed (Ed.), *Gendered realities: Essays in Caribbean feminist thought* (pp. 512–530). Kingston, Jamaica: University of the West Indies Press/Centre for Gender and Development Studies.

Lewis, L. (2004). Masculinity, the political economy of the body, and patriarchal power in the Caribbean. In B. Bailey & E. Leo-Rhynie (Eds.), *Gender in the 21st century: Caribbean perspectives, visions and possibilities* (pp. 236–261). Kingston, Jamaica: Ian Randle.

Lincoln, Y., & Guba, E. (2000). Paradigmatic controversies, contradictions and emerging confluences. In N. Denzin & Y. Lincoln (Eds.), *Handbook of qualitative research* (2nd ed.) (pp. 163–188). Thousand Oaks, CA: Sage.

Mann, J., Tarantola, D., & Netter, T. (1992). *AIDS in the world: A global report.* Cambridge, MA: Harvard University Press.

Marshall, A. (2011). Reclaiming the erotic power of black women. *Social and Economic Studies, 60*(1), 61–90.

Massiah, J. (1986a). Women in the Caribbean Project: An overview. *Social and Economic Studies: Women in the Caribbean (Part I), 35*(2), 1–29.

Massiah, J. (1986b). Postscript: The utility of WICP research in policy formation. *Social and Economic Studies: Women in the Caribbean (Part II), 35*(3), 157–181.

Massiah, J. (1998). *On the brink of the new millennium, are Caribbean women prepared?* Inaugural Lucille Mathurin Mair. Lecture, March 6, 1998. University of the West Indies.

Massiah, J. (2016). Setting the stage. In J. Massiah, E. Leo-Rhynie, & B. Bailey. *The UWI gender journey: Recollections and reflections* (pp. 3–10). Kingston, Jamaica: University of the West Indies Press/Institute for Gender and Development Studies.

Mathurin Mair, L. (1975). *The rebel woman in the West Indies.* Kingston, Jamaica: Institute of Jamaica.

Mathurin Mair, L. (1988a). Foreword. In P. Mohammed & C. Shepherd (Eds.), *Gender in Caribbean development* (pp. xi–xii). St Augustine, Trinidad: University of the West Indies, Women and Development Studies Project.

Mathurin Mair, L. (1988b). Women's studies in an international context. In P. Mohammed & C. Shepherd (Eds.), *Gender in Caribbean development* (pp. 1–9). St Augustine, Trinidad: University of the West Indies, Women and Development Studies Project.

Miller, E. (1986). *Marginalization of the black male.* Kingston, Jamaica: Jamaica Publishing House.

Miller, E. (1991). *Men at risk.* Kingston, Jamaica: Jamaica Publishing House.

Miller, E. (2004). Male marginalisation revisited. In B. Bailey & E. Leo-Rhynie (Eds.), *Gender in the 21st century: Caribbean perspectives, visions and possibilities* (pp. 99–133). Kingston, Jamaica: Ian Randle.

Mintz, S. (1955). The Jamaican internal marketing pattern: Some notes and hypotheses. *Social and Economic Studies, 4*(1), 95–103.

Mohammed, P. (2002a). Introduction. The material of gender. In P. Mohammed (Ed.), *Gendered realities: Essays in Caribbean feminist thought* (pp. xiv–xxiii). Kingston, Jamaica: University of the West Indies Press/Centre for Gender and Development Studies.

Mohammed, P. (2003). A symbiotic visiting relationship. Caribbean feminist historiography and Caribbean feminist theory. In E. Barriteau (Ed.), *Confronting power, theorizing gender. Interdisciplinary perspectives in the Caribbean* (pp. 101–125). Kingston, Jamaica: University of the West Indies Press.

Mohammed, P. (2004). Unmasking masculinity and deconstructing patriarchy: Problems and possibilities within feminist epistemology. In R.E. Reddock (Ed.), *Interrogating Caribbean masculinities: Theoretical and empirical analyses* (pp. 38–67). Kingston, Jamaica: University of the West Indies Press.

Mohammed, P., & Shepherd, E. (Eds.). (1988). *Gender in Caribbean development*. St Augustine, Trinidad: University of the West Indies, Women and Development Studies Project.

Mohammed, P., & Shepherd, C. (Eds.). (1999). *Gender in Caribbean development: Papers presented at the inaugural seminar of the University of the West Indies Women and Development Studies Project*. With a new Foreword by Elsa Leo-Rhynie. Kingston, Jamaica: Canoe Press.

Mokros, H. (2000). *Identity matters: Communication-based explorations and explanations*. Creskill, NJ: Hampton Press.

Nurse, K. (2004). Masculinities in transition. Gender and the global problematique. In R. Reddock (Ed.), *Interrogating Caribbean masculinities: Theoretical and empirical analyses* (pp. 3–33). Kingston, Jamaica: University of the West Indies Press.

Pargass, G. (2005). *Gender review and assessment of HIV/AIDS programming of selected National AIDS programmes in the Caribbean*. ECLAC Sub-regional Headquarters for the Caribbean and UNIFEM-Caribbean Office.

Parry, O. (2000). *Male underachievement in high school education in Barbados, Jamaica and St Vincent and the Grenadines*. Kingston, Jamaica: Canoe Press.

Peacocke N. (1998). Meditation on "the subject": Rethinking caring labour. In C. Barrow (Ed.), *Caribbean portraits: Essays on gender ideologies and identities* (pp. 194–207). Kingston, Jamaica: Ian Randle.

Prendergast, P., & Hylton, G. (2006). Bringing the male voice, perspective and issues to the gender agenda: The task of male organizations in the Caribbean. *Caribbean Quarterly*, 52(2/3), 14–21.

Ramkeesoon, G. (1988). Early women's organization in Trinidad: 1920s to 1930s. In P. Mohammed & C. Shepherd (Eds.), *Gender in Caribbean development* (pp. 357–360). St Augustine, Trinidad: University of the West Indies, Women and Development Studies Project.

Reddock, R. (1988). Feminism and feminist thought: An historical overview. In P. Mohammed & C. Shepherd (Eds.), *Gender in Caribbean development* (pp. 55–77). St Augustine, Trinidad: University of the West Indies, Women and Development Studies Project.

Reddock, R. (1998). Women's organizations and movements in the Commonwealth Caribbean. The response to global economic crisis in the 1980s. *Feminist Review*, 59, 57–73.

Reddock, R. (2003). Men as gendered beings: The emergence of masculinity studies in the anglophone Caribbean. *Social and Economic Studies*, 52(3), 89–117.

Reddock, R. (2004a). Caribbean masculinities and femininities: The impact of globalisation on cultural representations. In B. Bailey & E. Leo-Rhynie (Eds.), *Gender in the 21st century: Caribbean perspectives, visions and possibilities* (pp. 179–216). Kingston, Jamaica: Ian Randle.

Reddock, R.E. (Ed.). (2004b). *Interrogating Caribbean masculinities: Theoretical and empirical analyses*. Kingston, Jamaica: University of the West Indies Press.

Sedgwick, E.F. (2008). *Epistemology of the closet*. Berkeley, CA: University of California Press.

Shannon, K., Goldenberg, S., Deering, K., & Strathdee, S. (2014). HIV Infection in concentrated and high-prevalence epidemics: Why a structural determinants framework is needed. *Current Opinion in HIV and AIDS, 9*(2), 174–182.

Simon, B. (2004). *Identity in modern society: A social psychological perspective*. Malden, MA: Blackwell Publishing.

Thompson, W.A. (2015) "You sure aren't a real man!" Space, power, and possibilities for men in social care and gender studies. *Caribbean Review of Gender Studies, 9*, 77–94.

Wieringa, S. (2002). Essentialism versus constructivism. In P. Mohammed (Ed.), *Gendered realities: Essays in Caribbean feminist thought* (pp. 3–21). Kingston, Jamaica: University of the West Indies Press/Centre for Gender and Development Studies.

Young, K. (1988). Notes on the social relations of gender. In P. Mohammed & C. Shepherd (Eds.), *Gender in Caribbean development* (pp. 99–111). St Augustine, Trinidad: University of the West Indies, Women and Development Studies Project.

2.

Conceptualizing Sex/Gender Diversity
Considerations for the Caribbean

RHODA REDDOCK

This chapter challenges many common assumptions about sex/gender normalcy. It examines the concepts of sex/gender identity, diverse gender expression and gender variations or gender diversity, as well as the different ways in which these are experienced cross-culturally. Generally, in the discourse on gender and sexuality but also in everyday understandings, masculinity and femininity, male and female, are understood as binary opposites – to be masculine is to be not-feminine, to be male is to be not-female.

It can be argued that the male/female binary is one of the central thought patterns of Western culture. Ideologies deriving from it have become hegemonic throughout the world through colonial conquest, but more recently through a globalized media and popular culture. The masculine/feminine binary is probably one of the most powerful in Western philosophical thought. It is also an asymmetrical binary, which is a characteristic of many other binaries.

The sex/gender binary is a more recent construction. It emerged as a way of differentiating the socially constructed expressions of male/female differences – that is, masculinity and femininity – from the perceived biological and anatomical differences of sex. This dichotomy was initially brought into Caribbean feminist scholarship through the work of feminist social constructionists at the 1979 conference on the Subordination of Women organized by the University of Sussex. They used this term to facilitate an analytical and conceptual distinction between the biological differences of being "male" and "female" and the socially constructed, or socially determined, differences and meanings attached to "masculinity" and "femininity". These scholars established a conceptual distinction between "sex", seen as referring to biological differences, and "gender", seen as relating to the social differences between men and women. Kate Young (1988), a central figure of this school of thought, explained the concept of gender in this way:

> By using gender, we are using a shorthand term which encodes a very crucial point: that our basic social identities as men and as women are socially constructed rather than based on fixed biological characteristics. In this sense we can talk about

societies in which there are more than two genders (and in the anthropological record there are several such societies), as well as the historical differences in masculinity (femininity) in a given society. (p. 98)

Note on Concepts and Terminologies

A range of terminologies have emerged to address this complex area of human experience. What is important to note is that in many parts of the precolonial, premodern world, different concepts and terminologies existed that reflected indigenous ways of comprehending and experiencing sex/gender variation and diversity. Serena Nanda reminds us that cultures construct their sex and gender systems differently, and they do not always divide neatly into male and female, man and woman (Nanda, 2000, p. 1).

Wieringa and Sívori highlight the need to dislodge sexuality studies from its exclusively metropolitan perspective not just by "looking at these issues from different locations" but primarily by asking different questions and addressing the asymmetries of power involved in processes of globalization and colonialism (2013, p. 2). They also point to the great discrepancies between "Global North" and "Global South" definitions and understandings of sexualities and sex/gender identities. This language and the related conceptualizations, they argue further, reflect ongoing tensions between "increasingly powerful global discourses and local sexual ideologies and subjectivities" resulting in "an ethnocentric toolkit" with which scholars and activists from the South have to grapple (2013, p. 6). For example, in many scholarly contexts of the United States, the term "gender" is used to refer to women, while references to sexuality usually mean "gays" and "lesbians". Generally, in the Caribbean when researchers speak and teach about gender, they are referring to the social constructions of masculinity and femininity, and when they use the term "sexuality" they are referencing "the quality of being sexual" (Jackson, 2003, p. 4). This understanding and use of these terms in the Caribbean emerged from a specific historical and scholarly context, representative of the ways in which the concept "gender" was used in feminist scholarship. Similarly, the discourse on sexuality emerged as part of the politics and challenges to mainstream life and scholarship by gay and lesbian groups in North America.

These assumptions and meanings have been questioned, for example, by Richardson (2000) in her book *Theorising Heterosexuality*, when she observed:

Indeed, heterosexuality's naturalisation means that it is rarely acknowledged as a sexuality; as a sexual category or identification. By contrast, historically lesbians and gay men have been defined primarily as sexual beings, placed outside . . . or at the margins . . . of the normative boundaries of the social realm. As a result,

> homosexuality is defined primarily in terms of sexual identification, and very rarely
> are the social relations within which lesbians and gay men are embedded acknowl-
> edged. . . . In this sense, the notion of the social/sexual split is a sexualised notion,
> establishing heterosexuals as a socially inscribed class and lesbians and gay men as a
> sexually inscribed grouping. (p. 13)

In a similar vein, Nanda (2000) observed that "in contemporary Euro-American culture individuals are socially identified as if one's *sexual orientation* encapsulated one's total personality and identity" (p. 3). In other words, sexuality or sexual orientation has become the defining characteristic of sex/gender identity, and the terms used most commonly are: homosexual, heterosexual and bisexual. Wieringa and Sívori also point to the emergence of specific forms of "gay" and "lesbian" subculture as characterizing those definitions. Hetero- and homosexuality, they observed, are perceived as binary opposites permitting no transgression, even if temporarily (2013, p. 6). Relatedly, diverse forms of gender expression and sex/gender variation – commonly referred to as trans-genderism, transsexualism and intersex – have also come to be linked together under the umbrella of the acronym LGBTQIA[1] (lesbian, gay, bisexual, transgender, queer, questioning, intersex and asexual), which has been described as an ever-expanding alphabet soup (Petchesky et al., 2008, p. 1).

"Homosexual" emerged as a descriptive term meaning "of the same sex". Its emergence as an identity would come in the nineteenth century. This triad, while challenging the binary of male and female, sets up its own binary of heterosexual and homosexual. It is assumed that one is either one or the other or a combination of both. In North America, a clear pattern of behaviours, occupations, mannerisms and body language has emerged to be associated with male – and to a lesser extent, female – homosexuals, based largely on notions of masculine and feminine gendered behaviours. Each of these – homosexual, heterosexual and bisexual – is seen as a distinct and often mutually exclusive group with different lifestyles, cultures, and so on, giving rise to a sharp binary of "out" or "in". This vocabulary has now become accepted, normalized (or even naturalized) and transferred to other parts of the world. The North American terms "gay" for males and "lesbian" for females have achieved a popular usage that is almost coterminous with male and female homosexuals and today a preferred vernacular.

Although critical of the term "queer", Atluri (2009), on the other hand, reminds us that the term emerged to challenge this binary, and I would add this ever-expanding list:

> "queer" emerged as a radical term that sought to politicize a range of sexualities.
> Queer theory . . . in fact seeks to challenge succinct categories of sexuality and
> gender. Some argue that the main aim of queer theory as a body of scholarship is
> not to study gay and lesbian subjects or same-sex desire, but rather to deconstruct

heteronormativity as the benchmark of normalcy. . . . For that reason, the term continues to have value, particularly in relation to postcolonial sexualities. (p. 2)

Unfortunately, this understanding of the concept is not always recognized.

Sex/Gender Systems

Nanda uses the terms "gender variation" and "gender diversity" to "refer to the fact that cultures construct their sex/gender systems differently and that these systems do not always neatly divide into male and female, man and woman" (Nanda, 2000, p. 1). In her cross-cultural analysis of this phenomenon, she observed that sexuality or sexual orientation was not the main basis for sex/gender variation in many premodern and non-Western societies. The meanings surrounding gender variant behaviours and practices may have been quite different. Among the Native Americans, for example, Nanda notes that occupation and dress may sometimes have been more important in ascribing gender identity than sexual orientation or expression.

Following Rubin (1975) and Nanda (2000), I speak of the sex/gender system as "a set of arrangements by which the biological raw material of human sex and procreation is shaped by human, social intervention and satisfied in a conventional manner, no matter how bizarre some of the conventions may be" (Rubin, p. 165). In my understanding, sex is differentiated from sexuality, the latter being only one of the components of a sex/gender system. Although the concept of gender has been extremely useful in moving us away from biological determinism, as the feminist biologists have noted, it runs the risk of moving us away from bodies as well (Birke, 1999), a factor of which we are reminded by Butler (1999) when she stated that "bodies do matter" and argued: "sexual difference . . . is never simply a function of material differences which are not in some way both marked and formed by discursive practices. Further to claim that sexual differences are indissociable from discursive demarcations is not the same as claiming that discourse causes sexual difference" (p. 235).

Based on my dissatisfaction with the existing hegemonic construct, it is necessary to articulate conceptual formulations that would enlighten and not predetermine our emerging understandings of sex, gender and sexuality in the Caribbean using multiple sexual histories, including those of the premodern, colonial and contemporary Caribbean and the Global South more generally.

Sex/Gender Identity

It could be argued that sex/gender identity is probably the most fundamental trait for human beings. When children are born, they have no sense of themselves as sexed or gendered. But those around them do and relate to them accordingly. Identity therefore is a perception of oneself or a sense of self in relation to others. While human beings may understand themselves as sexed – that is, as biologically or anatomically male or female – and begin to recognize the gendered characteristics of behaviours that go along with their sex, their experience of themselves as sexual beings virtually goes unremarked until it is brought to their attention. This may be done negatively, as in being told by elders "don't do that", or encouragingly, as when Caribbean mothers and aunts wiggle baby boys' penises accusing them of being "just like" their fathers or of smiling when women enter the room – evidence that they "like woman"; in other words assuring themselves and others of their baby son's heterosexuality.

This becomes problematic when one's gender identity differs from one's biological sex, when behaviours or expressions are perceived as inappropriate for one's assigned sex. Western medical science shifted from earlier diagnoses of gender identify disorder to today's term, gender dysphoria, and a range of treatment options emerged: many developed by the famous psychologist and sexologist John Money. Money was also important for developing a protocol to be used when intersexed babies were born, and for decisions on gender re/assignment (Kessler, 2006).

It is also important to differentiate the sex/gender identity through which people develop a sense of themselves as sexed and/or gendered beings from politicized sexual identities that emerge when oppressed groups claim an identity as a basis of resistance and struggle. Such differentiation makes it understandable why in the Western/Euro-American context the identities of gays, lesbians, bisexuals, transgender, queer, questioning and asexuals would emerge under the same rubric. This is because a colonizing Europe, and later the United States, unlike other parts of the world, had developed a conscious and written (textual) and religious oppositionality to what I would call sex/gender variation and diverse gender expression. The process by which this situation developed is well documented (Greenberg, 1988).

Gender Expression

In addition to clear identities as male or female, people are also expected to behave and act or perform their perceived gender in ways appropriate to their sex. These expectations could differ from society to society. For many years, however, the distinction between sex and gender had not been definitively made: what is now called gender-appropriate behaviour was, in many societies, perceived as natural to a person's sex. Differences would arise when society had to grapple with people whose behaviours did not conform with the binary definitions. These variations in meanings and practice are captured by what Nanda (2000) called "gender variation". In some societies, such "nonconforming" people may be treated with ambivalence, fear, ridicule, awe or as possessing special significance. In Hindu India, for instance, categories such as the "hijra" or "koti" exist under which such persons might be classified, and indeed in other parts of South Asia and the Pacific, spaces exist for such groups that may have varying degrees of acceptance and ambivalence, for example, the fa'afafine[2] of Samoa. In other societies – for example, in much of the Global North until recently – the strict classification into binary opposites precluded such ambivalent spaces from emerging. The result often was that persons manifesting specific kinds of nonbinary gender markers would be hidden, made invisible or driven underground. For many of these marginalized persons, sex work often becomes their main means of economic survival.

Colonialisms, Sexual Cultures and Sex/Gender Diversity

The contemporary challenge to homophobia and heteronormativity has had its most visible manifestations in the North Atlantic world. This, in many ways, can be seen as a historical irony, as it was European colonialism that demonized and marginalized many forms of sexual and gender variation found in other parts of the world. In virtually every part of the non-Western world that European colonialists entered, they vilified, attacked, criminalized, demonized, pushed underground, and eventually closeted or made disappear existing forms of sex/gender variation. In most instances, these were practices, behaviours, parts of everyday life or rituals and ceremonies and not necessarily identities. Herdt (1993a), in his review of classic anthropological studies in Melanesia, especially in New Guinea, noted that what he called ritualized homosexuality was part of the sociocultural arrangements of that subregion of the South Pacific; yet these practices were downplayed and denounced by early anthropologists. In New Guinea, Herdt (1993b) identified a specific practice in which young boys were initiated into adulthood through fellatio with adult men, a process that was presumed to endow them with strength and manliness. For Herdt, this practice, which was a component of a larger framework of initiation processes starting around age nine, could be associated with the patriarchal specificities of this geo-ecological region. He associated this practice with an extreme fear of femininity, and a process of separating young boys from the feminine and establishing their manhood. In Sambia, New Guinea, where much of Herdt's research was carried out, there was no conceptualization of a homosexual, as would be understood today (Herdt, 1993, p. 5). While his work was pathbreaking, Herdt was criticized for imposing Western concepts of homosexuality onto a different cultural context. As noted by Anne Fausto-Sterling: "The anthropologist Deborah Elliston, for instance, believes that using the term homosexuality to describe practices of semen exchange in Melanesian societies 'imputes a Western model of sexuality . . . that relies on Western ideas about gender, erotics and personhood, and that ultimately obscures the meanings that hold for these practices in Melanesia'" (2000, p. 18).

Amadiume (1987), in her work among the Nnobi people of Western Nigeria, recorded the fluidity of gender identities that, when necessary, could be shifted from one sex to the other to serve instrumental reasons. She identified the phenomena of "male daughters" and "female husbands" and observed that as a result of Nnobi's flexible gender system, the institution of "male daughters" was "manipulated in the conflicts which arose as a result of the coexistence of principles of individual and collective ownership of land" (p. 32). At the time of her writing, in the 1980s, the head of the first obi (ancestral house or compound) of Nnobi, a minor patrilineage, was a seventy-year-old "male daughter" who, by this status, gained access to land. Amadiume (1987) documents the existence of "female husbands" – wealthy women who married wives as a means of developing lineages in their own right. She observed:

> As men increased their labour force, wealth and prestige through the accumulation of wives, so also did women through the institution of "female husbands". When a man paid money to acquire a woman, she was called his wife. When a woman paid money to acquire another woman, this was referred to as buying a slave, *igba ohu*, but the woman who was bought had the status and customary rights of a wife, with respect to the woman who bought her, who was referred to as her husband, and the "female husband" had the same rights as a man over his wife . . . . It was through this practice of marrying other women that the richest of Eze Okigbo wives obtained their wealth. (p. 46)

But the phenomenon of woman-to-woman marriage (which has been the basis of much contentious discussion and debate) was documented by Njambi and O'Brien (2005) in the 1970s for many different regions of West Africa, Southern Africa, East Africa and the Sudan (p. 45). They challenged Amadiume's instrumentalist understanding of that phenomenon, suggesting that there might have been other reasons for such marriages. Through interviews carried out in 1992 with women involved in woman-to-woman marriage households in one community among the Gikuyu (formerly known as the Kikuyu), the largest ethnic group in Kenya, the authors found that:

> The majority of the ahikania were middle-aged at the time of marriage, and two were in their early 30s. All of the ahiki, the women who accepted the marriage offer, were between the ages of 20–30 when they were married . . . the marriage ceremony

takes place in the same manner for woman-woman marriages as with woman-man marriages. In fact, there is no separate term to differentiate a woman-woman marriage from a woman-man marriage. As woman-woman marriages are not sanctioned by the various Christian churches in the region, kuhikania and uhiki continue to be performed through customary guidelines. (Njambi & O'Brien, 2005, p. 147)

Njambi and O'Brien also questioned the applicability of Amadiume's term "female husbands" in these situations, noting that the initiators of woman-woman marriages "do not identify their roles with maleness" (p. 147). While the existence of sexual relations was not always central to these relationships, Njambi and O'Brien argued that they were characterized by close emotional ties and love and not based solely on socio-economic factors like the acquisition of land or access to childbearing capacity.

In interviews with women in such unions, the authors found a range of possibilities and reasons for such marriages. In rejecting the term "female husband", Njambi and O'Brien cautioned against the imposition of Western understandings of family with its male-female binary onto African woman-woman marriages. Instead, they reported that the women used the words equivalent to co-wife or "partner in marriage" to refer to their partners (p. 158). Such marriage systems survived into the postcolonial period, although condemned by local Christian churches. Njambi and O'Brien referenced baptismal guidelines of the Catholic Church in Kenya at that time, which insisted that women in such marriages leave them immediately and completely or be denied the sacrament. Their children's baptism was also predicated on this. Relatedly, they cite a poll on these marriages carried out by Okongo in 1992 among the Igbo in Nigeria that found that 93.5 per cent of 246 women interviewed disapproved of woman-woman marriage, the result of decades of church pressures (p. 161).

The impact of Western, colonizing versions of Christianity in demonizing, destroying and silencing sex/gender variations of all kinds needs to be recognized. Today, the so-called West or North Atlantic is perceived as the champion of sex/gender diversity, while the so-called Third World or Economic South is perceived as a place of sexual backwardness, rigidity and narrow religious fundamentalism. Additionally, the models, understandings and conceptualizations of sexuality in the postcolonial world now emerge out of the struggles with a Christianity undergirded by the philosophy that sexual activity was acceptable for procreation and for pleasure only within certain parameters.

In contrast, according to Arnfred (2004), precolonial African societies, to some extent even today, distinguished between sex for reproduction (fertility) and sex for pleasure (sexuality); and as a result, nonreproductive sexual activity could take place relatively freely among non-married adults (p. 15). Examples of this include *uksoma* – non-penetrative thigh sex, which made it possible for young men and women in what is now KwaZulu-Natal in South Africa, to engage in sex before marriage without the fear of pregnancy. Similarly, same-sex relations were found to be widespread in Africa as practices but not the basis of fixed identities. They may have occurred as playful sex as a precursor to marriage or alongside heterosexual relationships as pleasure versus procreative sex. With the onset of colonization and Christianity, Arnfred (2004) noted that "Christian lines of thinking and Christian norms for social conduct gained an effective foothold" (p. 17). As a result:

> rules regarding sexuality and fertility coalesced into a single moral code, and norms for male and female sexual behaviours developed along different lines: for a man to have multiple sexual relations with women to whom he was not married became associated in positive ways to masculinity and manhood, *isoka* in Zulu contexts, whereas women were increasingly not allowed to have multiple sexual partners. (Hunter, cited in Arnfred, 2004, p. 17)

It is one of the great ironies of history that in 2013 the Nigerian House of Representatives passed a law banning same-sex marriages when these were acceptable in premodern times. The act "prohibits a marriage contract or civil union entered into between persons of same-sex, and provides penalties for the solemnisation and witnessing of same thereof" (Nigeria: Same Sex Marriage (Prohibition) Act, 2013,[3] 1). It also punishes anyone who enters into a same-sex marriage, or causes one to be celebrated, as well as anyone linked to the registration or support of gay organizations. With increasing knowledge about these precolonial forms and the rise of sexual rights movements globally, there have been two main types of responses from the Global South and those of Global South heritage in the North:

1. The attempt to view sexual and gender diversity and sexual rights as parts of a long and glorious gay and lesbian tradition. This was best reflected in the work of Audre Lorde (1984), who claimed African woman-woman marriage as a part of her heritage as an African American lesbian woman; and
2. A rejection of the fixed identities of the North in favour of what Wekker (1999, p. 125) referred to as multiplicitous sexualities. This is explored further below.

Conceptualizing Sex/Gender Diversity in the Caribbean

In a review of scholarship on Caribbean sexualities, Kempadoo (2009) noted that a growing scholarship on sexualities was emerging in the region, although this was still limited. For Kempadoo, sexual praxis – that is, how sexualities

are practised and expressed – emerged as the key theme in Caribbean scholarship on sexualities. She argued that in this region, "sexuality does not form
a primary basis of social identification and therefore the focus has been on
behaviours, activities and relations". Additionally, she noted: "the specification
of sexual identity groups often elides the very varied sexual arrangements in
the region, and can work to hinder broader understandings of how Caribbean
peoples relate sexually" (Kempadoo, p. 2). Atluri (2009) and others call for a
nuancing of the contemporary rhetoric of the homophobic Caribbean, arguing
that this "is frequently rooted in a neo-colonial paternalism which misses the
often-untranslatable way in which sexualities operate in non-Western contexts"
(p. 2).

One of the most significant contributions on this theme has been Wekker's
classic analysis of mati-work in articles based on her doctoral dissertation
(Wekker, 1993/1994, 1999) which have become a master narrative for postcolonial analyses of same-sex practice. In an earlier publication, Wekker (1993/1994)
described mati-work, an indigenous alternative approach to same-sex relations
among women in her native Suriname, contrasting it with attitudes among
African American lesbians in North America. She noted the early recording
of this phenomenon by a high-ranking Dutch official, A.J. Schimmelpenninck
van den Oye, who, in 1912, had this to say:

> I am referring to the sexual communion between women themselves ('matiplay'),
> which immorality has, as I gather, augmented much in the past decades, and alas!,
> penetrated deeply into popular customs. . . .
>
>   It is not only that young girls and unattached women of various classes make them-
> selves guilty of this, the poorest often going and living together in pairs to reduce the
> cost of house rent and food for each of them, but women who live with men, and even
> school girls, do the same, following the example of others. (Ambacht,1912, pp. 98–99,
> cited in Wekker, 1993/1994, p. 55)

Richard and Sally Price also documented this use of the term *mati* to refer to
men of the Saramaka Maroons also in Suriname, who had been shipmates in
the Middle Passage, and the term *sibi* to refer to a special friendship among
Saramaka women (cited in Wekker, 1993/1994, p. 56). Features of the mati
culture – a form of homosocial and homoerotic bonding among women that
is not exclusive, mentioned in older sources – have been preserved to this day.
These couples often involve an older and a younger woman who would typically have children and maintain ties with men, either as husbands, lovers,
brothers or sons (Wekker, 1999). In the early 1990s, Wekker observed:

> There were, for example, female couples who wore 'parweri': the same dress, women
> who embroidered handkerchiefs with loving texts in silk for each other: 'lobi kon'

(love has come) and 'lobi n'e prati' (love does not go away), women who courted each other by means of special ways of folding and wearing their anisa, headcloths, and finally the widespread institution of 'lobi singi' (love songs) . . . . It is furthermore, important to note that a mati career, for most women, is not a unidirectional path: thus, it is very possible that a woman takes a man for a lover, after having had several relationships with women. It is not unusual for a woman to have a female and a male lover at the same time. Nor does mati life imply restriction to one partner. (Wekker, 1993/1994, pp. 56–57)

In another text, Wekker (1999) contended that the notion of "identity should be problematised by scholars of sexuality as it carries heavy connotations of a static, core and unitary character, which is immutable and brings premature closure" (p. 120). In so doing, she considered mati as drawing heavily on what she perceived as the African heritage of the Creole Surinamese preserved in some religious and cultural traditions. Mati, she observed, unlike "gay" and "lesbian" identity, is not an exclusive category. It is a practice or possibly praxis and is normally spoken of in an active tense as doing mati-work. Mati practitioners, therefore, perceive themselves as engaging in behaviour as opposed to having an identity. This kind of sentiment is also evident in the original notion of *zami,* the French Creole term[4] for same-sex loving among women. In those parts of the Caribbean where the term zami was, or is, used, it was also part of an active rather than passive noun. People spoke of "making zami" or "to make zami", never of "being zami" until Audre Lorde made it her name (Lorde, 1982). Today zami has become an equivalent of lesbian.

Writing on southern Africa in the 1990s, Kendall (1999) reported on the widespread and normative character of erotic relationships among Basotho women of Lesotho, although none identified as lesbian (p. 157). Close and intimate relationships between married women locally called *mpho* relationships, were not conceived of as sexual by colonials, since no penis was involved. Husbands, according to Kendall, would often know about the mpho relationship, the wife's female lover sometimes having a status as a family friend. Woman-woman and woman-man relationships were conceived as differently constructed and thus not mutually threatening (cited in Arnfred, 2004, pp. 21–22).

Wekker proffers the term multiplicitous subjectivities in contrast to the dichotomous either/or hierarchical thinking of the Western system, in which one is either homosexual or heterosexual, with bisexuality "muddying the clear waters". In what Wekker (2006) called a creole (possibly African-influenced) universe, she argued: "A person is conceived of as multiple, malleable, dynamic and possessing male and female elements. Furthermore, all persons are inherently conceived of as sexual beings. . . . It is possible to talk about the self in masculine and in feminine terms, in singular and in plural forms, and in terms of third person constructions, regardless of the gender of the speaker" (Wekker, 1999, pp. 132–133). This approach is supported by Arnfred and other Africanist scholars who argue for "the importance of not only exposing dichotomies but also dissolving them – effectively making them evaporate in order to create a space for radically different lines of thinking" (Arnfred, 2004, pp. 8–9). Mati, sibi and zami all come from words for "friend" – mati from the Dutch *maatje* and *zami* from the French "les amis". Similarly, the word "friending" was used in Trinidad and Tobago and Grenada to describe a long-term non-married sexual relationship. This suggests that close and reciprocal friendship was at the core of these relationships.

But moving beyond colonialism, what is it that continues to nurture and feed contemporary homophobias that have become almost marks of national identity in some parts of the region? A number of propositions may need to be explored. The reconstructed power of fundamentalist religion is one factor, although this varies throughout the region. Linden Lewis observed that levels of tolerance ranged from St Thomas in the Virgin Islands, Trinidad and Tobago, and Barbados, where it was higher, to Jamaica and St Vincent and the Grenadines, where it tended to be lower (Lewis, 2003, pp. 109–114). One can suggest that the power of Protestantism in the latter and mainstream Roman Catholicism in the former may be one explanation, but, in all cases, the more recent US-based Pentecostal and evangelical religious influences may have exacerbated traditional prejudices and masked long-existing tolerances. As posited by Makeda Silvera for Jamaica (2008):

> Our foreparents gained access to literacy through the Bible when they were indoctrinated by missionaries. It provided powerful and ancient stories of strength, endurance, and hope, which reflected their own fight against oppression. This book has been so powerful that it continues to bind our lives with its racism and misogyny. Thus, the importance the Bible plays in Afro-Caribbean culture must be recognized in order to understand the historical and political context for the invisibility of lesbians. The wrath of God "rained down burning sulphur on Sodom and Gomorrah." (Genesis, 19:24) (p. 346)

In his ethnographic study in the anglophone Caribbean, Chevannes (2001) noted the strong sanctions in the region against male homosexuality, in particular among Afro-Caribbean communities, and provides a different explanation. He posited that the hostility towards male homosexuality among Afro-Caribbean males reflected the growing anxiety and insecurity about "achieving traditional terms of domination over women". He found much less anxiety in the Indo-Guyanese community of Overflow, where Indo-Guyanese

men, located in much clearer patriarchal family structures, were less challenged by the feelings of insecurity in relation to women (Chevannes, 2001,
p. 220). Living and working in Trinidad and Tobago, I suggest that much more
work is required in examining this issue.

Indo-Caribbean society, although highly patriarchal, also exists within
a tradition of androgynous deities and a more open acceptance of androgynous practice in social, religious and cultural settings. Nanda observed that in
India, despite the central importance of the "complementary opposition of the
sexes", there is an acknowledgement of a range of sexual variation, ambigui-
ties and transformations, such that "despite the criminalization of many kinds
of transgender behaviour under British rule and even by the Indian government after independence, Indian society has not yet permitted cultural anxiety
about transgenderism to express itself in culturally institutionalised phobias
and repressions" (2000, p. 28). Vertovec, writing on Trinidad in 1992, reported
on the presence of "traditional transvestite dancers" who danced with babies
as a mode of blessing and protection for children at the Sipari Mai[5] Festival
(Vertovec, 1992, p. 220). This practice is no doubt a legacy of the hijra tradition, which still exists in India (Nanda, 1993). In the existing context of ethnic
contestation in the Caribbean, however, the need for a strong Indo-Caribbean
masculinity to confront what is perceived as a hard Afro-Caribbean masculinity has necessitated a distancing from this androgynous tradition, although
it continues in subconscious and unconscious ways at different levels of society
(Puar, 2001).

Towards a New Understanding of Sex/Gender Variation

As we have seen, a binary or dichotomous structure of sex/gender identity
has characterized most societies, and especially those influenced by North
Atlantic colonialism and neocolonialism. Even where so-called third sex or
third-gender identities have existed, they often serve to reinforce the binary
as in the case of the hijras of India, who define themselves as "neither Man
nor Woman" (Nanda, 1993), or the bisexuals who see themselves as open to
sexual relations with both sexes. Even when transsexuals experience gender
identity conflict and seek reassignment, it can be argued that they too are
responding to the strong imperative for clear distinction between male and
female and the impossibility of existing in ambiguity. While this dichotomous
structure has been criticized, it continues to be a strong modifier of systems
of thought.

From the examples given above, it is clear that a great deal of sex/gender
diversity exists not only in relation to actual practices but also in the meanings

attached to the practices and relationships involved. In this situation, it may be better to conceive of sex and gender differences as continua between male and female and masculine and feminine with a range of possibilities in between, rather than as binaries. In teaching on this subject, I often ask my students to locate themselves along these continua. Interestingly, I have always found them happy to do this. In this way, they come to see themselves as variously constructed and to accept sex/gender diversity and variation. They are also able to unfix biological categories, unsettle the notion of deviance and of exclusions, seeing us all as deviant or normative in some way. This approach also has implications for rigid gender-ascribed behaviours that need to be challenged, behaviours such as violence in all forms, perceived as masculine, and the flight from the feminine that traps many Caribbean young men in hypermasculine behaviour that costs them their lives. It also draws our attention to young women, still seeing masculine behaviours as valued and who are increasingly engaging in public and social violence as a means of asserting themselves in peer-approved ways.

Conclusion

This chapter attempted a preliminary exploration of the complex and often taboo subject of sex/gender identity, variation and diverse gender expression. It began by acknowledging the hegemonic binary divisions between male and female, masculine and feminine, sex and gender, but noted that although these are very strongly held in Euro-American traditions as well as others, they do not reflect the complexity of the human sex/gender experience. Indeed, many African, Asian, Pacific and indigenous and pre-Columbian American societies had developed different gender categories and understandings in this regard. While the vocabulary of sex and gender identity categories challenged the dichotomy of sex/gender categorization, in many ways they are derived from these very structures and reinforce their binary character.

It was also found that although the distinction between sex and gender was a useful one in understanding masculinity and femininity, they were both closely interconnected in the construction of individual social identity. In concluding, a new framework for understanding the complexity of sex/gender variation is presented that goes beyond the constraints of existing binary and dichotomous systems of thought. An understanding of sex/gender diversity as continua therefore opens up possibilities for liberating humanity from many of its social constraints. As concluded by Petchesky et al. and the forum Sexuality Policy Watch in their 2008 paper rejecting the notion of sexual minorities – the freaks are all of us!

Notes

1. Recently A was added to mean all-sexual.

2. Some of these countries have now legally and/or socially recognized "third gender" categories, for example, Nepal, Vietnam, Pakistan and Samoa.

3. While this reference is titled 2013, it was signed off by the president of Nigeria in January 2014. As a result, all later references refer to this act as the Nigeria Same-Sex Marriage (Prohibition) Act 2014.

4. Derived from the French *les amis*. Winer (2009, p. 986).

5. Sipari Mai Festival takes place on the Thursday and Friday before Easter each year. It pays homage to the female Sipari ke Mai, the Hindu/Indo-Trinidadian interpretation of La Divina Pastora, a Roman Catholic statue located in the Siparia Roman Catholic Church. For more on this, see Vertovec. (1992, pp. 219–221).

References

Amadiume, I. (1987). *Male daughters, female husbands: Gender and sex in an African society*. London, UK: Zed Books.

Arnfred, S. (2004). Rethinking sexualities in Africa: Introduction. In S. Arnfred, *Rethinking sexualities in Africa*. Uppsala, Sweden: Nordiska Afrikainstitutet.

Atluri, T. (2009). Putting the "Cool" in Coolie: Disidentification, desire and dissent in the work of filmmaker Michelle Mohabeer. *Caribbean Review of Gender Studies, 3*. http://sta.uwi.edu/crgs/november2009/journals/CRGS%20Atluri.pdf

Birke, L. (1999). Bodies and biology. In J. Price & M. Shildrick (Eds.), *Feminist theory and the body: A reader* (pp. 42–49). New York, NY: Routledge.

Butler, J. (1999). Bodies that matter. In J. Price & M. Shildrick (Eds.), *Feminist theory and the body: A reader* (pp. 235–245). New York, NY: Routledge.

Chevannes, B. (2001). *Learning to be a man: Culture, socialization and gender identity in five Caribbean communities*. Kingston, Jamaica: University of the West Indies Press.

Fausto-Sterling, A. (2000). *Sexing the body: Gender politics and the construction of sexuality*. New York, NY: Basic Books.

Greenberg, D. (1988). *The construction of homosexuality*. Chicago: University of Chicago Press.

Herdt, G. (1993a). Ritualized homosexuality in the male cults of Melanesia: 1862–1983: An introduction. In G. Herdt (Ed.), *Ritualized homosexuality in Melanesia* (pp. 1–81). Berkeley: University of California Press.

Herdt, G. (1993b). Rituals of manhood: Male initiation in Papua New Guinea. In C.B. Brettell & C.F. Sargent (Eds.), *Gender in cross-cultural perspective* (pp. 82–92). Englewood Cliffs, NJ: Prentice-Hall.

Human Rights Watch. (2016). *"Tell me where I can be safe": The impact of Nigeria's Same Sex Marriage (Prohibition) Act*. http://us-cdn.creamermedia.co.za/assets /articles/attachments/65231_nigeria1016_web.pdf

Jackson, S. (2003). Heterosexuality, heteronormativity and gender hierarchy: Some reflections on recent debates. In J. Weeks, J. Holland, & M. Waites (Eds.), *Sexualities and society: A reader* (pp. 69–83). Cambridge, UK: Polity.

Kempadoo, K. (2009). Caribbean sexuality: Mapping the field. *Caribbean Review of Gender Studies, 3.* http://sta.uwi.edu/crgs/november2009/journals/Kempadoo.pdf

Kendall, K. (1999). Women in Lesotho and the (Western) construction of homophobia. In E. Blackwood & S. Wieringa (Eds.), *Female desires: Same-sex relations and transgender practices across cultures* (pp. 157–178). New York, NY: Columbia University Press.

Kessler, S. (2006). The medical construction of gender: Case management of intersexed infants. In V. Taylor, L. Whittier, & N. Rupp (Eds.), *Feminist Frontiers VII* (pp. 25–41). New York, NY: McGraw-Hill.

Lewis, L. (2003). Caribbean masculinity: Unpacking the narrative. In L. Lewis (Ed.), *The culture of gender and sexuality in the Caribbean* (pp. 94–125). Gainesville: University Press of Florida.

Lorde, A. (1982). *Zami: A new spelling of my name: A biomythography.* Berkeley, CA: Ten Speed Press.

Lorde, A. (1984). *Sister outsider: Essays and speeches.* Trumansberg, NY: Crossing Press.

Nanda, S. (1993). Neither man nor women: The hijras of India. In C. Brettell & C. Sargent (Eds.), *Gender in cross-cultural perspective* (pp. 173–179). Englewood Cliffs, NJ: Prentice-Hall.

Nanda, S. (2000). *Gender diversity: Cross-cultural variations.* Prospect Heights, IL: Waveland Press.

Nigeria Same Sex Marriage (Prohibition) Act, 2013. https://www.refworld.org/docid/52f4d9cc4.html

Njambi, W.N., & O'Brien, W. (2005). Revisiting woman-woman marriage: Notes on Gikuyu women. In Oyèrónkẹ́ Oyewǔmi (Ed.), *African gender studies: A reader* (pp. 145–165). New York, NY: Palgrave.

Petchesky, R., in collaboration with S. Correa, I. Saiz, & H. Baaghat. (2008). *Position paper on the language of "sexual minorities" and the politics of identity.* Sexuality Policy Watch. http://www.sxpolitics.org/wp-content/uploads/2009/03/sexual-minorities1.pdf

Puar, J. (2001). Global circuits: Transnational sexualities in Trinidad. *Signs: Journal of Women in Culture and Society, 26*(4), 1093–1065.

Richardson, D. (2000). Heterosexuality and social theory. In Diane Richardson (Ed.), *Theorising Heterosexuality* (pp. 1–20). Buckingham, UK: Open University Press.

Rubin, G. (1975). The traffic in women: Notes on the political economy of sex. In R. Reiter (Ed.), *Toward an anthropology of women* (pp. 157–210). New York, NY: Monthly Review Press.

Silvera, M. (2008) (1992). Man royals and sodomites: Some thoughts on the invisibility of Afro-Caribbean lesbians, in Thomas Glave (Ed.), *Our Caribbean: A gathering of Lesbian and Gay Writing from the Antilles* (pp. 344–354). Durham, NC: Duke University Press.

Vertovec. S. (1992). *Hindu Trinidad: Religion, ethnicity and socio-economic change.* London and Basingstoke, UK: Macmillan Caribbean.

Wekker, G. (1993/1994). Mati-ism and black lesbianism: Two ideal typical expressions of female homosexuality in black communities of the diaspora. In *SWI Forum,* Special Issue Vrouwen en Suriname, 10/2 and 11/1, pp. 52–65.

Wekker, G. (1999). What's identity got to do with it? Rethinking identity in light of the mati work in Suriname. In E. Blackwood & S. Wieringa (Eds.), *Female desires: Same-sex relations and transgender practices across cultures*. New York, NY: Columbia University Press.

Wieringa, S., & Sívori, H. (2013). Sexual politics in the global south: Framing the discourse. In S. Wierenga & H. Sívori (Eds.), *The sexual history of the global south: Sexual politics in Africa, Asia, and Latin America* (pp. 1–21). London, UK: Zed Books.

Winer, L. (2009), *Dictionary of the English-Creole of Trinidad and Tobago*. Montreal and Kingston, Canada: McGill/Queens University Press.

Young, K. (1988). Notes on the social relations of gender. In P. Mohammed & C. Shepherd (Eds.), *Gender in Caribbean development* (pp. 97–109). St Augustine, Trinidad: University of the West Indies, Women and Development Studies Project.

3.

The Variability of the Sexes from a Sociobiological Perspective

RONALD E. YOUNG

This article aims to clarify some of the issues surrounding the nature-nurture debate and to suggest a biologically guided approach to understanding and treating some of the controversies relating to gender/sex differences. It intends to present the complexity of the process of sex determination and to show the myriad opportunities for diversion from the targeted norms of standard male and female during the developmental process.

Sex differences are taken to refer to the complex constellation of physical differences, anatomical or functional (e.g., hormonal), associated with male-ness or femaleness. Gender is taken to encompass and be grounded in these sex differences, but to include, in addition, the behavioural and social features, whether generated by genetic programming, sociocultural conditioning or an inseparable amalgam of both. The WHO definition (http://www.who.int /gender/whatisgender/en/index.html) limits the application of gender to the assigned role, and this, of course, is what differentiates the concept of gender from that of sex.

Popular though not authoritative usage, however, tends to be looser (http://en .wikipedia.org/wiki/Gender). Statements such as "Gender is a continuum – no perfect bimodality exists: hair growth, vocal tone, breasts, clitoris/penis differ-ence, an Adam's apple, are all equivocal differentiators", which clearly focuses on physical differences; or "[There is] . . . no evidence that gender differences in neurophysiology are due to anything other than cultural conditioning", which focuses on acculturation; or "Gender is a label we give to people to keep things simple" – abound in articles on the Internet.[1] To a biologist, they at best over-state the case, or at worst are simply untrue. To some extent they may arise as a consequence of semantics. So if we say that "Gender is assigned social role versus sex which is biologically determined", then by definition, we may say that gender, the assigned behavioural roles of the sexes, is indeed not geneti-cally determined. There can, however, be no doubt that the willingness of indi-viduals to fit into socially defined roles, the contribution of these definitions to the success of the society that promulgates them, and hence the long-term viability of the sociocultural indicators adopted, will be built upon a physical/biological foundation. Certainly, evidence from studies on infants, both human (Pasterski et al., 2005) and monkey (Alexander & Hines, 2002; Hines & Alexander, 2008), although not without flaws, strongly indicate that there are early differences in behavioural preferences (choice of toys) between males and females, which could not be based solely or primarily upon acculturation, and which fall in line with the typical stereotypes of male and female inclinations. This suggests that differential choice of toys is contingent upon the basic biological differentiation between males and females rather than upon a completely flexible, culturally invented convention. It is hardly possible to completely disentangle the assignment of sociocultural gender roles from the basic biological differentiation on which this role definition must rest, but it would also be folly to disregard the important role that culturally developed conventions play in determining the precise manifestations of inherent, biologically programmed tendencies.

The important question then, is how the two – biological sex and gender, biologically programmed and culturally assigned behaviour of the sexes – relate to each other. This chapter proposes that aspects of our behaviour, including many nuances of personal interactions that hitherto appeared inexplicable, become readily understandable when analysed in the light of the principles of sociobiology: that is, in terms of the strategic advantages conferred upon individuals or families or communities of related individuals, in passing on genes that predispose them to develop certain anatomical, physiological or behavioural characteristics. We are, in this respect, more creatures of our genetics than was suspected prior to the insights of sociobiology. We should not, however, be misguided by this conception into a fatalistic view of the ways in which our genomes determine who we are. The Canadian neurophysiologist Donald Hebb, when asked what was more important, nature or nurture, is reported to have asked in return, "What is more important in determining the area of a rectangle, Length or Breadth?" (qtd. in Meaney, 2004). Genes express themselves through their interactions with the environment. They do not simply dictate that a characteristic should be so and have it happen but are involved in a continuous, bidirectional dialogue with the environment and with each other.

Animals, including humans, have developed quite complex and exacting mechanisms, discussed below, for ensuring the expression of two complementary phenotypes – male or female. This is contingent upon the fact that in order for individuals to out-compete others in passing their genes into the next generation through sexual reproduction, members of each sex have to advertise their desirability to the opposite sex and send clear signals concerning their identity. This does not presuppose a rigidly dichotomous distinction between a precisely defined male and female type. Indeed, each individual has to try to signal to potential mates just why he, she or it (these principles are as true for animals as for humans) is more desirable than potential competitors and may go to fanciful extremes in order to achieve this. One may think of tails of the peacock or the streamer-tailed hummingbird (but should also note that penguins on the other hand, are not usually sexually dimorphic in appearance). This inherently posits that a significant degree of variability must exist both in terms of the preferences of those being courted and the competitive offerings of the suitors.

Inevitably and importantly for the process of evolution, complex biological systems tend to be quite variable, producing genetically inheritable outcomes that form the basis for the vaunted "survival of the fittest" in terms of ability to pass on their genetic endowment into the next generation. The genetically programmed developmental processes that determine the multifaceted features characterizing the male and female sexes are, in fact, much more intricate than the basic relationships that can be portrayed in an article of this type and, in addition, may be subject to many environmental influences. The variations generated, therefore, will sometimes fall, actually or potentially, outside of the apparent organizational "intent" of the process. In nature, these genetic variations form the basis for innovation and evolution, with the acid test being only whether the variations in our genetic endowment are advantageous given the natural/social environment in which they occur. The incidence of any particular genetically governed variation, then, will rise or fall in the population based upon the reproductive advantage conferred upon those individuals *or groups* that carry the genes that engender the particular characteristic.

The Chromosomal Determination of Sex

In humans, sex is determined by whether individuals inherit from their parents a matching pair of sex-determining chromosomes (X chromosomes) or an asymmetrical pair, comprising one X and a much smaller Y chromosome, carrying several genes that are quite different from those on the partner X chromosome. Females, then, have two X chromosomes (XX configuration), which carry matching genes along their length, while males have one X and one Y chromosome (XY configuration). These X/Y chromosomes are called the "sex chromosomes".

Each of us has in each cell of our body 46 chromosomes – 23 pairs – with one of each pair coming from our mother and one from our father. For all pairs, except for the sex chromosomes as described above, the maternal and paternal chromosomes are similar in size and shape and carry matching genes governing particular characteristics. When you produce reproductive cells (eggs or spermatozoa), your corresponding maternal and paternal chromosomes are separated by an intricate mechanism (called reduction division), so that each reproductive cell produced by the division receives only one member of each pair – maternal or paternal – and a total of only 23 chromosomes, some from your mother and some from your father. Since females have 44 somatic plus two X (sex) chromosomes in each somatic (body) cell, each ovum or egg (reproductive cell) will have 22 "somatic" chromosomes and one X (sex) chromosome (22+X). Half of the millions of sperms in males will have 22 "somatic" chromosomes and one X (sex) chromosome (22+X); the other half will have 22 "somatic" chromosomes and one Y (sex) chromosome (22+Y). Therefore, when an egg is fertilized by a spermatozoon, the resulting cell will once again have 46 chromosomes: 23 from mother's egg and 23 from father's sperm. If the successful sperm was Y-bearing, then the resulting cell would be XY configuration (44+XY) and so would develop into a male. If it was an X-bearing sperm, then the fertilized egg would be XX configuration (44+XX) and so develop into a female. Since there are equal numbers of X- and Y-bearing sperms, this complex and exquisitely organized process ensures that, all other things being equal, half the children conceived will, on the whole, be female and half of them will be male, each with a random mixture of paternal and maternal variants of each gene, a process clearly evolved to ensure the continuity of the species. Despite the clearly targeted mechanisms, however, embedded in the complexity of the process is the potential for divergent outcomes. Some of these are nonviable and do not survive. Others are viable and tolerated to the extent permitted by the full biological context in which the variations leading to the divergence operate.

Occasionally, the well-orchestrated process of so-called "reduction division" (meiosis), ensuring that each egg produced by the division receives exactly one of each pair of matching chromosomes, goes astray, so that both members of a pair of X chromosomes end up in one of the eggs produced by the division (22+XX), with no X chromosome going to the other (22+O). If an egg of the first sort is fertilized by an X-bearing sperm, the resulting offspring will have the 44+XXX configuration (47 chromosomes) and will develop into a female; if the fertilizing sperm is Y-bearing, we will have a 44+XXY male. If the second type of egg (22+O) is fertilized, we would have a foetus with 45 chromosomes in all, with a configuration of either 44+XO (a female, with variable reproductive dysfunction, but sometimes very functional) or 44+YO (potentially male, but nonviable). Whenever a Y chromosome is present, whether there are one or many X chromosomes, the outcome is a male, although when extra X chromosomes are present along with a Y, there may be a degree of feminization (breast development, smaller genitalia, etc.). In the absence of a Y chromosome, a female develops.

So as we have seen, males generally have only one X chromosome, and females generally have two in each body cell. To avoid having a double-dose of X chromosome products in the female, only one of her two X chromosomes remains fully functional. Extra X chromosomes become at least partly inactivated or "heterochromatinized" to form a shrunken, deeply staining blob known as a Barr body. Normal XX females thus have a single Barr body in the nucleus of each cell; XXX females will have two since there are two extra X chromosomes. Normal males bearing XY chromosomes do not have a Barr body because they have only one X chromosome. However, XXY males, like normal females, will have one. This, then, has been used as a simple test to diagnose (e.g., in the context of athletics) so-called "genetic sex": males have no Barr body; females have one. Of course, as might be expected, many variations on these chromosomal configurations exist, and they are not restricted to the sex-determining chromosomes. One must note also that even with a given chromosomal configuration, the final, overt outcomes may vary considerably, suggesting that the link between genetic composition and final phenotype is simply not as rigorous as one might expect. The existence of chromosome inactivation, effects such as gene amplification or suppression, and variations in the extent to which these occur, based upon the particular composition of the genome and the specific environmental conditions, bring great complexity to the outcomes.

Underlying Mechanisms

But to focus simply on chromosomal variations is really to look at the surface without getting to the underlying mechanisms. Why does the presence of a Y chromosome result in the development of a male? We know that one of the unique Y chromosome genes, not present on the X chromosome and known as SRY (sex-determining region of the Y chromosome), produces a protein that activates other genes that control, among other things, the development of a testis and the production, in the testis, of testosterone and a substance known as anti-Mullerian hormone (AMH). SRY also appears to directly influence differential development in specific areas of the brain related to the regulation of movement and aggression (Dewing et al., 2006).

The human foetus in the early stages has the potential to develop either male or female reproductive systems. In the absence of a Y chromosome and its products (such as SRY protein), the bipotential gonads develop into ovaries; and in the absence of testosterone, the precursors of the male internal reproductive ducts degenerate before the end of the first trimester of pregnancy. In the presence of the Y chromosome – actually of the SRY protein and related products – the gonads develop into testes, which produce testosterone and AMH as well as sperms later at puberty. AMH causes the degeneration of the precursors of the female internal reproductive system, and testosterone promotes the development and differentiation of the male internal reproductive ducts and of male external genitalia.

In fact, the more potent stimulus for the development of male external genitalia is not testosterone itself, but a substance known as dihydrotestosterone, produced from testosterone by the enzyme 5α-reductase (5AR), which is present in certain tissues – such as those that may develop into the external male genitals. Dysfunction of this enzyme can cause genetic males (44+XY) to develop with normal but undescended testes and female-like external genitalia. The female internal ducts will still degenerate under the influence of the AMH from the testes, and male characteristics determined by testosterone, as opposed to dihydrotestosterone, will still develop. Such males will usually be perceived as females and brought up as females, but at puberty, the testosterone surge may, despite the weakly functioning 5AR enzyme, produce sufficient dihydrotestosterone to induce the development of normal male external genitalia and the descent of the testes. This produces a syndrome known as "Guevedoce" ("penis at 12", or "testicles at 12" in some interpretations) in the Dominican Republic, where this deficiency is relatively common in an isolated community (Imperato-McGinley, Guerrero, Gautier & Peterson, 1974). The cause for this increased incidence was ascribed to the spread of a random mutation in a group with an unusual degree of inbreeding, but Imperato-McGinley and her group also insightfully suggest that "heterozygotes may have a selective advantage which contributes to gene frequency". Some reports claim that these individuals do become functional males and have children, in spite of their early acculturation as females (Price et al., 1984) – an important "natural" experiment in the nature-nurture debate. Other evidence appears to suggest that in different cultural settings (e.g., in the United States), such males tend to develop sexual preference for males, emphasizing the point that neither genes nor environment exerts sole and unchallenged control over functional outcomes, but that an accepting cultural milieu can influence one's ability to adopt one role or another or to easily transit between roles. It is interesting to note, however, that in describing their sample of four persons with 5AR deficiency (the enzyme that regulates the production of dihydrotestosterone from testosterone), Price et al. (1984) noted that despite being raised in a culture that was not accepting of gender reversals:

The four men with 5α-reductase deficiency were reared as girls but had disturbances of gender role and identity during childhood. They all exhibited tomboyish behaviour, and at some stage between ages four and ten each came to feel that he was a male but nevertheless continued to play a female role for several years. Eventually, each of the four changed gender role to that of men and claimed unequivocal male gender identity. Each of the men has heterosexual orientation. (p. 1497)

This begs the conclusion that while dihydrotestosterone influences the development of external genitalia and hair distribution characteristic of males, testosterone or other Y chromosome products may act upon the developing brain to determine sexual orientation and preferences.

We have said that during the formation of the reproductive cells (ova and sperms), the members of the matched pairs of maternal and paternal chromosomes are separated so that each sex cell has one member of each pair – either the one from the mother or the one from the father, randomly assorted. This, in fact, is not quite true, because in the process of separation of the chromosomal pairs, the maternal and paternal congeners come together and exchange material. Part of the paternal chromosome carrying particular paternal variants of the genes in a given region of the chromosome interchanges with maternal segments of the chromosome pair, carrying maternal variants of the same genes. So the final chromosomes are no longer strictly maternal or paternal in origin. This ensures a more thorough mixing of maternal and paternal characteristics in the offspring. In the case of the sex chromosomes, a similar process may occur in females since the two X chromosomes have similar genes at similar locations, and interchange of material can take place without untoward consequences. In males, however, the quite dissimilar X and Y chromosomes have only a few genes in common, so that interchange of materials must be severely restricted.

Occasionally, however, a piece of a chromosome, carrying its characteristic genes, may break off and attach to another chromosome that normally should not carry the genes involved. This, of course, can lead to serious consequences. If, for example, a segment of the Y chromosome containing the SRY gene translocates to an X chromosome, then any potential XX female who happens to inherit the X chromosome with the SRY bit attached will have the developing gonad transformed into a testis under the influence of the SRY protein. We can thus end up, unusually, with an XX male (de la Chapelle, Hästbacka, Korhonen & Mäenpää, 1990) who, because the full complement of Y chromosome genes are not available, will sometimes not develop in the fully male pattern, displaying ambiguous genitals and perhaps some breast development; conversely, if the Y chromosome missing the critical SRY component is inherited, the outcome could be a 44+XY female (Fechner et al., 1993; Ellaithi et al., 2006).

As if this is not complicated enough, it should also be noted that, perhaps not surprisingly, the triggering hormones and factors that help to ensure typical sexual development (many not discussed here) may influence numerous targets and processes (related to secondary sexual characteristics) besides those involved with the internal and external genital precursors. They also target bone development, hair-growth patterns, brain dopamine levels and other functional and anatomical developments in the brain (Dewing et al., 2006), notably in the hypothalamus and related areas, which play an important role in regulating the nature and timing of hormonal secretions, and even susceptibility to certain diseases (e.g., schizophrenia and Parkinson's disease) differentially in males and females. Genes, in concert with appropriate environmental cues and contributions, help to ensure that hormones of required potency are produced in suitable concentrations at the scheduled times (note the case of "Guevedoce" above). All of this contributes to the many secondary sexual characteristics, structural and behavioural, that help to differentiate between males and females, and among males and females, and to provide the physical substratum for the differences between the sexes.

There are myriad feedback mechanisms that are geared towards ensuring that once a foetus is committed to become a male or a female, the developmental pathways are faithfully followed to keep the unfolding process on track. The very complexity of the process of sex determination, however, means that the final outcome is quite variable, and does not conform to an unequivocally dualistic construct of strict male or female. We have discussed some of the more extreme variations, but the consequence of the unimaginable combinations and permutations of variations that may occur among the innumerable processes that influence the final outcome means that what might be defined as "normal" maleness or femaleness comprise somewhat blurred, multidimensional modes around which there is significant variation. Through the stark lens of biological reality, not only the poles of male and female, but also the variations and intermediates thrown up by nature and the developmental process, are decidedly normal in the broadest sense, and also are existentially inevitable. The question we must face is exactly how we shall treat with this reality, and the consequences that we might face depending upon our decisions. We address some of these issues below.

Defining Markers of Normality

The existence of identifiable modal male and female characteristics that are biologically meaningful and relevant is incontestable. The fact, however, is that the boundaries that demarcate what is accepted as societally "normal" are quite arbitrarily placed and vary from time to time and from society to society, often for reasons that are difficult to fathom. In the final analysis, any attempt to rigidly define gender as an inflexible, dichotomous construct will have to face the real underlying biological variability, and the consequent discomfort of fit that will affect individuals whose biology does not allow them to find congruence with rigidly defined markers of normality. It should be noted, therefore, that the statement quoted in the introductory paragraph ("Gender is a continuum . . .") is simply an overstatement of the genuine variability of the sexes; its emphasis on continuity is misplaced, as is its reference to only physical attributes in relation to gender.

A significant population of persons, therefore, do not fall within the modal construct of the "standard" male or female patterns. The resulting disjoint between the reality of biological variability and any overly confining definitions of gender roles, attitudes and behaviours will have consequences – both for the individuals involved and for the society – and can take its toll in terms of psychological disequilibrium and physiological debilitation of immunological function (Trivers, 2011). We must, in the face of this, ask whether the existence of this group of persons with non-modal, intersexual characteristics is biologically tolerable. Is this not a waste of biological potential? Why does nature permit the existence of such variations, with presumably impaired ability to pass on their genes into the next generation? Why hasn't the developmental process been evolutionarily fixed to minimize such variations? To answer these questions, we need to engage the concepts of sociobiology, of "kin selection" and the broader concept of "inclusive fitness" (Hamilton, 1964a, b). I will not expand greatly upon any of these concepts, but in the next section I will try to illustrate some of the basic biological principles governing inheritance beyond the level of individuals, and influencing the frequencies of genetic variations in populations, using an example that is devoid of some of the more emotive aspects of gender determination. We will look also at how biology influences gender roles and how gender roles can in turn, through the evolutionary process, influence biology.

The Sociobiology of Sexuality: Gender Issues

Males and females are very different. Females produce a single, relatively large, fertile egg once per month. If this egg becomes fertilized, it embeds in the uterine wall and develops over a nine-month period, nurtured parasitically on maternal supplies. This is then followed by a period of maybe a year or so when the baby is fed, again from maternally supplied milk, with the process of suckling helping to further delay the ability of the mother to produce another egg. (This is another interesting genetically programmed outcome with clear survival advantage for the child and a delicate balance between the implications for the successful outcome of a given pregnancy, versus the evident biological advantage of being able to produce another child as soon as possible). From a purely physical perspective, therefore, a woman has a great deal invested in every child she has. It is in her interest to ensure that this investment is a good one and is not wasted. It is, then, not hard to see that a woman should be careful to ensure that the father who fertilizes her eggs has "good genes" and is likely to be supportive, and that her child is nurtured and cared for. She therefore needs to be quite selective of the male with whom she chooses to mate, judging to the best of her ability whether the characteristics he has, and will thus be likely to pass on to her children, will help them to better survive and reproduce successfully.

Males, on the other hand, produce millions of tiny spermatozoa and, at least potentially, can fertilize many eggs within a short spell. Because of their relatively minimal biological investment in the process, it may well appear that it would be biologically advantageous for males to adopt a strategy of fertilizing as many women as possible, who will invest in and raise his children for him, with minimal demands on him, while ensuring that other males do not fertilize these women, competitively pre-empting their time in gestating and rearing children that are not his. Both males and females, of course, adopt counterstrategies in response to their divergent basic "inclinations", and these, directed by a combination of genetic and social/environmental characteristics, give rise to thoroughly engrossing and intricately complicated characteristics of the mating rituals in our various societies. There are, in fact, many very good reasons why a male should be quite selective of his mates and should invest in ensuring that his children are protected, well nurtured and grow into competitive adults. Males, moreover, must advertise such propensities and any others (real or simulated) that can convince females, potential mates, that their genes are better than those of their competitors, making them a better choice as a mate and father for their children. It is for such reasons that males have evolutionarily been equipped with stronger bone and muscles and greater aggressive tendencies than women, through the evolved influence of the sex-determining hormones on bone, muscle and brain structure and function. But even this is an extremely simplistic scenario. In modern society, protecting, nurturing and ensuring the development of successful and competitive children involves rather more than simply fighting off predators and competitors. Features that might have primevally been critical for success may no longer be pertinent. In societies with extended families, additional factors come into play. For example, the question has to be asked whether, by investing in enhancing the success of a brother's or sister's children, an individual might be able to increase the probability that genes *like* his or hers (though not his or her own) will be successfully passed on through successive generations. Thinking along such lines allows us to see why the evolutionary process might not have been more rigorous in ensuring that the differences between the sexes are strictly defined and preserved. Because we share particular varieties of genes with our close relatives, a gene that diminishes the reproductive success of an individual can be biologically beneficial if that same gene allows for characteristics that improve the reproductive success of a sufficient number of relatives who may carry identical copies of the same gene, to counterbalance the negative effect in the individual (Hamilton, 1964a, b). This is referred to as "kin selection". An extreme example of this can be seen in worker bees who sacrifice their own reproductive ability to ensure that their sisters (with whom they share a rather large quantum of identical genes – more, in fact, than they would share with their own daughters) are extremely successful and can pass on their genes in copious numbers to the next generation (Hamilton, 1964b).

I here digress in order to share a simple example, not related to sexual differentiation, but that illustrates the way in which, given a particular environment, a characteristic that might inherently seem to be detrimental can actually be beneficial. We all carry the red pigment haemoglobin in our red blood cells. This allows us to pick up oxygen from the air and release it at the cells in our bodies, where we can literally slow-burn the sugars that we consume to produce the energy needed for all our activities. An essential part of the haemoglobin molecule is a protein specified by a particular gene. An error in this gene can cause a single amino acid in this protein to be replaced by a different one, producing a variant of haemoglobin called Haemoglobin-S that behaves differently from normal haemoglobin. It still picks up oxygen in the lungs and releases it at the tissues, but when it releases the oxygen, instead of retaining its usual properties, it becomes insoluble and crystallizes in the red blood cells, causing them to become misshapen – sickle shaped – and to block up the small capillaries in the tissues. The misshapen cells are quickly destroyed by the body so that we become anaemic and have to continuously produce more red blood cells – a drain on our resources. Now remember that we each have two copies of each chromosome – one from father and one from mother. If both copies have this variant gene, then all of our haemoglobin is defective, and we suffer from the condition known as sickle cell anaemia, which is characterized by painful crises and often, early death. If we inherit only one defective gene, then only half of our haemoglobin is faulty and the condition, known as sickle cell trait, is not so severe and we can function quite normally, although our red cells are still quite short-lived and the situation is not fully satisfactory. In most populations, because of the inherent disadvantages of Haemoglobin-S – primarily the relatively frequent failure of persons with sickle cell disease to survive to reproductive age – the gene occurs at a vanishingly low frequency. It so happens, however, that because of the relatively short life span of the red blood cells in this condition, the malaria parasite (which develops within the red blood cells) tends to be destroyed along with the cells, before they can come to maturity. In areas rife with malaria therefore, persons with the sickle cell trait – so-called "heterozygotes" with one defective and one normal gene – are protected from malaria and at the same time do not have the severe symptoms of sickle cell anaemia. Persons with normal haemoglobin are readily infected with malaria and may die early, as may persons with full sickle cell anaemia. Thus, because of the relative advantage conferred by the trait in heterozygotes, the incidence of the sickle cell gene rises considerably in populations intensely affected by malaria. A genetic variation, then, which seemed inherently a bad thing, has thus become a distinct advantage as a result of a critical environmental feature. Populations that moved from areas endemic for malaria to areas with little or no malaria still display relatively high incidence of the sickle cell gene; but with every generation, its frequency is falling, a subtle but clear illustration of the fact that evolution – a change in the genetics of our populations to better adapt us to our environments – is continuously in progress.

If we transpose the lessons learned from sickle cell anaemia to the admittedly more complex situation relating to gender differentiation, we can begin to understand just how intricate the interplay of genetic endowment and environmental circumstances can become. Again, the question of whether a particular characteristic is genetically or environmentally determined is not a simple one, and may even be irrelevant in the fullness of time. So too is the issue of whether a particular characteristic – genetically or environmentally pushed – is "good" or "bad". The essential thesis of this paper is that we must judge the efficacy of such characteristics by balancing the costs and benefits of structural and functional variations to individuals as well as to populations, in terms of their contribution ultimately to reproductive success. Especially in the face of rapidly changing circumstances and conditions, we must be careful about applying judgements that are based upon anachronistic conceptions of our present realities. But we must also guard against adopting crusading attitudes that prejudge propensities and predilections based upon philosophical or moralistic positions adopted without a deeper understanding of the biological and sociocultural conditions that govern the human condition and in which our definitions of who and what we are must be firmly rooted.

In *Deceit and Self-Deception*, referred to earlier, Trivers (2011) outlines the biological bases for many of these phenomena, and introduces the new dimension of internally or externally directed deception and its effects on our psychology and physiology – cautioning us to be particularly careful in interpreting and analysing issues bearing upon our own self-concept, because, often for our own good, we have difficulty being objective about such matters. We have a strong propensity to dismiss or gloss over findings that appear contradictory to our preferred positions, and to seize upon findings that are supportive, as vindication of our correctness. But Popper (2002 [first published in 1935]) long ago cautioned that understanding of phenomena progresses best when scientists formulate clear hypotheses, logically predict what the consequences of these hypotheses should be, and through critical experimentation or interrogation of reality as it exists seek to knock down or disprove these favoured hypotheses and the deductions to which they lead. This central principle that should guide our search for an objective understanding of reality is too often forgotten. We ignore these warnings at our own peril.

Lessons from Sociobiology

What then have we learned from the admittedly detailed, but still woefully limited, foregoing review? My purpose was not simply to force you to revisit and extend your high school biology. It was rather to allow you to apprehend directly the complexity of the process of sex determination and to see the myriad opportunities for diversion from the targeted norms of standard male and female during the developmental process. We must then superimpose upon this the environmental influences that involve the issues of group dynamics and self-identification with "in" or "out" groups, and the many ways in which the biological and social forces can help or hinder reproductive success measured in terms of passing our genes (or genes like ours) from one generation to the next. This is further complicated when the importance of sexual behaviour as a social organizer is recognized – not only as a human artifice, but as a basic biological attribute that we share in common with animal societies (de Waal, 1995). For the present purposes, we should clearly see that variations in sexual drive and orientation can arise in so many ways that it is fruitless to try to classify all sexual variations in a unitary fashion and to hem them in through rigidly prescribed gendering. It is as wrong to try to lump all variations in sexual proclivity into a single bag as it would be to assert that "all whites are voracious exploiters" or that "all blacks are kind and generous". This is a matter of the individual human right to be judged upon individual actions and the consequences – positive or negative, to the society and to other individuals – of these actions. We must understand that where variations are tolerated biologically at relatively high frequencies, it will usually mean that these variations do make some contribution, however subtle, to the overall success of the population. We need, therefore, to be much more fine-grained in our treatment of variations from the accepted norms, in the definition of what comprises an accepted norm, and be willing to differentiate between those variations that are real threats to social order and those that are not. To return to Hebb's reported assertion, behavioural preferences of individuals are based upon a vast number of factors, some biological, some social; some driven by biological imperatives, others motivated by social choice or cultural channelling that cannot be wholly independent of the biological underpinnings. Whatever the particular combination of factors determining sexual preference, any individual case must be judged on its own merits and demerits, and not painted with a broad brush. And here we speak not just of sexual preference, but of just about any human characteristic that you might choose. We all strive to fit in or differentiate ourselves from various groups in our societies with varying degrees of success: the sports buffs, the party people, the intelligentsia or the sufferers. We may find ourselves identified with a particular group as a result of social pressures, family history and/or biological propensity; we may succumb reluctantly, revolt against the classification, embrace the role wholeheartedly or we may find ourselves pathologically conflicted. It is no different with sexual orientation/gender identity, and a humane society must be sensitive to these highly textured nuances and accept the variations that form the substrate of our society's ongoing richness and potential evolution towards a more robust and equitable condition, better suited for facing changing and uncertain futures.

Note

1. I have refrained from quoting the sources of these statements since I refer to them merely as indicative usages – samples that can readily be accessed – and not as authoritative sources to be supported or refuted.

References

Alexander, G. M., & Hines, M. (2002). Sex differences in response to children's toys in nonhuman primates (*Cercopithecus aethiops sabaeus*). *Evolution and Human Behavior, 23*, 467–479.

De la Chapelle, A., Hästbacka, J., Korhonen, T., & Mäenpää, J. (1990). The etiology of XX sex reversal. *Reproduction Nutrition Development, 30*(Suppl 1), 39s–49s. DOI 10.1051/rnd:19900704

De Waal, F. (1995, March). Bonobo sex and society. *Scientific American*, 82–88.

Dewing, P., Chiang, C.W.K., Sinchak, K., Sim, H., Fernagut, P., Kelly, S., . . . Vilain, E. (2006). Direct regulation of adult brain function by the male-specific factor SRY. *Current Biology, 16*, 415–420. DOI 10.1016/j.cub.2006.01.017

Ellaithi, M., Gisselsson, D., Nilsson, T., Abd El-Fatah, S., Ali, T., Elagib, A., . . .
Fadl-Elmula, I. (2006). A del(X)(p11) carrying SRY sequences in an infant with
ambiguous genitalia. *BMC Pediatrics, 6*, 11–15. DOI 10.1186/1471-2431-6-11

Fechner, P.Y., Marcantonio, S.M., Jaswaney, V., Stetten, G., Goodfellow, P.N., Migeon,
C.J., . . . Bard, P.A. (1993). The role of the sex-determining region Y gene in the
etiology of 46, XX maleness. *Journal of Clinical Endocrinology and Metabolism,
76*(3), 690–695.

Hamilton, W.D. (1964a). The genetical evolution of social behaviour. I. *Journal of
Theoretical Biology, 7*, 1–16.

Hamilton, W.D. (1964b). The genetical evolution of social behaviour. II. *Journal of
Theoretical Biology, 7*, 17–52.

Hines, M., & Alexander, G.M. (2008). Monkeys, girls, boys and toys: A confirma-
tion letter regarding "Sex differences in toy preferences: Striking parallels between
monkeys and humans". *Hormones and Behavior, 54*(3), 478–479.

Imperato-McGinley, J., Guerrero, L., Gautier, T., & Peterson, R.E. (1974). Steroid
5-alpha-reductase deficiency in man: An inherited form of male pseudohermaphroditism. *Science, 27*(1470), 1213–1215.

Meaney, M. J. (2004). The nature of nurture: Maternal effects and chromatin remod-
eling. In J.T. Cacioppo & G.G. Berntson (Eds.), *Essays in social neuroscience* (pp. 1–14).
Cambridge, MA: MIT Press.

Pasterski, V.L., Geffner, M.E., Brain, C., Hindmarsh, P., Brook, C., & Hines, M. (2005).
Prenatal hormones and postnatal socialization by parents as determinants of male-
typical toy play in girls with congenital adrenal hyperplasia. *Child Development, 76*,
264–278.

Popper, K. (2002). *The logic of scientific discovery* (First published 1935, Springer,
Vienna; first English publication 1959, Hutchinson). London, UK: Routledge.

Price, P., Wass, J.A.H., Griffin, J.E., Leshin, M., Savage, M.O., Large, D.M., . . . Besser,
G.M. (1984). High dose androgen therapy in male pseudohermaphroditism due to
5α-reductase deficiency and disorders of the androgen receptor. *Journal of Clinical
Investigations, 74*, 1496–1508.

Trivers, R. (2011). *Deceit and self-deception: Fooling yourself the better to fool others.*
London, UK: Allen Lane (Penguin).

4.

"Male and Female Created He Them"
Calling for a New Discourse on Gender and Sexual Diversity in the Jamaican Church

ANNA KASAFI PERKINS

On 29 June 2014, according to police estimates, twenty-five thousand people converged on Half Way Tree Square, a central and important gathering point for Kingstonians specifically, and Jamaicans generally, for a rally organized by the Jamaica Churches Action Uniting Society for Emancipation (Jamaica CAUSE). The rally urged "Jamaicans to stand up for strong and healthy families, righteousness and justice as well as to resist the homosexual agenda and the repealing of the buggery act" (Skyers, 2014). At the event, church leaders and allies warned the country about the impending loss of religious freedom, particularly as a result of criticizing homosexuality. The event came on the heels of and in direct response to the controversial "Bain case", in which the University of the West Indies terminated the contract of Professor Brendan Bain, who had led the Caribbean HIV/AIDS Regional Training Network (CHART). The termination followed concerns expressed by a coalition of Caribbean community-based organizations regarding testimony Bain had given on behalf of the church in a Belize court case challenging that country's laws criminalizing anal sex.

In the latter half of 2015, as talk in Jamaica turned to general elections, Jamaica CAUSE held a second rally. On 27 September of that year, tens of thousands of supporters of the movement gathered again in Half Way to warn politicians not to capitulate to international pressure to repeal the law criminalizing anal sex. At this rally, like the previous one, strong appeals to nationalism and calls for defence of Jamaica's sovereignty were made, with people dressed in national colours and event organizers leading recitation of the national pledge and the singing of the national anthem. In this, the previous demonstration and other similar more current engagements, denunciations of homosexuality were raised to the level of national duty, with the church acting as herald and warrior willing to engage in battle (see Perkins, 2016).

Against the backdrop of these public displays regarding the threat that LGBT activism posed to Jamaican society, this chapter attempts a socioreligious analysis of the Jamaican church's conventional attitudes towards gender and sexual minorities. It explores the relation and interplay between Jamaican cultural proscriptions against LGBT identity and expression, and traditional interpretations of Christian Scriptures. As is clear from media representations in Jamaica, the treatment of LGBT matters forms an important part of the church's discourse on gender and sexuality in the country. Further, discussions about LGBT issues in the island, regardless of the perspective, are invariably approached through the prism of religion. However, while the chapter highlights how Christian discourse has contributed significantly to shaping current, often-negative views of minority gender and sexuality in the country, it also seeks to identify within the Christian tradition a more affirming approach to the examination of LGBT people and their gender and sexuality expression. In this regard, the chapter sets out to capture within the far-from-homogeneous Christian faith, approaches that can be marshalled in beginning a more justice-oriented discourse with and around gender and sexual minorities in the church and society and, in so doing, to "give more regard for the human condition" (Major-Campbell qtd. in Baxter, 2013). Of note is that while these resources do not always reside in the official pronouncements and positions of the various Christian denominations found in Jamaica, there are increasing signs, particularly from within the established churches, of a more compassionate approach towards LGBT issues.

Binaries in Gender and Sexuality

Nelson (2010) argues that religion is an ambiguous mix of creative and destructive influences. This is particularly evident in its dealing with human sexuality, which is a major preoccupation of most religions. To this end, religious belief influences – positively or negatively – a range of decisions about sex-related issues (Crawford, Rawlins, McGrowder & Adams, 2011). To begin, orthodox Christian perspectives on gender and sexuality are based on a neat male-female binary, proffered as having been divinely ordained. The Jamaican religious and social landscape reflects this understanding, with ideas about gender and sexuality being divorced from the complex realities of identity, orientation, desire and practice (Nanda, 2000). Accordingly, homosexuality, usually of the male-male kind, is rejected as simply a perversion of the divine order, commonly reflected in the saying, "God made Adam and Eve not Adam and Steve!" (Buckley, 2012). Tafari-Ama (2006) captures the link between social perspectives on non-heterosexual sexuality in her groundbreaking study of sexual politics, violence and culture in the Jamaican inner city. In explaining the deep cultural prohibitions against homosexuality and non-vaginal sex in inner-city communities, she draws on the role of the church as the main institution that defines the parameters of Jamaican social mores. She writes: "Penile penetration of the vagina is perceived as the all-time and only normal way to have sex. This outlook is also institutionally reinforced, because in Jamaica, the predominant Judeo-Christian ethic influences many other institutions of socialisation such as the education system, the family and popular culture. These institutions are therefore important channels for the transmission of the ideology and practices of heterosexism" (p. 275). Munroe (1991) confirms this view, identifying the church as one of the main institutions to which Jamaicans attach significant value. Roughly 75 per cent of Jamaicans profess to be Christians (STATIN, 2011). Indeed, the popular declaration that Jamaica has more churches per square kilometre than any other nation in the world explains, at least at face value, the extent to which "church life and religious beliefs permeate so many aspects of daily life, both reflecting and shaping gender ideologies and relationships" (Fox, 2010, p. 118).

The strong influence of the church on the sexual attitudes and behaviour of their members and on definitions of appropriate social norms is well documented (Gutzmore, 2004; Gaskins, 2013). Even where people are not "practising" Christians, the manner in which Christian values have penetrated the society leads to certain beliefs going unquestioned. Crawford et al. (2011) remarked that Christian faith potentially influences a range of decisions on sex-related issues among Jamaican adolescents. They found, for example, that religious belief and practice were positively associated with less permissive attitudes towards matters such as extramarital sex, and noted correspondingly lower rates of nonmarital sexual activity among this group. Similarly, in exploring the role of faith-based organizations (FBOs) in the fight against HIV and AIDS, and the stigma and discrimination associated with them in Jamaica, Bernard (2011) found that the "belief systems held by Jamaican FBO leaders present[ed] opportunities and threats to partnerships between their organizations and the Ministry of Health and other partners in the national HIV response" (p. 47) – again the ambiguous face of Christian religion in Jamaica.

Baptist pastor and *Gleaner* columnist Devon Dick (2000) comments on the importance of Christianity in shaping mores in the country when he points out that the church, by using the tool of evangelism as the major means of encouraging proper values, "has transformed Jamaica into a country wherein Christian values are pervasive" (p. 58). Dick clarifies what he means by "proper values" when he identifies them as existing under a "system based on respect for life, people and property, family life and *healthy sexual practices*" (p. 52, emphasis added).

The focus on the dominant heterosexual binary and its overt rejection of same-sex couplings is accompanied by a rejection of all forms of behaviour or expressions that do not conform to the dominant gender-pairing norms of male and female, man and woman, masculine and feminine. However, the socially designated "perversions" associated with them such as bisexuality, transvestism, and transsexuality tend to be subsumed under the umbrella of homosexuality, to the detriment of them all. On the extreme end of this characterization of homosexuality as perversion is the conflation of "perverted heterosexual violence, such as rape or incest, with same-sex desire, establishing a continuum of criminality in which same-sex desire is the apotheosis of a range of violences [sic] including murder, robbery, dishonesty, lying, rape, domestic violence, adultery, fornication, [paedophilia] and incest" (Alexander, 1997). Charles (2011) calls such conflation of homosexuality and a range of negative cultural practices such as paedophilia "anchoring", which creates and reinforces in the public mind a sense of revulsion to all who might be classified as "deviants".

Christianity and LGBT Questions

National Surveys and Attitudes to Same-Sex Matters

Over the last several years, a number of studies have been conducted to test attitudes towards members of the LGBT community in Jamaica. The first, commissioned by J-FLAG, was a national survey of attitudes towards same-sex relationships conducted by Boxill, Martin, Russell, Waller, Meikle and Mitchell in 2011. One of the findings of this study was the pervasiveness of Christian-influenced values that condemned same-sex sexual practices as unhealthy. The survey found that negative views of homosexuality tended to be greatest among Jamaican males, non-university-educated persons, those who listened mostly to dancehall and reggae music and those in lower socio-economic groups. By contrast, females and university-educated persons were found to be slightly less homophobic. Antipathy towards gays and lesbians, whose orientation and culture were often loudly denounced, was demonstrated in the lyrical, cultural and sometimes physical violence deployed against members of the LGBT community (see Hope, 2006). Of significance, the study noted that the strongest objections to the decriminalization of buggery were raised on religious grounds, and the participants in the focus groups liberally quoted the Bible, especially Leviticus 18, referring to the sinfulness of same-sex acts as the basis for their opposition to homosexuality. Over 80 per cent of those surveyed claimed to attend church and deemed male homosexuality to be morally wrong. Boxill et al. were careful to note, however, that the connection between dancehall music and religious affiliation as predictors of homophobia was statistically weak and a matter of probability. Therefore, the relationship identified did not mean that all members of a group would behave in the same way. Nonetheless, in speaking to the impact of religion on homophobic attitudes among Jamaicans, they concluded: "Based upon the results of the survey and focus groups there can be no doubt that religion plays a significant role in determining attitudes towards homosexuality. However, statistically speaking there is no evidence from this survey that attending church or religious activities drives anti-homosexual attitudes or behaviour. The precise role of religion in regard to attitudinal formation towards homosexuality is complex and requires further study" (p. 34). While confirming the impact of such factors as religion on levels of antipathy towards homosexuality, the most important finding from Boxill et al. was that strong negative perceptions and attitudes towards homosexuality cut across all social classes, genders and social groups in Jamaica. Marshall's (2011) study among Jamaican female university students intersects well with that of Boxill et al., revealing that condemnation of LGBT persons was typically bolstered by reference to the Bible.

In 2012, Boxill, Galbraith, Mitchell and Russell identified an apparent shift in religious attitudes towards gay people. They noted, "religious persons are seemingly becoming more tolerant, but positive attitudes towards homosexuals are still more likely found in less religious individuals" (p. 3). The study concluded that there was very little difference between the results of the 2011 and 2012 studies.

The Bible, Gender and Sexuality

LGBT Male and Female Created He Them

Biblical injunctions frame responses to issues of gender and sexuality in Jamaica, particularly in relation to the LGBT community. Important aspects of the national discourse on gender find their root in the patriarchal stories in the Hebrew Scriptures. The same is true for the condemnation of same-sex sexual activity, particularly that between men. More liberal leaders in the Jamaican church argue that biblical interpretations underpin attitudes to gender variance and homosexuality in Jamaica because stories in the Bible are taken by many as literal truth or history. Indeed, two perspectives hold "true" in Christian circles in Jamaica: God is male (father, man, judge, king); and He, the male god, created human beings male and female, the apex of the order of creation. The "naturalness", that is, the divinely ordained nature, of this fact is confirmed by interpretations of the two creation stories in Genesis, which are usually read as one (Genesis 1 and 2).

Same-Sex Intercourse

Given that social and legal proscriptions against homosexuality in Jamaica are overdetermined by the Judaeo-Christian Scriptures, it is important to investigate the source of these proscriptions. Same-sex intercourse is specifically outlawed in the Holiness Code (Leviticus 17–26), a purity code to distinguish the Israelites from the Canaanites (Wright Knust, 2011). Leviticus 17–26 is called "the Holiness Code", by scholars, as it asserts "you shall be holy". The Holiness Code prohibits particular forms of intercourse at particular times or in particular ways. For example, intercourse with animals, parents, siblings, daughters-in-law, a neighbour's wife, menstruating women, a man (the target of the text is understood to be male), and so on is expressly forbidden. What is common to these illicit sexual acts is the emission of semen into an inappropriate receptacle (one that is unclean, the property of another man, incapable of producing children). The punishment for these activities is outlined in Leviticus 20: lying with a man as with a woman is an abomination punishable by death (Leviticus 20:13), and this is the language used by some Jamaicans, especially in popular music culture, to express their disapproval of male homosexuality, as will be discussed below. Ironically, while sleeping with a woman during her menstrual cycle is also prohibited and punishable by banishment from the community, this and other prohibitions from the Holiness Code are not part of the Jamaican discourse around "unhealthy sexual practices", although significant prohibition exists around sex during the menses (Perkins, 2017).

Creation

In the first story of creation, God creates male and female at the same time and says, "Be fertile and multiply" (Genesis 1:27–28). This story is often conflated with the second one, told in Genesis 2, where God creates man (the Hebrew word is *Adamah*, which means "earth being" and is the generic reference to human being; however, it is understood that the archetypal human being is male, so the word is translated "man". The man is never named, although in common biblical interpretation he is called Adam.). God places the man in the Garden of Eden. His loneliness prompts God to create a suitable partner ("help-meet") for him using one of his ribs. This partner is called "woman" because she is bone of the man's bone and flesh of his flesh. "That is why a man leaves his father and mother and clings to his wife, and the two of them become one body" (Genesis 2:24). Christians who take this text literally see it as the basis on which heterosexual marital relations are ordained according to divine plan. Key ideas arising from these stories include the view that the Divine Male made the female human being subordinate to the male, given that she was fashioned from one of his ribs and for his comfort. This is captured in the use of the term "helpmeet", that is, a "fitting" helper, in the King James translation of the biblical text. A corollary of God's creation of gendered humanity therefore is the idea that the woman, who is named "Eve" by the man, meaning "mother of all living" (Genesis 3:20), was male property. In these stories, the heterosexual and patriarchal identity of all human sexual relations is assumed and canonized. As will be seen below, these interpretations are read into the first story in Genesis 1, although they arise from that in Genesis 2.

In a 2013 *Gleaner* commentary, outspoken cultural critic Carolyn Cooper questioned the dominant gender binaries arising from interpretations of Genesis (Cooper, 2013b): "If you think there are only two genders, you're not living in the 21st century. You are stuck in the dark ages, at the very beginning of time, in the Book of Genesis, King James Version: 'Male and female created he them.' That was then. These days, gender is much more complicated. It comes in multiples" (p. A9). Tongue firmly in cheek, Cooper called the beginning of time (Genesis time) the Dark Ages. Acknowledging the two stories of creation recorded in Genesis, Cooper wonders aloud whether the Divine declaration in Genesis 1:27 ("God created man in his own image, in the image of God created he him; male and female created he them") might not actually have meant that every human being is both male and female as is the God who created them. In so doing, she finds "support" for "multiples" of gender (gender variance) in the very story that is used to undergird the dominant binaries Christians invoke. Moving to the "completely different account of the origin of human beings in Genesis 2:7" (p. A9), she further questioned the creation of woman from the rib of the man. She dismissed the story as "clearly a male fantasy" in which the basic facts of biology were inverted by insecure patriarchal males.

The Fall

The second story of creation is more detailed. The man, at the instigation of the woman, disobeys God's command not to eat the forbidden fruit (not apple). They are both punished for this disobedience in very gendered ways: the woman is punished with pain in childbirth and sexual desire for and subjugation to the man; the man has to undertake hard work to survive:

> To the woman he [God] said: "I will intensify the pangs of your childbearing; in pain shall you bring forth children. Yet your urge will be for your husband and he shall be your master.
>
> To the man he said: "Because you listened to your wife and ate from the tree of which I had forbidden you to eat, Cursed be the ground because of you! In toil shall

you eat its yield all the days of your life. Thorns and thistles shall it bring forth to you, as you eat of the plants of the field. By the sweat of your face shall you get bread to eat. Until you return to the ground, from which you were taken; for you are dirt, and to dirt you shall return." (Genesis 3:16–19; New American Bible translation)

The procreative mandate that is at the base of the first story provides support for the establishment of a social order that privileges the male (heteropatriarchy) and normalizes heterosexual relations (heteronormativity) when it is linked to the punishment for the Fall in the second story. It is conceivable, then, that any practice or behaviour that does not lead to procreation and turns on its head the gender hierarchy inherent in patriarchal relations is to be seen as contrary to divine order. This heteronormative and heteropatriarchal perspective of the Judaeo-Christian Scriptures has impacted the development of Jamaican culture in a fashion that allows for limited consideration of gender and sexuality variance in the norms of society. Indeed Charles (2011) maintains that "public interrogation of the heterosexual hegemony is not tolerated in Jamaica. Jamaica is a heteronormative place where heterosexuals exercise hegemonic control over homosexual presence" (p. 15).

Cross-Dressing

The Bible further demarcated and distinguished male and female gendered identities through clothing. Males and females, respectively, are prohibited from dressing in clothing specific to the other gender: "A woman shall not wear a man's garment, nor shall a man put on a woman's clothing; for anyone who does such things is an abomination to the LORD, your God" (Deuteronomy 22:5). This is usually the verse quoted "to label male cross-dressers as sinners in need of repentance" (Little-White, 2007). Yet little attention is paid to female cross-dressers. Indeed, this prohibition is taken literally in regard to cross-dressing males as is clear in the treatment of cross-dressing and transvestite males in Jamaican society (Cooper, 2013a).

Sodom and Gomorrah

Homosexual activity and its condemnation ostensibly enter the biblical text in the form of the proposed homosexual gang rape of the visitors by the men of Sodom and Gomorrah that was punished by God (Genesis 19). Paradoxically, heterosexual rape appears not to receive the same wholesale condemnation as the Genesis text and other "texts of terror" like Judges 19:1–30 demonstrates (Trible, 1984). In the Sodom and Gomorrah story, Lot offers the citizens bent on homosexual rape of two of his guests his own virginal daughters to do with as they please. The would-be-rapists refuse and attempt to harm both Lot and his guests only to be blinded and their cities eventually destroyed. A similar story is told in Judges 19, with a Levite's concubine being the sacrifice offered to the men of the town who intended to sexually assault the visitor. In this story, the concubine is not as fortunate as Lot's daughters. When the men of Gibeah demand that the visiting Levite be thrown out to them, his host said to them: "No, my brothers, do not be so wicked. Since this man is my guest, do not commit this crime. Rather let me bring out my maiden daughter or his concubine. Ravish them, or do whatever you want with them; but against the man you must not commit this wanton crime" (Judges 19:23–24). Eventually, the concubine is tossed out to the men by the Levite to save himself. The men rape, torture and leave her for dead on the doorstep. In these patriarchal heterosexist stories, the rape and abuse of women are viewed as normal and natural, more to be countenanced than the "wicked" act of so treating a male. The value of the male is such that he may not be reduced to the role of the female as would happen if the would-be rapists had been given their way. In the case of the concubine, her rape causes no outrage, but her death, signalling the loss of her property value to the Levite, leads to mass murder of the men of Gibeah (Judges 20). Notwithstanding the multiple social facts present in these stories, their readings typically lock in on the supposed homosexuality of the perpetrators, not the proposed homosexual rape or the actual heterosexual rape, to the point where, since the nineteenth century, Sodom has "given" its name to the abominable crime of "sodomy".

In analysing the texts, Trible (1984) notes the strong link between patriarchy and heterosexism in these stories, in which the women "satisfy the gamut of heterosexual preferences. One is virgin property; the other, seasoned and experienced" (p. 74). The humanity of women is not countenanced – they are property, objects, tools to be captured, betrayed, raped, tortured, murdered, dismembered, scattered. The interconnectedness of both forms of oppression is captured in the term heteropatriarchy.

The Abomination

Anderson-Fletcher, in her book *The Dance of Difference: The New Frontier of Sexual Orientation* (2011), tells of growing up in Jamaica and learning to fear persons who were bisexual, gay or lesbian. According to her, adults spat out the word "homosexual" with such venom it made her shiver. Her first introduction to attitudes towards homosexuals came at the age of seven; she overheard her gentle, churchgoing father say to a friend, "Those men are an abomination. They should be killed!" (p. 1). She writes of her shock at hearing his words and wondering who these men were and what they had done to make her father so angry. She remarks that the moment stayed with her because the venom and hostility in her father's voice were unmistakable and frightening. These she identifies as the opening shots in her negative programming regarding homosexuality. Later, she accepted the notion that heterosexual people were morally superior to homosexuals (see also Gutzmore's description of his experience in Gutzmore, 2004).

Anderson-Fletcher's reference to her father's otherwise gentle persona as well as his churchgoing status are of note in a context like Jamaica, which is so often described as a dangerous space for gays and lesbians. It can be argued that her father's hostility and hatred of gay people, which she identifies as homophobia, is a direct part of his identity as a Christian. Even his words echo the Levitical descriptions of male-male intercourse: "You shall not lie with a male as with a woman; such a thing is an abomination" – the same verse quoted in the Boxill focus group (Leviticus 18:22). This biblical idea of abomination is also echoed in the Jamaican law that criminalizes male-male sex. The Offences Against the Persons Act, of which the church was fully supportive at its drafting in 1864 (Charles, 2011), legally defines "the unnatural offence" and outlaws "the abominable crime of buggery" (Sections 76 and 77). Such condemnations are echoed daily in the lyrical and physical violence directed at gays and lesbians. Dancehall music, in particular, targets homosexual men ("battyman"); many songs promote hatred of gays and lesbians and advocate killing and beating them. Dancehall artistes like Capleton, Elephant Man, T.O.K., Konshenz, Queen Ifrica, Vybz Kartel, Beenie Man, Bounty Killer and Buju Banton have collectively produced over 200 songs referred to as hate or "murder" music (Jamaica Forum for Lesbians, All-Sexuals and Gays, n.d.). Perhaps the most notorious of these is Buju Banton's "Boom Bye Bye", which declares: "Boom Bye Bye inna batty bwoy head . . . di nasty man dem haffi dead" (literally, "shoot the faggots in their heads . . . these nasty men must die"). The consonance between the violence of popular culture and the admonishments of the church is evident in the 2009 declaration by then political ombudsman and high-profile religious leader Bishop Herro Blair that there were two things that he would never allow anyone to do to his "boys and that was [sic] to turn them into homosexuals and give them drugs" (Jamaica Forum, n.d.). Similarly, Wellesley A. Blair, administrative bishop for the New Testament Church of God in Jamaica and the Cayman Islands, in an interview with the Gleaner on 28 February 2007, proclaimed "sodomites who are caught should be beaten . . . when the court orders lashing, some of those sodomites who are caught and some of the criminals, should be brought in the square of Half-Way Tree and be lashed and send them home" (J-Flag, 2011, p. 19). This consonance between the religious and popular music sentiments is telling.

Christian Interpretations: Examples

The widespread understanding of the divinely created gender binary and its meaning for male-female relationships range beyond the verses in Genesis. Among them are passages that prohibit same-sex relations: Leviticus 20:7–21; Romans 1:24–27; 1 Corinthians 6:9–11. Small's sentiments echoed those of many Christian communities across Jamaica. Then-moderator of the Moravian Church in Jamaica, in a 2 November 2003 letter to the editor of the *Gleaner*, expressly joined the debate in response to several articles in the paper dealing with the issue of homosexuality (Thompson, 2003). In outlining his church's position on the issue "at this time" – he appeared to leave open the door for a change in that position – he recounted the Moravian Church's 1982 resolution: "Be it resolved that this synod condemns the evil practice of homosexuality and recommends that a consultative body comprising the church and government be set up to provide counselling and advice in eliminating this evil from the society" (Thompson, 2003). Thompson then cited the 1995 synod as remaining firm in its resolution. In an intriguing penultimate paragraph, which may be attributed to Thompson himself, there is an amelioration of tone, where the position is not condemnation but treatment for deviant tendencies: "The church takes a caring rather than a condemning attitude to such persons and oppose [*sic*] any form of violence against them" (Thompson, 2003). This is a clear shift in tone from the 1982 resolution. Nonetheless, heterosexual and patriarchal identity continues to be assumed and canonized.

The Anglican Communion in the West Indies put out a Provincial Statement on Same-Sex Unions, 25 April 2013. In the statement, the bishops denounced a trend they identified as coming from outside the developing world, and the threat it posed to developing nations: "[I]n which matters related to human sexuality have been elevated to the level of human rights and are being promulgated as positions which must be accepted globally. Frequently, failure to conform by developing nations like our own, results in the threat of various sanctions, including the withholding of economic aid" (Church in the Province of the West Indies, 2013, para. 2). The bishops spoke against the backdrop of announcements that Britain would cut aid to countries like Jamaica, which continued with discriminatory laws against gays. They framed the issue in the context of global domination by the North versus respect for national sovereignty of countries from the South, religious values, and cultural traditions. (This is an ironic position as it can be argued that the influx of religious right/conservative groups and leaders into the Caribbean in a bid to do battle for the public square and to reclaim traditional family values against "the homosexual agenda" is another form of domination from the North not countenanced by the church. See Perkins, 2016.) The bishops emphatically claimed for the Caribbean "the right to affirm our cultural and religious convictions regarding our definitions of that most basic of social institutions, marriage" (2013, n.p.). They urged Caribbean governments to resist the pressure from the United Kingdom and expressed concerns about the redefinition of gender. They contended that there was:

a re-definition of gender to accommodate gay, lesbian and transgendered [sic] people, and the creation of a plurality of definitions which leaves the issue of gender to self-definition, thereby dismissing traditional definition of male and female. Additionally, there is the passage of legislation among a number of metropolitan nations whereby marriage is defined as a human right in which any two persons may be joined, inclusive of persons of the same-sex. The 'marriage' of persons of the same-sex is justified as a human right on the basis of marital equality with heterosexual unions. (Church in the Province, 2013, para. 3)

The West Indian bishops' rejection of nontraditional notions of gender seemed tied to their desire to protect traditional teachings about marriage as being between a man and a woman. To accept the possibility of same-sex unions was interpreted as calling into question the divinely ordained marital binary reflected in the Judaeo-Christian creation stories. The bishops claimed for themselves the right to defend a purpose of marriage aligned with orthodox doctrinal teachings, contending that the church was to teach its members about the source and purpose of marriage and to solemnize matrimony. The government, in their eyes, did not have a role in defining "that most basic of social institutions" but rather to protect it as well as the men and women in it.

In defending heterosexual marriage, the West Indian bishops quoted a Church of England document on civil partnerships stating that marriage was "a creation ordinance, a gift of God in creation and a means of His grace". In outlining the parameters of this ordinance, the bishops stated that marriage was "a faithful, committed, permanent and legally sanctioned relationship between a man and a woman" and one that was "central to the stability and health of human society". Accordingly, this kind of relationship must be seen as continuing "to provide the best context for the raising of children" (Civil Partnerships: A Pastoral Statement from the House of Bishops of the Church of England, 2005, para. 2, cited in Church in the Province, 2013, para.5).

Reliance on this document by the West Indian bishops was ironic because of the original purpose it served. The Church of England, in its initial efforts to grapple with the tensions resulting from new perspectives on same-sex practices, used the document as a means of balancing the pastoral need of lesbians and gays with those of traditionalists wishing to remain faithful to the conventional definition of marriage. In this regard, the document reflected an attempt to promote civil union as a viable option for dealing pastorally with non-heterosexually-oriented people who were unable to live in celibacy. In this way, a compromise would be reached where the church would serve its gay and lesbian faithful without doing damage to the traditional view of marriage. The English clerics therefore seemed to be open to some form of partnership for same-sex couples, which makes their perspective on nonnormative sexuality appear more nuanced than that of their West Indian counterparts.

Other Christian Approaches

Thus far, this chapter has examined Christian approaches to gender and sexuality variance that have been generally negative. However, these interpretations are not the entire story of the Jamaican church's attitude to gender minorities. Jamaican Christianity is by no means monolithic. More nuanced positions exist and have managed to emerge even in the Jamaican context typically described as extremely homophobic.

Anglican canon Ernle Gordon responds directly to the inaccurate use of the Bible to criticize homosexuality. Gordon confirms that "it is incorrect (theologically and biblically) to associate the story of Sodom and Gomorrah with homosexuality . . . and it is incorrect to associate the language of homosexuality with the language of the Greek in I Corinthians 5" (Anderson, 2003, para. 5). Sean Major-Campbell, also from the Anglican Communion, is critical of the way the church addresses questions relating to gender and sexual minorities, which he attributes to inadequate biblical interpretation. Not afraid of controversy, Major-Campbell shocked many in Jamaican church circles when in December 2014, he washed the feet of two lesbians and a transgender man in a service to commemorate International Human Rights Day at his Christchurch parish in Vineyard Town, Kingston. As a church "insider", Major-Campbell is in a unique position to point to the destructive impact of Christianity on members of the LGBT community:

> When the subject of homosexuality is addressed in the church, it would be helpful if the approach sought to wrestle honestly with searching questions versus using the Bible to beat people over their heads. The culture is versed in the various rhymes, songs, and Bible verses which encourage hatred and murder [of persons who are perceived as homosexual]. What is needed is more regard for the human condition, with its many unanswered questions – some of which are not sufficiently addressed by the Bible. (Major-Campbell in Baxter, 2013, para 8)

Major-Campbell attributes the misunderstanding of homosexuality and the mistreatment of LGBT people to the interpenetration (and perhaps mutual reinforcement) of Christianity, culture and even education in Jamaica. In his prescription, the often-satirical Anglican cleric challenges a fundamental tenet of many Jamaicans – that the Bible contains answers to all of life's questions. In so doing, Major-Campbell calls for a revisiting of the Christian tradition beyond a reliance on the Bible in order to treat more honestly with matters such as homosexuality and, by implication, gender nonconformity.

Spiritual Theory and "Scientific" Theory

The condemnation of homosexuals has often led to persons being "dismembered" – that is, excluded from fellowship – from church, according to Stephen-Claude Hyatt, ordained minister and former guidance counsellor at Jamaica College, who shared three cases in local congregations of which he was aware (2000). Hyatt admitted that there were individuals in church, including pastors, who wrestled with their sexuality. He questioned: "As the church of God, are we to condemn them for actions which they may or may not have had control over, or assist them in dealing with and overcoming same?" (para. 24). Such persons, in his estimation, were not to be condemned or rejected; rather he called upon the church to minister to them to help them overcome what he qualified as sinful temptations to which they were subject. He made a clear distinction between persons who experienced same-sex attraction and those who acted on it. He likened homosexual activity to heroin addiction, which he saw as a difficult habit to break. According to him, prolonged counselling, deep prayer and much anguish were the remedies for homosexual addiction. In Hyatt's estimation, homosexuality was curable, because it was a disorder that could be explained scientifically. Unlike many others, he attempted to understand the nature of sexual orientation: "As far as I am concerned, it would be irresponsible both ways, for us to cast aspersions and judgments about people's sexuality, without seeking first to understand same" (2001, p. C7).

Michelle Smith, a pastor preaching at the Shalom Missionary Church in Grants Pen, confirms Hyatt's perspective through her own experience of moving from "lesbianism to grace" (title of her book). Smith claimed that her experience has taught her that homosexuality is not innate and "that a change in thoughts and divine intervention is [sic] a sufficient remedy to rescue those caught up in the lifestyle" (Thaffe, 2011, para. 4).

Former head of the Seventh-Day Adventist Church and now governor general of Jamaica Sir Patrick Allen acknowledged that homosexuality is present in all areas of society, including within the churches. He concurs with Smith that gays are capable of living a "normal life" if they accept Jesus. Allen, unlike Smith, believes that even if homosexuality "was a genetic behaviour, there were ways for gays to refrain from acting out their desires" (Davis, 2001). He notes, however: "It is not our desire to call down blood and fire on people. . . . I have seen people who were once homosexuals now living normal Christian lives" (Davis, 2001).

Hyatt's approach can be seen as salutatory as it does not follow the expected condemnatory approach to homosexuality. It calls the church to a more inclusive approach to all persons as is often heard among more mainline denominations such as the Anglican Communion. In calling for a different perspective, Hyatt counters the "spiritual theory" explanation proffered by some in evangelical circles, which he discussed a year after the article referenced above, in a *Gleaner* online special feature on gays in Jamaica (Hyatt 2001). Spiritual theory sees homosexuals as demon possessed and therefore in need of exorcism by the laying on of hands. Hyatt dismisses this theory as the most subjective of all explanations of homosexuality as it is not based on any form of research or testing. He writes:

> [R]ather, it is based purely on interpretation of scripture, which varies as well as feelings, biases, convictions and a need to condemn. Many Church leaders and members hold this viewpoint, and would rather beat the life out of an individual, be it by the tongue or with an object, all under the guise of exorcism and godliness, than searching for realistic explanations. In order to support this point, individuals use scripture, in particular the Hebrew Scripture (Old Testament), to support their beliefs and actions. Let me be quick to state that there is nowhere in scripture which supports the practice of homosexuals, nowhere which calls us to be merciful or accommodating. However, there is no verse that stipulates that homosexuality is the greatest and unpardonable sin. (Hyatt, 2001)

However, even Hyatt's "scientific" approach joins the "spiritual theory" of Smith and others to paint homosexuality as a disorder, disease, sinful affliction, or addiction amenable to treatment and cure.

The approaches espoused by Hyatt and Smith and others of their ilk about the curability of homosexuality are contested by recent developments in the evangelical church as discussed by Ian Boyne (2013). In June 2013, after thirty-seven years of operation, Exodus International, a United States–based conservative interdenominational organization that led the charge for reorienting same-sex attraction and advocated reparative therapy, closed its doors with an apology to the gay and lesbian community. The president of the organization admitted that 99.9 per cent of those treated by Exodus did not achieve any real change in their same-sex attraction as neither did he, "a formerly active homosexual" (Boyne, 2013, para. 5).

Act versus Orientation

There are other church approaches to homosexuality that eschew forced conversion therapy, ideas of demon possession or the need to overcome sinful temptation. Former Roman Catholic archbishop of Kingston Charles Dufour pointed to his church's position on homosexuality when he remarked: "We do not regard homosexuality as natural behaviour, but we say you are to respect the person. Respect, do not kill the person, do not stab the person. You must show respect to the person. . . . We have always maintained that stance and we will never change that" (Thaffe, 2012, para. 11). Roman Catholics distinguish sexual orientation from sexual activity Roman Catholic deacon and newspaper columnist Peter Espeut outlines:

> First of all, we distinguish between homosexual 'orientation' and homosexual 'practice'. Everyone in the world, whether single, married or celibate, has a sexual orientation. Most have a heterosexual orientation, feeling drawn to be involved in intimate human and sexual relationships with persons of the other gender (in Greek, 'heteros' means 'other, another'). Some have a homosexual orientation, feeling to enter intimate human and sexual relationships with persons of the same gender (in Greek, 'homoios' means 'same as, like'). Individuals are not morally responsible for their orientation, since it does not flow from 'free choice' and therefore, having any particular orientation cannot in itself be sinful or virtuous. It is how we act on our orientation which can be either sinful or virtuous. (Espeut, 2003, p. 4)

In this way, Espeut presents an approach that manifests the distinctions between tendency and practice, with the former being free from moral judgement.

Baptist pastor and theologian Trevor Edwards expresses this in terms of the orientation/practice dichotomy: "There is a place in the church for accepting all persons regardless of gender, race or sexual orientation. (But) accepting someone who is thus oriented does not mean that his/her homosexual practices must be embraced. A distinction must be made between an orientation, that is, a tendency and behaviour or practice which is a choice" (Anderson, 2003, para. 14). Dick noted that in discussing the question of homosexuality, the church's position on the issue: "has been to support those with homosexual tendencies without condoning the lifestyle. Church leaders believe that the complementarity of the man/woman relationship is the correct mode of sexual behaviour [sic]. However, tolerance for consenting adults, rather than imprisonment, has been advocated as a concession to a behaviour lifestyle that is an affront to societal norms" (2000, p. 55).

The language of act and orientation/tendency does not find support in the Scriptures, some would argue, as the Bible supposedly sees all persons as heterosexual, so the prohibitions are against persons perceived to be acting against what is assumed to be their true nature. Espeut, who is theologically trained, does not countenance this. He further argues:

> Whatever our sexual orientation, our sexual lives have to be ordered, channelled in acceptable directions. Traditional Christian teaching is that the only appropriate context for sexual intercourse is in lifelong marriage between a man and a woman. Heterosexuals who sexually exploit others, abuse children or who force others to have sex with them (rape) are out of control, and are in need of counselling and pastoral care. Traditional Christian teaching is that there is no appropriate context for homosexual sex, no morally appropriate way to act on a homosexual orientation. Although all homosexuals are loved by God, homosexual acts are not. Persons who have a homosexual orientation should be welcomed as full members of Christian churches, and they should seek to keep their sexual lives in order; should they fail, they will be in need of counselling and pastoral care. (2003, p. 4)

Questioning Act versus Orientation

What the "tendency versus lifestyle" approach encapsulates is the "hate the sin, love the sinner" perspective, which draws a distinction between person and act. This seems to provide a middle ground between the standard rejection of persons with same-sex attraction and their unconditional acceptance. Jakobsen and Pelligrini (2004) argue that in practice "love the sinner, hate the sin allows people to take positions that are punitive toward their fellow citizens, while at the same time experiencing themselves as being not simply ethical, but compassionate and even tolerant of difference" (p. 1). Considering that such professions of tolerance are mixed with stern moral judgements, the line between what is to be loved and what is to be hated is movable and clearly contradictory, and can work to justify hatred rather than undercut it (Jakobsen and Pelligrini, 2004).

Furthermore, tolerance creates an "us-versus-them" relationship; the very construction of an "us" leaves out a "them" – LGBT people – and sets up a relationship in which "we" tolerate "them". The "we" who tolerate are considered generous, Christian even, and open-minded; yet this allows for an exclusionary view of the world as the tolerance it preaches involves defining others as outsiders. Calling for tolerance does not represent a full inclusion into society of those tolerated but is more a "grudging form of acceptance in which the boundary between 'us' and 'them' remains clear, dangerously clear" (Jakobsen and Pelligrini, 2004, p. 52). Rather than producing justice and freedom, tolerance, the product of this love-hate relationship, is exclusionary and hierarchical.

Towards a Conclusion

Nanda posits that because of the centrality of sex, gender and sexuality to individual identity in modern Western societies, "it is difficult to dislodge our ideas, and more so, our feelings about them" (Nanda, 2000, p. 1). Undoubtedly, Christians in Jamaica hold very strong views about homosexuality that run the gamut from an uneasy tolerance to rejection and denunciation of person and practice. For many Jamaicans, those strongly held ideas have been deeply coloured by the Judaeo-Christian tradition. From the perspectives surveyed, two broad categories are discernible. The first is based on more fundamentalist readings of Scripture such as Genesis and Leviticus that see sex/gender as a divinely instituted binary – male or female – and/or oppositional – hetero-sexual or homosexual. The second set of perspectives presumes to distinguish between the nonheterosexual/non-cisgender person and the acts related to their orientation or gender identity. The first set of perspectives is more typi-cally evangelical and the latter more mainline in their orientation. The first set of readings remains thoroughly heteropatriarchal and heteronormative and appears to leave no space for sexual/gender diversity. The second set creates categories of "sinners", leaving sin anchored in the sexual/gender identity of LGBT people.

The homology that exists between popular culture and Christianity on the issue of homosexuality has caused Gutzmore to charge that the "moral and religious legitimacy of the fundamentalist ideological imperative is in danger of evaporating, leaving in its place nothing more sacred or spiritual than self-righteous and even blasphemous people irrationally wrapping their will to mistreat, murder even, their fellow men in a cloak of very questionable godli-ness" (2004, p. 128). In the Jamaican context, the sex/gender variant group that is often at the receiving end of much condemnation and varying forms of violence are gay men, although gender-variant females are subjected to viola-tions like "corrective" rape. Underlying expressed Christian concerns about homosexuality are commitment to supporting improved male-female relation-ships and family life. However, when buttressed by decontextualized biblical and theological warrants, these seemingly unassailable commitments lose their force. As Canon Ernle Gordon outlined in a 2003 *Gleaner* Editor's Forum: "I believe we have to have a new theology in the church and we have to be careful of the Fall/Redemption theology that is judgmental, patriarchal, colonial and anti-woman" (Anderson, 2003, para. 2).

What seems necessary is a more just and holistic approach to the question of difference, informed by science. To this end, a truly democratic conversa-tion will be needed, one in which the voices of those who are not the dominant group are not crowded out or condemned by the state on behalf of the church. The first step in achieving this is for the church to embark upon a more honest and critical (re)reading of Scripture that questions conventional readings that deny the dignity and value of human persons, especially gender-variant ones.

References

Alexander, M.J. (1997). Erotic autonomy as a politics of decolonization: An anatomy of feminist and state practice in the Bahamas tourist economy. In M.J. Alexander & C. T. Mohanty (Eds.), *Feminist genealogies, colonial legacies, democratic futures* (pp. 63–100). New York, NY: Routledge.

Anderson, G. (2003, October 12). Churches differ on homosexuality. *The Gleaner*.

Anderson-Fletcher, S. (2011). *The dance of difference: The new frontier of sexual orientation*. Bethesda, MD: Pearson.

Anglican Bishops of the West Indies. (April 2013). *Provincial statement on same sex marriage*. April 2013. Unpublished manuscript.

Baxter, M. (2013, July 31). Anti-gay hypocrisy: Jamaica destined to become tolerant of homosexuality, says clergyman. *The Gleaner*. http://jamaicagleaner.com /gleaner/20130731/lead/lead1.html

Bernard, G. (2011. June). *Final research report qualitative research focus group study among faith-based organizations*. USAID 3532-HE-2010-AA: Submitted to the Ministry of Health and Environment National HIV/STI Programme.

Boxill, I., Galbraith, E., Mitchell, R., & Russell, R. (2012). *National survey on attitudes and perceptions of Jamaicans towards same sex relationships. A follow-up study*. Department of Sociology, Psychology and Social Work, University of the West Indies, Mona.

Boxill, I., Martin, J., Russell, R., Waller, L., Meikle, T., & Mitchell, R. (2011). *National survey on attitudes and perceptions of Jamaicans towards same sex relationships*. Department of Sociology, Psychology and Social Work, University of the West Indies, Mona.

Boyne, I. (2013, June 23). Culture clash on homosexuality. *The Gleaner*. http://jamaica -gleaner.com/gleaner/20130623/focus/focus2.html

Buckley, B. (2012, January 8). Church picking on gays. *The Gleaner*. http://jamaica -gleaner.com/gleaner/20120108/cleisure/cleisure2.html

Charles, C.A.D. (2011). Representations of homosexuality in Jamaica. *Social and Economic Studies, 60*(1), 3–29.

The Church in the Province of the West Indies. (2013, April 25). Provincial statement on same-sex unions. https://www.thinkinganglicans.org.uk/6024-2/

Cooper, C. (2013a, August 4). Dressed for murder. *The Gleaner*. http://jamaica-gleaner .com/gleaner/20130804/cleisure/cleisure3.html

Cooper, C. (2013b, December 15). LGBTQIA – The new sex alphabet. *The Gleaner*, p. A9.

Crawford, T.V., Rawlins, J., McGrowder, D.A., & Adams, R.L. (2011). The church's response to sexual reproductive health issues among youths: Jamaica's experience. *Journal of Religion and Health, 50*(1), 163–176. https://www.ncbi.nlm.nih.gov /pubmed/20559735

Davis, G. (2001). Homophobia still high in the church. *A go-Jamaica feature.* http://jamaica-gleaner.com/pages/gay/homophobia.html

Dick, D. (2000). *Rebellion to riot: The Jamaican church in nation building.* Kingston, Jamaica: Ian Randle.

Espeut, P. (2003, November 12). Not an "alternative lifestyle". *The Gleaner*, p. 4.

Fox, D. (2010). *Cultural DNA: Gender at the root of everyday life in rural Jamaica.* Kingston, Jamaica: University of the West Indies Press.

Gaskins J. (2013) "Buggery" and the Commonwealth Caribbean: A comparative examination of the Bahamas, Jamaica, and Trinidad and Tobago. In *Human rights, sexual orientation and gender identity in the commonwealth: Struggles for decriminalisation and change.* Institute of Commonwealth Studies, School of Advanced Study, University of London, pp. 429–454.

Gutzmore, C. (2004). Casting the first stone! Policing homo/sexuality in Jamaican popular culture. *Interventions: The International Journal of Postcolonial Studies*, 6(1). 118–134.

Hope, D. (2006). *Inna di dancehall: Popular culture and the politics of identity in Jamaica.* Kingston, Jamaica: University of the West Indies Press.

Hyatt, S.C. (2000). Homosexuality and the role of the church: The church living outside the realm of reality. *The Gleaner.* http://old.jamaica-gleaner.com/gleaner/20001013/news/news6.html

Hyatt, S.C. (2001, August 13). Sexual orientation: Critiquing the theories, looking at the realities. *The Gleaner*, p. C7.

Jakobsen, J.R. & Pelligrini, A. (2004). *Love the sin: Sexual regulation and the limits of religious Tolerance.* Boston, MA: Beacon Press.

Jamaica Forum for Lesbians, All Sexuals and Gays. (J-FLAG). (2011). *Focus right: Young people and human rights – A factsheet on the rights of lesbian, gay, bisexual and transgender youth.* http://www.jflag.org/wp-content/uploads/2011/06/Focus-Right-LGBT-Youth-Human-Rights-in-Jamaica.pdf

JFLAG survey finds Jamaicans don't want their children taught by gays. (2016, April 11). *The Gleaner.* http://jamaica-gleaner.com/article/news/20160411/jflag-survey-finds-jamaicans-dont-want-their-children-taught-gays

Little-White, H. (2007, June 3). Who is a cross dresser? *The Gleaner.* http://jamaica-gleaner.com/gleaner/20070603/out/out6.html

Major-Campbell, S. (2013, June 8). Bugger off! Keep the law! *The Gleaner.* http://jamaica-gleaner.com/gleaner/20130608/cleisure/cleisure3.html

Marshall, A. (2011). Reclaiming the erotic power of black women. *Social and Economic Studies*, 60(1), 61–90.

Munroe, T. (1991). The impact of the church on the political culture in the Caribbean: The case of Jamaica. *Caribbean Quarterly*, 37(1), 83–97.

Nanda, S. (2000). *Gender diversity: Cross-cultural variations.* Prospect Heights, IL: Waveland Press.

Nelson, J. (2010). Where are we? Seven sinful problem and seven virtuous possibilities. In M. M. Ellison & K. Brown Douglas (Eds.), *Sexuality and the sacred: Sources for theological reflection* (pp. 95–104). Louisville, KY: Westminster John Knox Press.

New American Bible. (1987). (Revised Edition). Catholic World Press/World Bible Publishers.

Perkins, A.K. (2016, April). Evangelical Christianity and social change in the Caribbean: A battle for/in the public sphere? *Journal of Eastern Caribbean Studies* (Special Issue on Religion in the Caribbean), *41*(1), 13–46.

Perkins, A.K. (2017). "Shi wi use har blood tie him": A theological interrogation of cultural beliefs about menstruation and female [im]morality in Jamaica. In Nicholas Faraclas, et al, (Eds.), *Memories of Caribbean futures: Reclaiming the precolonial to reimagine a postcolonial languages, literatures and cultures of the greater Caribbean and beyond 2*. Puerto Rico/Curaçao: University of Curaçao: 349–359.

Skyers, Javene. (2014, June 30). Thousands rally against tossing out buggery act; shout out for clean, righteous living. *Jamaica Observer*. http://www.jamaicaobserver.com /news/no-to-homo-agenda_17050490

Statistical Institute of Jamaica (STATIN). (2011). *Jamaica population and housing census.*

Tafari-Ama, I. (2006). Blood, bullets and bodies: Sexual politics below Jamaica's poverty line. Kingston, Jamaica: Multi Media Communications.

Thaffe, N. (2011, August 31). Homosexuality is wrong. *The Gleaner*. http:// jamaica-gleaner.com/gleaner/20110831/lead/lead93.html

Thaffe, N. (2012, June 3). Scandal, migration have weakened the Catholic Church. *The Gleaner*. http://jamaica-gleaner.com/gleaner/20120625/lead/lead7.html

Thompson, Livingston. (2003, November 3). Moravians' position on homosexuality. *The Gleaner*, A10.

Trible, P. (1984). *Texts of terror: Literary-feminist readings of biblical narratives*. Philadelphia, PA: Fortress Press.

Wright Knust, J. (2011). *Unprotected texts: The Bible's surprising contradictions about sex and desire*. New York, NY: HarperOne.

5.

Taboo and Obligation
Normative Pressures on Sexuality and Gender in the Caribbean and the Rise of Hard Masculinity

DAVID PLUMMER

There are many challenges facing the modern world. These include greater interconnectedness, unprecedented population growth, population mobility and changing social values. It is inescapable that these challenges will require communities and governments to be adaptable. Failure to do so will almost certainly have serious social consequences. Fortunately, this unprecedented period of change has coincided with a growing recognition of the importance of human rights. There is no doubt that it is through mutual respect and safe-guarding human rights that the challenges facing humanity can be success-fully negotiated. But the Caribbean is no stranger to change or, on occasion, to revolution. There have been dramatic shifts in the past, to which the region has responded, sometimes well and sometimes with a struggle. The challenge for the future will be to ensure that the winds of change are met in a peaceful and constructive way. This is one of the motivating themes behind this paper.

Changes in the status of men and women – gender – will inevitably be part of global social change. Indeed, they have been under way in the region for some time (Reddock, 2004). Changes in the status of women are evident in new patterns of education and employment, although they still have a long way to go. But as we will see, changes in the status of women entail changes for men too. Some of these have not been positive, and we men must shoulder much of the responsibility for this. In general, young men have not adapted well to changing educational demands, men "enjoy" poorer health status, men regu-larly take risks and place themselves in harm's way, and we predominate in acts of violence and crime (Parry, 2000; Parry, 2004).

About the Caribbean Masculinities Project

This chapter reports on the findings of the Caribbean Masculinities Project, which set out to document the experiences of young Caribbean men in their transition from childhood to manhood: in the family, at school, in peer groups, on the street and out of school. Altogether, 138 detailed interviews were conducted in seven Caribbean countries and one territory: Anguilla, Grenada, Guyana, Jamaica, St Kitts and Nevis, St Lucia, St Vincent and the Grenadines, and Trinidad and Tobago. Purposive sampling was undertaken to identify participants who were in positions to promote understanding of the social and cultural constructions of gender in the region. The data analysis used an adapted grounded theory approach with the aim of generating a better explanatory framework for gender patterns in the Caribbean. Steps were taken to ensure that the framework that emerged was adequate, meaningful and had relevance to society more generally. These steps included adding cases until saturation occurred, including diverse, variant and negative cases; and relating the findings to those of other researchers. A diverse sample was recruited, which incorporated a range of variables including race (principally mixed race, African and East Indian descendants); socio-economic background; geographic location (garrison communities, rural and urban, seven countries and one territory); religion (Catholic, Protestant, Hindu and Moslem); and academic background (early school leavers, school completers and tertiary educated). In addition, participants went beyond simply giving accounts of their own experiences – they also acted as lay field observers and provided data on complex social systems that they interacted with and that encompassed many additional participants (such as persons in villages, communities, schools and peer groups). Using a strategic approach to sampling (known as theoretical sampling) allowed us to build a rich and highly relevant database that can be used to explore and map emerging social trends, interpret those trends and make them intelligible.

Male Dominance as a Key Social Reference Point

Male domination has long been recognized by researchers as a recurring characteristic of human gender arrangements (Connell, 1987). This notion is explicit in both activist writings and academic research; it is also the implied basis for important critical concepts such as "the patriarchy", "hegemonic masculinity" and "heterosexism", all of which assume male domination as a prerequisite. Moreover, male dominance, in one form or another, is a recurring (but not inevitable) finding across cultures and through history. Indeed, a rich body of literature, research and the tradition of feminism itself have arisen in large part as a movement to redress the habitual subordination of women through social arrangements that routinely institutionalize male dominance. It is this norm of male dominance that I will take as the entry point to this analysis of gender relations in the Caribbean.

Given that male dominance is the default position in many societies and cultures, and given the pre-eminence of dominant masculinity in gender relations as a result, it should not be surprising to find that dominant masculinity(s) constitutes a key reference point from which wider gender relations are triangulated. Indeed, male dominance does not stand alone. Dominance can only exist in relation to something that is subordinated. There is, in fact, a binary relationship at work here: one end of the binary is dominant masculinity while the other is subordinate femininity. This binary relationship has important implications for how people view the world, how they approach life, how social relations are constructed and how society functions.

At first glance, binaries such as masculine/feminine appear to be relatively straightforward because everything seems to boil down to two distinct alternatives. In that sense binaries simplify our view of the world and narrow our options in life. If you accept the binary rules, then you are left with only two choices: masculine or feminine. Binaries can therefore act to restrict choices, to mark out what is acceptable and remove from consideration what is out of bounds. However, this straightforward appearance is deceptive; it grossly oversimplifies gender and conceals an extensive and complex system of power and social control. It is easy to forget that these binary rules do not need to be observed and people can choose not to subscribe to them.

It is also in the nature of binaries that they can – and do – give rise to great complexity (think of the extraordinary complexity of the digital world built entirely on a binary code consisting of combinations of 1 and 0). In order to understand gender arrangements better, it is necessary to explore how this complexity arises from a system that depends on only two options: masculine and feminine. To do this we will focus on five key qualities of the gender binary, which collectively serve to generate complexity and entrench power and, in the case of gender, male dominance. First, while binaries sometimes convey a superficial appearance of symmetry ("equal opposites"), they are never symmetrical – one side always enjoys privilege over the other. That is to say, the assumption of male supremacy has traditionally allowed men to enjoy precedence over women in many walks of life – domestic, education and career. Second, the two parts of a binary are mutually exclusive and "relational"; that is to say that if a particular characteristic is considered masculine, it cannot by definition be feminine, and vice versa (unless something changes). In this regard, masculinity relies on femininity to define what masculinity is, and the same is true in reverse – without one pole of the binary, gender itself would not only be meaningless, it would cease to exist. Third, despite appearances and popular dogma, there is a wealth of evidence to show that masculinity is not a fixed, permanent, unchanging quality. Gender is known to have varied enormously over time and in different cultural settings, and continues to do so. For example, during early colonial times, dominant males wore elaborate clothing that included lace trim and wigs, something that would not be considered appropriate for males now. Moreover, being a respected gentleman was considered proper for men in the past, whereas respect has quite different connotations now, more akin to being feared and certainly not gentle. Fourth, thus far we have only considered the "simple" closed binary of masculinity versus femininity, but to further add to this complexity, rather than having a single "opposite" in femininity, in people's minds, masculinity seems to have many "opposites". Not only is woman considered the "opposite" of man; but being a man is also commonly assumed to be the "opposite" of being a boy, or a homosexual, or a transsexual, an emasculated male, or a broken man who has failed to prove his masculinity or has somehow betrayed it or lost it. In all of these cases, the binary that makes these seeming paradoxes logical is not the binary between masculine and feminine, but another less obvious binary: the binary between masculine and everything that is considered un-masculine. Fifth, binaries can be "mapped" onto each other. By mapping, I mean that one pole of a binary can become related to a pole of a second binary, and this affects the meaning of the whole binary system. For example, if masculinity is considered to be superior and desirable, then femininity can easily be assumed to be inferior and undesirable; or if masculinity is seen as inherently healthy and good, then effeminacy can easily be assumed to be intrinsically degenerate and evil; or if the epitome of masculinity is strength, then any softness shown by a male can be assumed to be a betrayal of masculinity and/or a sign of homosexuality that deserves correction and/or punishment; if masculinity is equated to physical prowess, then academic performance can easily be assumed to be something for girls or "batty boys", but not something "real men" would want to be associated with.

In each of these cases, the masculine/feminine gender binaries "map" onto other binaries such as good/bad or hard/soft or strong/weak or safe/risky and so on, and this creates complex webs of implied meaning. While these binary associations have become "naturalized" and are routinely accepted, it should be noted that they rely on flawed logic and false binaries: there is no intrinsic reason why a homosexual should be seen as un-masculine (in many traditional cultures, homosexual practices were considered the epitome of masculinity); likewise, there is no intrinsic reason why if masculinity is highly valued, femininity should be disparaged. They can both be valued and/or both be bad, for that matter; there really is no reason why they should be thought of as opposite. Similarly, being manly is usually considered to be a "good" outcome for boys and unmanly is "bad", and being "hard" is considered manly and "soft" is unmanly, and thus "soft" boys are bad and "hard" men are good. The problem with this reasoning is that a sensitive, loving "soft" man may make an ideal husband and father, which is definitely not bad; while a hard, aggressive male could be a terrible partner, and this is definitely not good. The explanation for why these "opposite" associations are so readily accepted in everyday life is because they accord with people's preconceived ideas – their prejudices; people want to believe them.

Socially Constructed and Changing Gender Roles

The above analysis should not be taken to imply that all men are dominant, or that men are always dominant, or that there is no possibility for change, or that there is little chance of creating better, fairer, more equitable societies. Research and analysis have also revealed considerable evidence that masculinity is not fixed (Connell, 1995). Unlike a person's biological sex, which is usually established before birth, gender is little more than a set of social conventions, albeit a resilient, elaborate and powerful set that we all subscribe to. These social conventions deeply influence how we speak, how we dress, how we groom ourselves, how we gesture, how we posture, how we act, the roles we take in life, and how we relate to one and other. Gender is best thought of as an elaborate web of social expectations rather than something that is biologically preordained.

The fact that the rules of gender have their basis in social convention raises the possibility that these conventions might change as society changes. This is exactly what has been found in historical and cultural analysis: different forms of masculinity have come to dominate societies at different points in history and in different cultural contexts (Connell, 1987; Connell, 1995; Gilmore, 1990).

But it is not simply the case that gender shifts have occurred slowly over long periods of time, during the great epochs of history or with the rise and fall of civilizations. What we found in the Caribbean Masculinities Project is that gender conventions can shift surprisingly rapidly and dramatically. The education of Caribbean boys is a case in point. Data and analysis on the intakes of new students at the University of the West Indies consistently show that in recent years the number of females enrolling at the university far exceeds the number of males (Figueroa, 2004; Plummer, 2013; Reddock, 2004). This was not the case a few decades ago when the situation was reversed. It seems that Caribbean boys no longer value the opportunity to get educated as their predecessors did. There is accumulating evidence that this has to do with shifting gender norms: education no longer boosts your status as a man among your peers; on the contrary, being too educated and articulate nowadays can undermine your reputation of being a "real man".

To drive this point about the variability of gender norms even further, it is worth noting the evidence that gender conventions can commonly vary in everyday life depending on the context. Thus, while it is generally not accept-able for men to cry, it is perfectly acceptable for them to get emotional and even to cry in the event of a great sporting triumph – something they could not get away with after a fight. Likewise, it is not uncommon for sporting teams to hug and even kiss on the sports field, but this would be frowned upon on the street. In other words, gender arrangements can shift sometimes quite dramatically and quickly both in different contexts and as the result of social change.

Modern-Day Rites of Passage

The transition from childhood to adulthood is a critical time for consolidating a gender identity (Gilmore, 1990; Van Gennep, 1960). While children gener-ally have a clear idea from an early age whether they are a boy or a girl, the transition to adulthood is when that gender identity matures and is realized in its fully developed form. Most traditional cultures attached such significance to this transition, especially the passage to manhood, that a range of rituals and ceremonies developed around this period – presumably to emphasize its importance, to orchestrate the process and to ensure it conforms to prevailing social norms. These events are known as "rites of passage".

In the modern world, traditional rites of passage have largely given way to modern approaches to development. Yet the imperative attached to becoming a "real man" is arguably as powerful as ever. It is not surprising, therefore, that alternative arrangements might arise to compensate for the loss of traditional rites and to guide young people through this complicated transition to adult-hood (Plummer, 1999). At the same time, social and economic changes have seen a reduction in the role played by the traditional custodians of the rites of passage (older adults from the family and clan). Changes such as the need for (both) parents to work, a decline in communal and village living and long commuting distances and working hours have all reduced the involvement of older relatives in the journey to adulthood. On the other hand, schooling has come to play a leading role in the child's life during these crucial developmental years, and this includes providing a modern arena for the transition from child-hood to adulthood. The role that schools play in this transition will be affected by how schooling is organized and conducted. For example, at the time of the Caribbean Masculinities Project, Trinidad had a system of "shift schooling" where half of the pupils attended school in the morning and the other half attended in the afternoon in order to accelerate universal access to education. While this is an admirable goal, a side effect was to leave pupils without super-vision for significant periods of time every day. This gap extended even further when parental working hours and commuting times are also long.

At the school level, other factors contribute to further reducing adult involvement, especially in boys' development: males are now a minority among schoolteachers in many parts of the Caribbean, and teachers increasingly have to maintain greater distance from children to avoid suggestions of impropriety, especially male teachers and especially when it comes to developmental issues. The net effect of these changes is that during this crucial period of development, many children have minimal mentoring and supervision for significant periods of time (Plummer, McLean & Simpson, 2008).

In short, adult-free power vacuums have opened up during this crucial stage of development. However, strictly speaking, it is not correct to say that children go altogether unsupervised. The presence of a power vacuum in children's lives creates an opportunity for peers to step in and fill the gap (Plummer & Geofroy, 2010). The result is that the transition to adulthood is increasingly being orchestrated by peer groups. The old system of vertical mentoring – by older adults – is being overtaken by horizontal mentoring by peers – kids bringing up kids. The kids themselves have developed their own rules to govern the rites of passage, many of which are embedded in youth culture. Unfortunately, when it comes to gender identity, this means that the standards of manhood against which boys are being measured are dominated by the prevailing standards of the peer group. For many peer groups, physical prowess is what determines the pecking order, and the everyday rules can resemble the "laws of the jungle". Kids can easily be left with little choice but to conform to the expectations of peers, and it is a small step before some peer groups start to resemble a gang. This is especially true for boys from poorer "garrison communities" who have much less private space at home to escape to and are forced to spend most of their time growing up on the street in the company of peers. It is here that physical prowess is king – even more so if it is exercised collectively in a gang that is fully armed.

Earning a Reputation

It is useful to consider gender roles as being akin to a public performance, something that is done for social approval. In social situations, gender roles take on heightened importance, while in private settings the rules can be safely ignored. Take, for example, the well-known gender convention "real men don't cry", which is generally observed in public but not in private. The imperative to possess a gender identity that meets with social approval is an accomplishment that dominates adolescence. Ultimately a key aspect of gender identity is to establish a reputation for yourself. There are two important issues that affect this accomplishment that we will consider, both of which relate to a gender identity being very much a social achievement: first, opportunities are needed for boys to act out gender roles and adopt them (considered in this section); and second, which audience the enactment is for (which we will return to later).

In the first case, in order to establish their masculine reputation, boys need opportunities to rehearse and perform their gender roles (Gilmore, 1990). Everyday life offers a range of opportunities to do this: on the sporting field, in the street, through a souped-up car (if he has one) and through sexual performance, to name a few. On the other hand, there are social arenas where boys are no longer able to "prove" themselves like they once could, perhaps because these are no longer considered exclusive male domains and performing well in these fields proves little in terms of gender. In the Caribbean (and elsewhere), one such domain is education. Education is a particularly important case because, as was mentioned above, in recent historical times schooling has come to meet an important need for both boys and girls in the passage to adulthood that traditional rites of passage once met.

The Caribbean has an impressive track record of men's academic and literary accomplishment, including Nobel Prizes, and at the time, such educational outcomes and intellectual leadership were compatible with dominant standards of masculinity. However, there is a growing body of evidence that suggests this may no longer be the case (Figueroa, 2004; Plummer, 2013). While achieving high grades in education is still something that boys can do if they are so inclined, gender patterns in education are changing, and this seems to be impacting boys' inclination to do well in class. The problem for gender identity is not so much that education has been "feminized" as some authors complain, but paradoxically, that there is greater equality of opportunity in education (Miller, 1986; Parry, 2000; Parry, 2004). While this is entirely as it should be and an admirable achievement, the problem for boys is that academic performance was once a much more important vehicle for establishing a reputation for manhood (at least as far as the classroom goes), whereas now it is something that boys and girls can both do well at.

The result of these changes is that boys are faced with having to look elsewhere for opportunities to establish their masculine credentials. For this purpose, there remains one key domain that cannot be equalized and continues to offer a means of demonstrating manhood and of asserting one's reputation: the biological differences between males and females.

Retreating to the Male Body

Although gender is recognized as being a set of social conventions, biological differences do, nevertheless, provide the foundations on which these conventions can be constructed. First among these opportunities is physical difference, in terms of physical build, facial appearance, hair distribution and, of course, genital details. Overlaid on these basic physical differences are additional layers of socially defined gender differences concerning appearance and grooming: hairstyles, shaving patterns, muscular development and dress codes.

Appearance offers the foundation for further differentiation based on performance: the way the body is used and what it symbolizes serves to further distinguish men from women. How the physical body is postured, gait, the meaning ascribed to certain seemingly minor gestures and styles of speech, all convey profound gender meaning. Physical appearance is equated with strength, and strength, in turn, is equated with courage and bravery as well as aggression and risk-taking. The use the male body is put to, what sports it plays, what risks it takes whether it is an "outdoors" body that is well acquainted with physical labour, also speaks volumes about the masculinity of the "owner" (Willis, 1977).

In contrast, this "retreat to the body" as a reliable vehicle for defining one's gender implicitly sets up a new binary: if masculinity is typically defined in physical terms, then intellectual accomplishment is susceptible to being seen as soft and of little (if any) value when it comes to establishing one's masculinity. Indeed, much of the data from the Caribbean Masculinities Project shows that during the school years, being smart, getting good grades, being studious, trying hard in class, obeying teachers, speaking standard English, being conscientious about learning and so on can serve to define a boy as soft and unmanly and to be a liability that invites teasing and bullying. This teasing invariably involves suggestions that the boy is gay, through labels like "batty", "buller" or "antiman" (Crichlow, 2004; Plummer, 2014; Plummer & Geofroy, 2010; Plummer, McLean & Simpson, 2008).

Youth Culture, Peer Groups and Gender Policing

As I argued above, having a "satisfactory" gender identity is a social obligation that can be usefully understood as being analogous to a performance. Of course, a performance is nothing without an audience, and this raises a key point: who is the performance for? You will recall above that gaining a gender identity is an achievement of the transition from childhood to adulthood that has traditionally been orchestrated through various rites of passage. As I pointed out earlier, the steady shift in the rites of passage has entailed a reduction in the formal role played by senior adults (vertical mentoring) and an increase in the unofficial role played by peers (horizontal mentoring) (DuBois & Karcher, 2005; Lewis, 2008). These changing roles have resulted in shifts in the audience that the performance is for. The balance seems to have shifted in favour of peer groups being the principal audience, and thereby being the principal fount of masculinity, its arbiter of standards and its scrutineer – and all at arm's length from the wider adult world.

But how can young peers of roughly the same age and experience be the principal source and arbiter of masculinity? Surely kids have to learn the gender rules somewhere? These questions are indeed challenging, and the answer has typically been that the rules originate from parents and teachers, including the common complaint that bad behaviours are the result of bad parenting and poor schooling. However, data from the Caribbean Masculinities Project along with previous research reveals another explanation: with growing autonomy of the role of peer groups in the development of young people, the rules are being passed down from older peers to younger ones. Usually this happens during the school years where kids in senior grades pass codes and practices on to kids in lower grades in locations that are generally not under adult control: in the school ground, in graffiti, in how they use curse words, in music, on buses going to and from school and on the streets, the "block" and in the shopping mall. I have previously used the term "rolling peer pressure" to describe this phenomenon (Plummer, 1999).

Rolling peer pressure offers an explanation and a mechanism whereby adolescent codes of conduct can be passed from generation to generation with little, if any, adult intervention. This process also explains how peer groups can develop, perpetuate and modify their codes in rich, complex and enduring ways: in symbols, dress codes, musical genres, grooming and bling, sports and sexual behaviours. Indeed, this system of semiautonomous practices is so rich and resilient that it can rightly be considered a living dynamic culture: youth culture. With the combination of the growing influence of peer groups in the passage from childhood to adulthood and of boys resorting to biology as a reference point for masculinity, it is possible to explain how and why a narrowing and hardening of masculinity might occur.

The consequence of resorting to biology as a reference point for masculinity is that physical characteristics such as musculature and strength come to define manhood (at the expense of alternatives, such as being a gentleman or an intellectual). While physical characteristics have always been part of how masculinity is defined, with boys forsaking education in growing numbers, these physical characteristics gain in prominence considerably. It is therefore perhaps not surprising to find that in recent years, there has been a remarkable growth in the amount of money being poured into men's sport, and there has been a rise of male body culture, including tattoos, expensive grooming and elaborate hairstyles, bodybuilding and striptease. Our research also found that the standards of male clothing are shifting in Jamaica and nearby countries. Until recently, the archetypal clothing for Caribbean adolescents was baggy and casual, whereas tight, body-hugging clothing was considered to be a sign that a boy was gay.

More recently, there has been a shift towards tight clothing as being the definitive masculine clothing, and, according to our informants, the justification for this was that it allowed young men to show off their body and their "goods".

This renewed emphasis on physical masculinity also has symbolic dimensions. Not only is physical development of the body emphasized, but how that relative physical advantage is used is also significant. Physical prowess is easily equated with power in general, and this can be acted out in aggression, risk-taking, not to mention ascribing greater value to manual work over intellectual pursuits. Being strong, tough, hard, risky, aggressive, "respected" and feared are all iconic of modern masculinity(s). This ethos also extends into the sexual domain, where sexual performance is highly valued. Indeed, in Jamaica the term "one burner" is used to disparage men who are faithful to their women (Bailey, Branche, McGarrity & Stuart 1998). Using this term, it is possible to suggest that there was something wrong with a man's masculinity and to raise the possibility that he may even be gay. Paradoxically, therefore, by exerting pressure on men to "prove themselves", we found that this style of homophobic insinuation contributed to the HIV risk of *heterosexual men* (Plummer, 2010; Plummer, 2014). Conversely, being thoughtful, intellectual, favoured by teachers, obedient towards parents, respectful of the law, and faithful are considered "soft" and generally not a respected part of modern manhood. On the contrary, boys who display such qualities are often suspected of being gay and are targeted with homophobia and bullied.

An underlying theme of this chapter is that gender is an intensely social phenomenon, acted out in a multitude of ways according to complex codes. These codes are passed from generation to generation of young people often with very little adult involvement. On the other hand, the codes are not fixed and are subject to the vagaries of social change. Much of this transition occurs under the auspices of the peer group, which promulgates the rules and benchmarks and arbitrates over success and failure. The focus on physical masculinity gives advantage to the most aggressive boy, especially in relation to the peer group pecking order. Moreover, the obligation to secure a mature gender identity – a reputation for being a "real man" – introduces a competitive tone to the process. The peer group plays a central role in scrutinizing and policing the emerging manhood of peers and in punishing transgressions (Plummer, 2005; Plummer, 2014; Plummer & Geofroy, 2010). Gender is a collective endeavour and male peer group solidarity is a key aspect of the gender code. The Caribbean Masculinities Project identified a number of cases where gender transgression and peer group betrayal were punished, often with considerable brutality including injury and death. In many cases, the line between being a peer group or a gang is merely a matter of definition.

Standards of Hard Masculinity and Taboos on Softness

The growing emphasis on hard, physical masculinity has wide-ranging consequences. This particular configuration of masculinity is, in fact, part of a binary. The other side of the coin, which is implied in the valorization of hard masculinity, is a taboo on softness. According to our data, this taboo on softness goes hand in hand with deeply held misogynistic and homophobic taboos. What the Caribbean Masculinities Project found was that deep homophobia in the Caribbean was more often related to anxieties about gender transgression than about what people do in bed. For example, boys learned homophobic words from a very early age – generally before puberty, before they became sexually active, before their own gender identity was worked out and mostly before they knew what homosexuality really was. This way of using these terms was the norm, and using homophobic words to target sexual activity was rare and usually not based on any concrete evidence. In other words, the most usual reason for using homophobia was to target attitudes and characteristics that didn't measure up to the standards of hard masculinity rather than anything sexual (Plummer, 2014).

Based on these observations, homophobia appears to be used as a powerful way of policing manhood, and it conveys the impression that punishment for nonconformity is somehow justifiable and should be severe (Plummer, 2005). Indeed, it is not uncommon to hear of homophobic attacks, including murder, being justified by the Bible and as being God's work (and it is rare to hear "religious" leaders saying otherwise, despite the brutality). Paradoxically, these justifications even seem to be used by those who are otherwise not religious or who readily break the Ten Commandments themselves. This leads to the likely conclusion that religious justification for homophobia is merely an excuse, and that the real driver of this phenomenon runs deeper. In my opinion that driver is gender – specifically the taboo on gender transgression and presumably the threat this poses to male solidarity. For this purpose, the soft, well-spoken, gentle "battyman" symbolizes everything that hard, physical masculinity is not supposed to be: he is a demonized scapegoat par excellence for the ugly side of conservative gender politics (which would explain why conservatives in particular are so obsessed with homosexuality).

Towards a Model for Understanding Gender in Changing Times

The observations outlined above have significant implications for society and for social stability. If we accept that the prevalent forms of dominant masculinity constitute a key frame of reference for gender relations, and that gender arrangements are not fixed but are instead relational, then we have a basis for: (1) understanding contemporary gender patterns better; (2) insight into how these arrangements can change; (3) anticipating how points of friction can emerge and (4) the (anti)social consequences that might result.

The relational nature of the masculine-feminine gender binary means that when one part of the equation changes, there will inevitably be a reciprocal change in the other. For as long as a rigid gender binary holds, then it would seem that there are only two choices: (1) characteristics that come under the umbrella of masculinity cannot (for the time being) be considered feminine and vice versa or (2) qualities that are shared equally by both no longer have gender significance. While this formulation almost certainly oversimplifies more complex realities, it is, nevertheless, useful for anticipating the pressures that binaries impose on young people during their transition from childhood to adulthood, especially during volatile times. In essence, there is a balancing act underway, and in present times the balance seems to be shifting: boys are increasingly defining their manhood in physical terms rather than through brainpower (with the exceptions of being street-smart or a criminal mastermind). But the problem that faces boys is not that education has been feminized, but that it no longer has much utility for defining their masculinity, so they are looking elsewhere for guidance. The distinctive physical changes of maturation provide a more secure basis for ways to define their masculinity. The result is that boys are increasingly walking away from formal education and resorting to narrow, physical definitions of manhood to "prove" themselves (Ghaill, 1994; Plummer, McLean & Simpson, 2008; Willis, 1977). There is a risk that boys will increasingly use physical, aggressive and risky ways of negotiating life if they continue to deprecate academic and intellectual prowess. In the entirely reasonable drive for equal opportunity, education has been opened up to both boys and girls. Nor is it the case that girls have been unduly favoured; they have simply had their traditional disadvantage addressed. Moreover, it is definitely not the fault of girls if all they want is to do well at school. On the contrary, what we are witnessing is an unexpected response of male peer groups during times of change.

The dual obligations – to eschew softness and to embrace hard masculinity – create a powerful pressure for boys to act out their manhood in hypermasculine ways. Such acting out can be risky, aggressive and often antisocial. Yet many young men see it differently. For them, acting out in hypermasculine ways is intensely pro-social as a way of conforming to the collective rules of masculinity and the laws of the peer group (Plummer & Geofroy, 2010). Risk-taking has become a rite of passage where boys can prove their bravery and live up to the "no fear" and "live fast, die young" credos of modern manhood. From their perspective, rather than failing society, boys are gaining status in the eyes of those who matter most – their peers. Defying authority is very much part of the package because this is a way of affirming allegiance with everything the peer group stands for. It is a way of earning status – of gaining stripes – and of moving higher in the pecking order. For some, proof of their masculinity lies in their willingness to be violent and even to kill. Under these conditions, violence and crime can be seen as an obligation of honour rather than a shameful transgression. It is part of the rules they grew up with, and we shouldn't be surprised when it becomes a reality. In a very real sense we "reap what we sow", to paraphrase the late Barry Chevannes (see Chevannes, 1999).

Unfortunately, there will be casualties along the way. The first is the boys themselves. Not having the benefit of education and higher qualifications puts them at severe disadvantage for life. The pressure to compensate by acting out in hypermasculine ways will expose boys to cultures of risk-taking and consequent harm. For women, the growing educational and employment gap will impact relationships. Moreover, the great successes in girls' education will be at risk in societies where there is a growing underclass of men. Finally, there are those who do not fit the gender rules neatly, and with the hardening of masculinity, you can expect to see a more intense scapegoating, resulting in misogyny and potentially savage homophobia – something that has become increasingly evident in Jamaica and elsewhere in recent years. Of course, these changes will not be uniform. They will vary by country, class and different circumstances, but this should not obscure the fact that when there is a divided society with deep intolerance, everyone loses.

Conclusion

Conventional explanations for homophobia and misogyny have generally invoked the idea of "heterosexism" as an explanation. However, this formulation seems to be far too mundane and abstract considering the great depth of feeling associated with these phenomena that can often culminate in lynch mobs, brutal assaults and savage murders. As a consequence, one of the aims of the present study was to arrive at more fulsome explanations of the way that gender works and to explain why the issue is so deeply cathected. Such powerful, almost primal responses suggest that any explanation had to consider deeply indoctrinated attitudes, intense taboos and the workings of power. For me, "heterosexism" just does not cut it as an adequate explanation. Choosing the lens of dominant masculinity was deliberate, as it seems to speak to the above issues and is richly supported by the research data. At the heart of this analysis is another binary: masculine obligation and taboo. The combination of taboos on softness and an obligation to be a "real man", coupled with shifts in how masculinity is being defined, are resulting in significant social pressures. These can be best summarized as:

Obligation on everyone to project a socially acceptable gender identity;

Growing valorization of hard, risky, aggressive, physical, dominant masculinity (obligations of manhood);

Growing deprecation of soft, safe, caring, intellectual, subordinate masculinity (masculine taboos);

Attribution of negative qualities to women and failed males (immature, emasculated, weak, soft men);

Embodiment of rejected qualities in a convenient scapegoat, seemingly ready-made for the purpose (the "buller", "antiman", "batty man");

The combination of taboos on softness and the obligations of manhood drives a vicious cycle of pressure on boys to act out their masculinity in hypermasculine ways.

While this chapter uses data collected as part of the Caribbean Masculinities Project, it is increasingly clear that similar trends are occurring to varying degrees around the world and the findings are neither Caribbean-specific nor race-specific (Messerschmidt, 1994; Willis, 1977). We have seen the impressive gains made by Caribbean women (the good news) and a rise of virulent and often brutal homophobia (the bad news). Moreover, what the research also showed is that some boys shine through despite these pressures and they succeed brilliantly even, sometimes, in fields that are now considered to be "feminized". Clearly the dynamics outlined above can only be taken as a model to assist our understanding; in the real world, individual agency, good teachers and parents counterbalance these trends, and social and cultural variations will also influence the outcomes. The future would appear to be bleak in communities where these dynamics are allowed to go unchecked. Ultimately, societies that support their young people during key developmental transitions, who promote a greater variety of role models for them, who value and view diversity as a strength and who embrace human rights will be best equipped to deal with the challenges of a modern world.

Acknowledgements

The author would like to thank the Commonwealth, UNESCO and the University of the West Indies for their support. He would also like to thank the participants, individuals and organizations who assisted with recruitment for the Caribbean Masculinities Project and to acknowledge the invaluable assistance of Joel Simpson; and of Ian McKnight and the late Robert Carr in the Jamaican arm of the study.

References

Bailey, W., Branche, C., McGarrity, G., & Stuart, S. (1998). *Family and the quality of gender relations in the Caribbean.* Mona, Jamaica: Sir Arthur Lewis Institute of Social and Economic Research.

Chevannes, B. (1999). *What we sow and what we reap: Problems in the cultivation of male identity in Jamaica.* Kingston, Jamaica: Grace Kennedy Foundation.

Connell, R.W. (1987). *Gender and power.* Cambridge, UK: Polity.

Connell, R.W. (1995). *Masculinities.* Sydney, Australia: Allen and Unwin.

Crichlow, W.E.A. (2004). History, (re)memory, testimony and biomythography: Charting a buller man's Trinidadian past. In R.E. Reddock (Ed.), *Interrogating Caribbean masculinities: Theoretical and empirical analyses* (pp. 185–222). Kingston, Jamaica: University of the West Indies Press.

DuBois, D., & Karcher, M. (2005). *Handbook of youth mentoring.* London, UK: Sage.

Figueroa, M. (2004). Male privileging and male "academic under-performance" in Jamaica. In R.E. Reddock (Ed.), *Interrogating Caribbean Masculinities: Theoretical and empirical analyses* (pp. 137–166). Kingston, Jamaica: University of the West Indies Press.

Ghaill, M. (1994). *The making of men: Masculinities, sexualities and schooling.* Buckingham, UK: Open University Press.

Gilmore, D.D. (1990). *Manhood in the making.* New Haven, CT: Yale University Press.

Lewis, T. (2008, July 5). No role models for black youths. *Trinidad and Tobago Express.*

Messerschmidt, J.W. (1994). Schooling, masculinities and youth crime by white boys. In T. Newburn & E.A. Stanko (Eds.), *Just boys doing business: Men, masculinities and crime* (pp. 81–99). London, UK: Routledge.

Miller, E. (1986). *The marginalization of the black male: Insights from the development of the teaching profession.* Kingston, Jamaica: Institute of Social and Economic Research.

Parry, O. (2000). *Male underachievement in high school education.* Kingston, Jamaica: Canoe Press.

Parry, O. (2004). Masculinities, myths and educational under-achievement: Jamaica, Barbados and St Vincent & the Grenadines. In R.E. Reddock (Ed.), *Interrogating Caribbean masculinities: Theoretical and empirical analyses* (pp. 167–184). Jamaica, Barbados, Trinidad &Tobago: University of the West Indies.

Plummer, D. (1999). *One of the boys: Masculinity, homophobia and modern manhood.* New York, NY: Haworth Press.

Plummer, D. (2005). Crimes against manhood: Homophobia as the penalty for betraying hegemonic masculinity. In G. Hawkes & J. Scott (Eds.), *Perspectives in human sexuality.* Melbourne, Australia: Oxford University Press.

Plummer, D. (2010). HIV + masculinity = risk: Exploring the relationship between masculinities, education and HIV in the Caribbean. In J.F. Klot & V-K. Nguyen (Eds.), *The fourth wave: Violence, gender, culture and HIV in the 21st century.* New York, NY: Social Science Research Council.

Plummer, D. (2013). Masculinity and risk: How gender constructs drive sexual risks in the Caribbean. *Sexuality Research and Social Policy, 10*(3), 163–174.

Plummer, D. (2014). The ebb and flow of homophobia: A gender role theory. *Sex Roles,* *71*(3–4), 126–136.

Plummer, D. & Geofroy, S. (2010). When bad is cool: Violence and crime as rites of passage to manhood. *Caribbean Review of Gender Studies, 4,* 1–17.

Plummer, D., McLean, A., & Simpson, J. (2008, September). Has learning become taboo and is risk-taking compulsory for Caribbean boys? *Caribbean Review of Gender Studies, 2.*

Reddock, R.E. (Ed.). (2004). *Interrogating Caribbean masculinities: Theoretical and empirical analyses.* Kingston, Jamaica: University of the West Indies Press.

Van Gennep, A. (1960). *The rites of passage.* Chicago: University of Chicago Press.

Willis, P. (1977). *Learning to labour.* Westmead, UK: Saxon House.

6.

"Bring It Cross?"
Sexuality and "Passing" in Jamaica

MOJI ANDERSON

"You have to walk, you have to take the public bus, you have to go where majority straight people is because you don't have no cars, so you have to [be] under disguise majority of the time. It is really difficult sometimes, but you have to just get used to it. It's a thing that you must do."

"A so me stay and a so mi bawn, and nobody cyaan get it out a me." (That's how I am and how I was born, and no-one can change me.)

"Mi box up mi face [I put on makeup] but . . . the [straight people] dem don't notice."

"To display or not to display; to tell or not to tell; to let on or not to let on; to lie or not to lie; and in each case, to whom, how, when and where." (Goffman, 1963, p. 42)

This chapter examines how some gay and transgender Jamaicans navigate and negotiate their environment. Analysis of the narratives of twelve focus group participants[1] shows that they have developed a variety of ways to cope with the hostile environment that demands what Rich (1994) called "compulsory heterosexuality". One way is, unsurprisingly, frequent performances of heterosexuality; another is a refusal to engage this performance; a third falls somewhere in the middle of these two poles. These behaviours comprise crucial everyday micro-politics that have important consequences at the macro level. The decisions the participants in this study make about how to appear and act have serious implications – not just for their well-being, but for the place of homosexuality in Jamaica and the development of Jamaican heterosexual masculinity.

Erving Goffman's (1959, 1963) theorization on stigma and impression management is used as a starting point in this chapter to understand the respondents' behaviours. Goffman (1963) was concerned with how people "manage information about [their] failing" (p. 42). He found that one of the ways they do this is by moving across boundaries of gender, race and sexuality (*inter alia*) to counter the visibility of their "spoiled identity". This "passing" is a "performance . . . 'socialised', molded and modified to fit into the understanding and expectations of the society" (Goffman, 1959, p. 35) in order to escape stigmatization. To Goffman (1959), performance is a necessary part of daily life: everyone performs and all identities are staged. Autobiographical literature and research on Caribbean sexualities have established the importance of passing, or "masking" (Murray, 2002), for avoiding social death (Crichlow, 2008; Glave, 2008; King, 2014).

"Being in the closet" is the metaphor typically used to describe passing among homosexuals. Thus, "closet practices" are a "response to repressive strategies aimed at maintaining a norm of heterosexuality by excluding homosexuality from public life" (Seidman, Meeks & Traschen, 1999, p. 11). Recent work has suggested, however, that this Euro-American idiom does not travel well to the Caribbean. King uses La Fountain-Stokes's (2009) notion of the "open secret" derived from his work in Puerto Rico to reject the closet's "mandate of constant revelation" in favour of "a mandate of discretion, which is not (always) the same as hiding" (2014, p. 64). Moore (2014) argued that in the Caribbean "queerness is about *practice* rather than a hardened identity that must be attained for legitimacy" (p. 11; emphasis in original). That is, it is about what people *do*, rather than what they *say*.

The narratives of the participants in this study show that an important aspect of living in Jamaica is deciding on whether and how to pass as heterosexual. This decision-making is relevant in a context in which some participants said being gay is "like being in a prison without bars". Researchers agree with this, saying that homophobia is encoded in Jamaican masculinity and notions of citizenship, and can manifest in verbal abuse, physical assault and even murder (Carr, 2003; Chevannes, 1993; Lewis & Carr, 2009; Schleifer, 2004; White & Carr, 2005). Scholars have said that anti-gay sentiment is embedded in Jamaican society, from popular culture (particularly dancehall music, Jamaica's most popular music form) to national legislation[2] (Gutzmore, 2004; Hope, 2006, 2010; Lafont, 2009).

Passing: How?

"You Have to Man It Up"

As Goffman (1963) said, passers have to be "alive to aspects of the social situation which others treat as uncalculated and unattended" (p. 88). Thus, the respondents are participant observers par excellence. They are confident in

Table 6.1. How to "rough it up"

"Manning up . . ."	Description/Example
Facial expressions	"Yu naw too pree inna fi him face [but] you screw up all of your face [you don't stare at him, but you make a mean face]."
Speech	"Yo pussy, a weh you ah do? Mi wi shoot yu, yu nuh [Hey (expletive), what are you doing? I will shoot you, you know]!"
Body language	Participant: "stand up like this like a man in the corner" [demonstrates]
	Interviewer describing the participant's demonstration: "Your hands are in your pockets or you fold your arms and you put your foot up against the wall."
Approach to women	"If you see a girl pass they expect you to look at her and lust or make a remark to her."

their knowledge of the cultural symbols and societal expectations surrounding masculinity crucial for credible performances (Goffman, 1963, p. 45) because "we grow up in this country, we know what they expect, we know everything, we know what to do". They know the pitch of the voice, the facial expression, the precise position of the cap on the head, the (lack of) movement of the hips, the placement of the hands and the language that tells the people on the bus, on the road or elsewhere, that they are heterosexual, and often, Jamaica's hyper-masculine "gangster" or "thug". Two participants explained how to create this "façade":

> [P1:] Mi wear [a] do-rag or the stocking cap and den mi wear one cap [I wear a cap] and twist it around . . .

> [P2:] and let go your hair [i.e., it is not styled in braids, cornrows etc.] . . .

> [P1:] and mi wi tek out mi shirt out a mi pants [I will take my shirt out of my pants] and just look normal . . . or sometime mi wi put it inna mi pants [sometimes I will put it in my pants].

Table 6.1 lists other cues that participants hope their audience will accept "on faith" (Goffman, 1959, p. 58).

These participants are concealing what Goffman called "stigma symbols" (1963, p. 43), those signs that would identify them as the reviled homosexual. Kimmel (2002) says that proper masculine behaviour concerns "negative rules about behaviour. Never dress that way. Never talk or walk that way" (p. 105), and so on. Accordingly, they said that roughing it up meant they could not, for example, wear tight clothes or intricate hairstyles, speak in a high-pitched voice or Standard English (instead of Jamaicans' first language, Jamaican Creole), or swing their hips.

There are two particularly important elements of Jamaican male hetero-sexuality to which men must adhere. The "anti-homosexual heterosexuality" necessary for authentic manhood in Jamaica and elsewhere (Chevannes, 1993; Cowell, 2011; see also Kimmel, 2002) is often demonstrated in ostentatious expressions of homophobia. All respondents claimed to know of men who regularly engaged in verbal and sometimes physical abuse of putative homo-sexuals although they were themselves gay. One told the story of "what you would call one of the regular gyalist [ladies' man] . . . bad boy [who] would hurl abuse at [gay men]. One night he was at a gay party and when he saw his [most recent] victim he head for the bathroom. The victim went straight in there and said, 'Come out! You remember me?!'"

As suggested in the quote above, the respondents know that another crucial aspect of being a Jamaican man is to be a "gyalist": to have a great deal of sex with a great many women (Chevannes, 1993; Anderson, 2009). Therefore, "you must be seen with these amount of girls per month, like a quota system". And it is not always enough just to be seen: "I had sex with a girl so when I went home and they ask me I tell them everything in an effort to remove some suspicion." If they cannot fulfil this requirement, they must devise a credible reason, such as the participant who claimed to be Christian to justify "celibacy", that is, the lack of sexual relationships with women.

Passing: Why?

"If the public should know, or any panty a show, is straight judgment."
(If the public were to find out, or any female underwear is visible, there
will definitely be gay-bashing.)

Goffman (1963) stated that people pass "[b]ecause of the great rewards in being considered normal" (p. 74). The most important reward for normalcy is escaping "judgement" (see Carr, 2003 for a discussion of homophobic violence in the Jamaican context). Respondents report verbal abuse and much worse. Two described being confronted by a mob of over a hundred people and being rescued by police officers, who berated them at the police station.

They "monitor" their behaviour because they believe they are under intense surveillance. As one complained, people are constantly on the lookout for stigma symbols: "[I]t supposed to be a man's job who loves men, not a man that loves women, to be watching a man 24/7. [He] can tell what you wear this morning, see which car pick you up, which colour man came to the house last night, what he was wearing." Passing does not only protect the participants themselves. They are well aware of "the tendency for a stigma to spread from the stigmatized individual to his close connections" (Goffman, 1963, p. 30).

They know that "if you as a straight man [are] walking with an effeminate man, guess what? 'Well, a 'im man' [well, that's his boyfriend]" and therefore pass to avoid their heterosexual friends being deemed homosexual by association.

Passing: Where?

"I know when and where to . . . let out my hair."

Goffman (1963, p. 42) pointed out that it was crucial to know where passing was necessary. When the participants are in what they feel is a safe environment – "in we likkle corner" (our own space) – they "drop our hair . . . pull up dem frock tail and dem stocking" (let down our hair, wear dresses and stockings). Although passing is a performance for the public, there are "likkle corners" in the public domain. Participants generally agreed that "when you're going on the road . . . you try to fix up yourself like a man", but some said that they could be "a little more flowery" in the more prosperous part of Kingston ("uptown"), because people there were more "disciplined" and less likely to "cause much of a scene". Downtown, where the capital's poorer residents live and "the slightest thing ticks them off . . . I'll be like, 'yow'" (*yow* is a greeting between men, said in a deep voice). There are "likkle corners" even within downtown, however: clothes stores and beauty salons whose proprietors cater to gays, for example. Still, the respondents pointed out that travelling to these shops had to be done with minimal interaction with the public (by taking a taxi, for example).

Successful Incomplete Passes

"They have a little feminish inna dem still." (They are still a little feminine.)

Passing is a dialogic process that depends on others' assent and consent to the cues presented for validation of the performance (Goffman, 1959; Renfrow, 2004). In some cases, the participants try and fail at passing. A young respondent tried changing haircuts and "dress[ing] the thug way" but "it still don't work out . . . some man always see mi and seeps [calls out to] me". However, for the most part, the cracks in the "façade" are by design. For example, one participant wears braids although aware of this hairstyle's potential as a stigma symbol. This respondent's performance of other tropes of heterosexuality are intended to shed doubt on the meaning of the braids, because by itself the hairstyle does not "determine whether I am gay or not". Another participant's "swinging" walk remained unchanged, because there is "just one walk for me. [People might] say, 'how that boy walk so' ['why does that boy walk like that']? But at least they only can say that but they not sure." They are therefore depending more on others' uncertainty than on their assent and consent for a successful performance.

As the two examples above suggest, there are fairly complex calculations to be made for a successful incomplete performance. For example, the respondents know that their behaviour and their appearance should not both bear stigma symbols. One warns, "your dressing cannot match your swinging attitude. You might act girly or effeminate but you can't wear a pencil-foot Lees [skinny-legged brand name] jeans and a woman blouse and a woman pump." Another "walk[s] like a man" but wears makeup: "Mi box up mi face [I put on makeup] but it is only those who around me can notice it, but like the [straight people] don't notice that I am wearing makeup."

Language can also be mobilized for partial engagement. When in groups, the participants recode words to express homosexual desire in the presence of unsuspecting heterosexuals. Thus, "two guys walking coming, you could say, 'girl, the chile in the red [redacted][3] big, eeh?' And im naw go find out because you say [redacted]. In fi wi world we know weh we a talk bout." ('Girl, the guy in the red has a big penis, doesn't he?' And he won't realize because you said [redacted]. In our world we know what we're talking about.)

Cracks are also engineered in the fulfilment of heterosexuality's "gyalist" criterion. Students invite both men and women to their university dorms, but "try to balance" their relative numbers so that observers cannot finish the sentence, "a pure man come a him room, so that mean seh . . .". (Only men come to his room, so that means. . . .)

This could be what Goffman (1959) is referring to in his discussion of the various discrepancies between appearance and reality in impression management. Perhaps these participants have chosen, as he puts it, to "forgo [their] cake and eat it too" (p. 41). That is, although they know and follow most of masculinity's "negative rules" (Kimmel, 2002, p. 105), contrary behaviour is "indulged in secretly" (Goffman, 1959, p. 41) because of the satisfaction it brings them. Thus, the respondent who "walk[s] like a man" also engages in "secret consumption" (ibid., p. 42) of makeup.

The Toll of Performing

"Like you in this shell and you just want to break out."

Goffman (1963) argued that the negative effects of passing are incorrectly "assumed" (p. 87). Some of the participants disagree: monitoring their behaviour and appearance, as well as contending with others' surveillance and reactions, is "exhausting". It is especially stressful when the sharp-eyed audience perceives gaps in the performance that escape the respondents themselves, such as when a participant and friends in a fast food restaurant were received with a hush and whispering by the other patrons even though they had thought they were "just going about our regular way, not out there singing".

Added to the fatigue and stress described above is one of the psychological repercussions discussed by Renfrow (2004, p. 500): dissonance resulting from denial of self. One participant attributed the discomfort to the knowledge that "within yourself that's not how you want to [behave]. It's a lot of strain, a lot of lie, living in denial in order to stay alive." Another expressed existential angst, saying, "You become the lie."

Passing the Other Way

"Not even the straight man can identify them as a man."

So far, the discussion has concerned passing for a heterosexual male. But there are others who are attempting to pass for heterosexual females, convincing heterosexual men through a variety of tricks that they are women. In their "drags" – "lace" (the lace-front hair weave popularized by the African American performer Beyoncé), high heels, skimpy clothing, their bras stuffed with tissue and their underwear with buttock padding, and high-pitched voice ("Mi throw out one of the bass pon one of the speaker dem" [I turn down the bass on one of the speakers]) – they draw pride and affirmation from their success. As one said, "When you say, 'me did trick one boy', you feel good inna yourself. Me is a man and me dress like woman and man a call to me." (When you say, "I tricked a guy", you feel good inside. I am a man dressed like a woman, and men are calling to me.) Arousal of a heterosexual man is a ringing endorsement of their success – sex with him even more so.

The following story shows one participant's partial success, subterfuge techniques and the penalty for playing this high-risk game:

> I see this guy and say, "Oh my God you are very sexy; I like you" and him a look pon me [he looks at me] from head to toe and him say, "How half of you sound like man and half of you sound like woman?" So I say, "I am a woman" and him say him would like to feel my pum pum [vagina]. I just hurry up and tucked it [penis] under, and [he] feel, [but] you can't make him over-feel [feel too much]. As him touch it I say "oh" [and] laugh and make him draw weh [away] him hand. And then him take out him dick and me start to have oral sex with him. And him shub [shove] him hand inna my breast, and draw out the tissue. [I] hold on pon [onto] him penis and try run [interjection from another participant: "cause him nuh (doesn't) want you bite him"]. It was very risky, because him take up some big stone and a come after me.

Participants even knew of someone who had sex with heterosexual men without being discovered, using an inventive combination of douches, lubricants and duct tape.

To Be Real . . . Freedom Fighters?

"They are so forceful and without any fear."

Some respondents refuse to pass or to stay in their "likkle corner". They reject the invisibility that passing offers, and instead stake a claim for the visibility of alternative identities and sexualities. They are Goffman's (1963) "social deviants", who live "in collective denial of the social order" (p. 143) and believe that "the life they lead is better than that lived by the persons they would otherwise be" (p. 145). Those who display their alternative sexuality overtly are called "real", which suggests, as they said, that for them it is not a performance but a natural expression of their self that they should not have to deny. Said one participant defiantly, "I just be myself. I don't want to blend in", while another said, "I always say, we nah guh hide [we're not going to hide] to please no one."

These "flamboyants" engage in what many observers call "flaunting". They wear makeup, dress in tight, revealing (often women's) clothing, display very "feminish" gestures, and even in some cases express their homosexual desire in public. They might sit on each other's laps, braid each other's hair, and call to men on the street: "wah gwaan, big hood [what's up, you well-endowed man]!"

Some of their peers think that by "sprinkling rainbows" too aggressively on the Jamaican public, flamboyants are increasing homophobia. They agree with Goffman's (1963) description of social deviants as a severe threat to the status quo that must be contained. However, the flamboyants construe their refusal as a matter of claiming universal human and civil rights. One said, "I will live my life personally how I feel to live my life, just like how I woulda feel fi do [how I would feel about doing] the job cleaning for the night." Others said that flamboyants envisioned themselves as pioneers in a political movement: "Nobody is willing to take a stand for them, so them a now [now they are] the Nelson Mandela, Marcus Garvey, Nanny of the Maroon[4] . . . dem a make statement fi di gay community say, 'we are here' [they feel they are making a statement on behalf of the gay community: "we are here"]."

An older participant described flamboyants as predominantly younger men "throwing a tantrum [saying], 'listen, I am here, I am not leaving, I'm here to stay'".

The flamboyants have other ways of claiming their visibility and neutralizing critics: by playing on the very homophobia they are critiquing. When one respondent and friends hear homophobic dancehall lyrics, for example, they "make noise"– that is, they dance and sing along. If any heterosexual men complain, they say, "'wah gwaan, girl! [how are you doing, girl!]' because when someone hear you call them 'girl' [others will] think you know them from somewhere". They are thus implicating in their putative immorality those who would condemn them. The lesson no doubt to be learned by potential critics is to allow them their behaviour, distasteful as it may be, to avoid guilt by association.

The participants do not only protect themselves in discursive ways. One was "always prepared for anything, whether you have a knife or a machete in the corner". Another defensive strategy was to be in public alone, as onlookers were more likely to say, "chuh, a suh 'im act already" (oh well, that's just how he is).

Other participants refuse to pass but are less overt in their denial – they do not engage in flamboyant behaviour but carry recognizable stigma symbols, such as their manner of walking or talking, the clothes they wear, and so on. Their refusal to pass can be a frustrated response to the psychic toll of performing. One sometimes lets the performance wane: "I can't bother with that anymore . . . it's tiring, so I'm just being myself." Or they may also simply realize that their performance is imperfect and stop trying, as another said: "I've given up now because I've tried everything . . . how I walk, how I talk, not drawing attention to myself, and people still" discerned the stigma symbols.

Complicating/ed Homophobia

Although every participant could give multiple examples of homophobic incidents and was well aware of the general imperative to pass, the narratives also reveal a degree of acceptance of homosexuals in Jamaican society. One respondent actually denied that Jamaica was homophobic, claiming that most anti-gay expressions in Jamaica were spouted by homosexuals fearful of the "ripple effect": the negative repercussions of homosexuality's move into the public sphere. Another was confident that homophobia would soon disappear: the influence of North American media's increasingly frequent and sympathetic portrayals of homosexuality was encouragement to be "more bold [and] more OK with me". A third participant believed that Jamaicans' distaste of hypocrisy led them to prefer honesty surrounding sexuality: "people will more appreciate you if you don't hide it. I think even Jamaicans hate liars."

This attitude might explain why when a respondent walked past a group of men with friends, the men, having identified them as gay, merely said, "a fi dem life . . . mek dem have fun" (it's their life . . . let them have fun). The transgender participants who had sex with ostensibly unaware heterosexual men said that some of the latter knew their sexual partner was biologically male, but were so aroused that they ignored the fact. Another respondent recalled that high school classmates' teasing ended after a display of self-defence against an attempted judgement: "One person said, 'Well, if he's gay he's just gay – let's leave him alone.'"

Perhaps most surprising are the accounts of safe spaces in the ghettos, typically considered the crucible of the hypermasculine archetype in Jamaica. Many participants had first- or second-hand stories about people known to be gay surviving and even thriving in the inner-city communities. As the last example above also suggests, people who had earned others' respect seemed more likely to be allowed some leeway. One participant's fellow community members said, "im gay but im nice" (he's gay but he's nice). In another, the "nine-night" (wake) of a gay teacher and longtime resident was "blocked" by his gay friends (that is, the partiers, some in their drags, sprinkled rainbows).

Nevertheless, there were limits to this tolerance. The participant who believed it was better to be honest still did not feel comfortable being honest with acquaintances. Those who enjoyed some acceptance were well aware that the tolerance would soon evaporate if they were to "bring it cross [cross the line]", or make visible their same-sex desire. Thus, "as soon as you start carry guy come there [into the community] and them know seh you suh [they know you're gay], you're going to get the judgment". Similarly, a participant who blew kisses at male co-workers in jest knew that "there was no way I can actually kiss the guys them – you'll get beaten".

Bringing It Cross?

The small body of research and autobiographical accounts of the experiences of LGBTQ people in Jamaica echoes the stories told in this chapter. While the literature shows that men often feel compelled to "pass" by performing the hypermasculine ideal (Glave, 2008; King, 2014; Powell, 2008), it also concurs with the participants' narratives that suggest the Jamaican attitude to homosexuality is less than straightforward. In fact, almost two decades ago, Williams (2000) called it "a badly kept secret that Jamaica has a perceptibly vibrant gay population" (p. 106). Lafont (2009, p. 113) pointed to the "level of immunity" that well-off LGBTQ Jamaicans enjoy. The dancehall scholar Hope (2006, 2010) has noted the difference between the public expression of homophobia and the private tolerance of homosexuality, while West and Hewstone's (2012) quantitative research showed varying degrees of homophobia in Jamaica, and that contact with queer Jamaicans is associated with less prejudice. One of Moore's (2014) respondents demonstrated the importance of both contact noted by West and Hewstone (2012) and respect noted in the present study, saying that people in his community accepted him as a gay man because they "know you, and *know that you are a nice person*" (p. 120; emphasis in original).

Events on the ground provide added evidence. Although in 2008 Prime Minister Bruce Golding, leader of the Jamaica Labour Party (JLP), declared that he would not allow gays to serve in his cabinet, his opponent in the 2011 general elections, Portia Simpson-Miller, not only publicly disagreed with that stance, but swept to a landslide victory. Furthermore, in 2018, Golding's successor and Jamaica's new prime minister, Andrew Holness, stated that "sexual orientation is not a criterion" in his decision on cabinet membership and that Jamaican "culture is evolving" vis-à-vis homosexuality (Virtue, 2018). More evidence resides in the staging of Pride Week celebrations over the last few years without major incident. These examples suggest that shrouding Jamaica in a blanket of homophobia (viz. Padgett in *Time* [2006] asking rhetorically whether Jamaica is "the most homophobic place on earth?") obscures the nuances of Jamaicans' perceptions and navigations of and around homosexuality.

This assumption has also been questioned in other parts of the Caribbean.[5] Although similar dynamics of policing, passing and performing exist in the region, Murray (2009a) noted that the degree of sexual diversity in Barbados, for example, "renders problematic . . . depictions of uniform regional homophobia" (p. 3). Crichlow (2008) recalled that in his youth certain expressions of homosexuality were accepted by older Trinidadian women (p. 113). And King (2014) pointed to the protective function of factors such as social status, gender expression and geographic location for Caribbean LGBTQ people.

King and others have posited that the key dynamic driving queer navigation of life in the Caribbean is discretion; however, they have rejected the assumption that this necessarily implies greater homophobia. To them, rather than the Euro-American "closet", there is the "open secret", where an individual's nonheteronormative sexuality is known but not confirmed and s/he is able in many cases to live a fulfilling life (King, 2014, p. 63; La Fountain-Stokes, 2009). King quoted a Jamaican activist who said that "the real problem is not *being* a homosexual but *confirming* that one is a homosexual" (2014, p. 73; emphasis in original). She argued for an alternative epistemology whose lack of "explicit revelation" (2014, p. 64) does not imply self-hatred, as Euro-American queer thought would have it. Rather, it renders "coming out" unnecessary, and in fact is transgressive for challenging heteronormative rules of behaviour and identification (King, 2014). Murray (2002) agrees with the problematic nature of the Euro-American assumption that coming out is a necessary rite of passage. He stated that the lack of public disclosure is born of pragmatism, not hypocrisy, and is a compromise that protects family reputation, *inter alia* (p. 113). Although not engaging discretion directly, Moore (2014) decried the "homohegemony"

(p. 128) of Euro-American LGBTQ and called attention to the "different ways of being queer that are located within an African-diasporic/Afro-Caribbean tradition of queerness as praxis" (p. 127), such as mati-work in Suriname.[6]

According to King's (2014) argument, people living the open secret are not passing. They appear to be in a liminal place: betwixt and between fixed, socially recognized and legitimated identities. But she also states that a minority of people are able to flout the putative limits of discretion, under the protection of the above-mentioned factors. The present study has provided examples of this openness – and, it appears, without those buffers. It has also shown that the limits themselves are sometimes pushed. Even the participant who knew not to "bring it cross" challenged the dictates of the open secret by making sexual jokes with men. If it is true that "public gender transgression is more problematic than private homosex" (King, 2014, p. 69), these participants are freedom fighters indeed.

There are many examples of flamboyants sprinkling rainbows in the Jamaican newspapers, reported in salacious detail (e.g., Hines, 2012; Walker, 2013). In Jamaica and elsewhere, hypervisibility has typically been imposed upon non-gender-conforming people as a means of stigmatization (Moore, 2014) and/or to serve political purposes that may or may not be in their best interests (Shakhsari, 2012). While most have shied away from this hypervisibility in the interest of self-protection, flamboyants actively engage it. Hypervisibility becomes an indicator of their own agency, a presentation of their ideal, true self and their "human-ness", just as Moore (2014, p. 88) found for denizens of the dancehall. Hypervisibility can therefore be construed as a reaction "against a dominant culture that regularly holds [those engaging it] up for ridicule" (Bristow, 1989, p. 71), as Bristow understood the deployment of "camp" (broadly speaking, the US analogue to "flaunting") in the United States.

Passing: Revolutionary or Conservative?

From one perspective, the ramifications of passing are negligible: passing performances assist in the maintenance of the boundaries of acceptable gender and sexuality within Jamaican society. Thus, the performers are the ultimate losers, as they follow the rules that reject them. At best, then, as Renfrow (2004) argues, passing is negotiation, not subversion. Johnson (2002) points out that the heteronormative order can in fact be bolstered by inclusion of the "'good' gays and lesbians who are prepared to pass as heterosexual citizens" (p. 330).

This point has been made by observers of the Caribbean as well. Murray (2002) cautions that what he calls "masking" "contributes toward the ongoing public and governmental silence and erasure of alter-sexualities" (p. 114).

Playing *"le jeu de l'homme Martiniquais"* (the game of the Martinican man) (Murray 2002, p. 112) demonstrates what Williams (2000) said gays in Jamaica have long known: that "there is no legitimacy as a gay person or a gay community" (p. 108). This might explain why the flamboyant – the "'bad' gays" (Johnson, 2002, p. 330) – refuse to play the game. They are angling for a new game with new rules that assert their legitimacy. Hence the rejection of this group by both those who want to pass, and by wider society.

However, passing can also be seen as transgressive, because it "threatens to throw into chaos a societal system based on the perceived difference between self and others", as Inness (1997, p. 161) states, discussing lesbians' passing strategies. That is, passing unsettles the boundary between heterosexual and homosexual, and thereby has "the potential to wreak havoc" (Inness, 1997, p. 161). The fact that the audience is being tricked by those who should by rights be ostracized and alienated is additional subversion. As Alexander (2004) noted, passing as straight could in effect "de-center . . . as it remaps" (p. 396). Passing as female has similar, and perhaps greater, potential: those in their drags engage in "deconstructionist social protest" (Gamson & Moon, 2004, p. 50) by unsettling not just heterosexual/homosexual, but male/female as well.

The most potentially radical iteration of passing is the participants' successful incomplete passing. In this technique resides the possibility of slowly but inexorably changing what it means to look and behave like a heterosexual Jamaican man. That is, the "made-up" performance of the participant who "walks like a man" might redraw heterosexual masculinity, given that it is validated by a heterosexual audience. Thus, although they themselves may not realize it, this is another means of resistance and subversion, albeit much subtler than that of the flamboyants.

Moore (2014) described a phenomenon similar to successful incomplete passing in her discussion of those she called men who have sex with men (MSM) in the dancehall. She argued that they become "invisible", or "indecipherably different" (p. 125) in the dancehall through "a doubled effort to queer the dancehall space and the strategic deployment of heterosexual signifiers in an attempt at misdirection" (p. 108). Thus, in the dancehall, as with the participants in the present study, the bounds of heterosexual masculinity are extended through MSM engagement. Further, the very hyper-heterosexuality of the dancehall creates a "blind spot": all dancehall participants are assumed to be heterosexual *because* they are in the space (p. 92). Paradoxically, that allows MSM to function within it, without worrying about intense surveillance, because putative stigma symbols are re-signified by their fellow partygoers. Thus, Moore (2014) says, "through strategic performances of the self, [MSM] may access the space under the cover of heterosexual assumption" (p. 92). This subterfuge is facilitated by what she asserts is the queerness of the dance-hall itself; she uses "queer" to mean gender-nonconforming behaviour, such as "hyper-adornment" (p. 53), not necessarily same-sex desire (see also Ellis, 2011). Perhaps blind spots exist outside the dancehall as well, in public (typically heterosexually, if not hyper-heterosexually, coded) spaces, which could allow for the reinterpretation and manipulation of stigma symbols described by successful incomplete passers. In this way, homophobia *enables* queerness (Moore, 2014).

Queering has not been limited to the dancehall. More than ever, straight (particularly working-class) men have been appropriating putatively gay male or feminine aesthetics. They pay close attention to their personal grooming and fashion, wear earrings and the like. In truth, the boundary dividing Jamaican male heterosexual and homosexual aesthetics has been blurring for a while, explained by some as the result of the influence of international media and local role models (Ellis, 2011; Figueroa, 2004; Hope, 2010; Moore 2014). Thus, what two decades or so ago would have been obvious stigma symbols now adorn heterosexual men: shaped eyebrows, tight pants, bright, matching clothes and elaborate hairstyles. For that reason, braids alone do not automatically brand one a homosexual anymore.

This recalls the conclusion that Crespo Kebler (2003) drew from her exploration of Puerto Rican lesbians' lives. She argued that their "identities arise from the dissonant and contradictory messages contained in the norms of heterosexuality they appear to negate" (p. 190). In a similar way, Jamaican alter-sexualities can take advantage of the paradoxes and complications inherent in the dictates of Jamaican male heterosexuality to form and re-form their own *and* heterosexual male identity.

Strategically, Essentially, Constructivists?

The respondents' narratives stimulate consideration of queer theory's insistence on constructivist over essentialist views of sexual and gender identity. The assumption that identity is an innate, fixed essence has been contested by the constructivists' argument that identities are "inter-subjectively negotiated social and historical products" (Epstein, 1996, p. 145, cited in Gamson & Moon, 2004, p. 48; Irvine, 1994). They rightly posit that construction opens the possibility of subversive re- and/or deconstruction (viz. Butler, 1990). However, the narratives suggest that both perspectives are important in identity theorization and politics (Irvine, 1994; Johnson, 2002).

We have seen that the flamboyants believe they are "real". This appears to be contrary to the "realness" espoused by participants in ballroom culture:[7] for the latter, realness aims to "disguise their gender and sexual nonconformity" in the outside (heteronormative) world (Bailey, 2011, p. 380; Caldwell, 2009).[8] For the passers (towards heterosexual maleness or femaleness) as well, emically an authentic identity does exist. They would therefore argue against Goffman's (1959) idea that all identities are staged, and certainly against Butler's position that there is no self preceding social discourse, just a body performing "a stylized repetition of acts" (1990, p. 140). The men are clear that, *pace* Bristow (1989), they do have a crucial "existential essence" (p. 61) that they choose to display or conceal. As Prosser (1998) said, there are those who "seek very pointedly to be nonperformative, to be constative, quite simply, to *be*" (p. 32; emphasis in original). Although he was writing about transsexuals, his argument applies to the respondents who make such statements as, "it's not so much of acting girly: it's just being me". Another participant had learned this after many failed attempts at walking like a heterosexual man: "I ketch the walk [I do the typical male walk] and then . . . you just see the hip them start sway [the hips begin to sway]. . . . Is just you."

Renfrow (2004) would agree, saying that the very act of passing demonstrates that there is an authentic self ironically highlighted in the very performance, by showing the person what s/he is not. For some transgender participants, passing the other way brings them closer to the truth, the real self that they know they are. Thus, some "like to dress like female because they feel that they *are* female" (emphasis added). To recall Renfrow, the authentic self is highlighted by showing the person what s/he *is*.

Queer theorists might argue that the participants are engaging in "strategic essentialism", the "strategic use of a positivist essentialism in a scrupulously visible political interest" (Spivak, 1988, p. 13). For the flamboyants and the participants in their drags this seems likely: their "realness" and their "femaleness" become resources to be engaged in a push for recognition and visibility.

At the same time, this "realness" and "femaleness" must be performed, which requires engagement with notions of particular identities. While they make a claim for essence, it is clear that participants' identities are also social constructions, the product of "historical and political circumstances under which subjectivities are continually created" (Irvine, 1994, p. 241). Their identities are therefore "self-creations . . . on ground . . . laid out by history" (Bristow, 1989, p. 61).

Murray (2002; 2009a) would agree: he points to the swirl of discourses that form Caribbean queer identities in the context of colonialism in a unique combination of the local and the global. The respondents' identities are forged

by long-standing legislative prohibitions, long-established ways of being homosexual in Jamaica, changing aesthetics of heterosexual masculinity, louder
internal and external pro-alternative sexualities voices and so on, which create
particular notions and expressions of other sexual identities. Moore (2014)
details the various historical and contemporary forces and discourses that have
shaped heterosexual and nonheterosexual Jamaican identities. For example,
she argues that colonial and legislative discourses attempted to homogenize
and discipline queer identities and black sexualities to create a compulsory
heterosexuality and therefore shape how sexualities are understood and
engaged (p. 68). She also discusses how Euro-American LGBTQ organizations
and discourses have increasingly influenced the way heterosexuals and nonhet-
erosexuals perform and perceive queerness (p. 107), through the dissemination
of Northern queer aesthetics and notions of "'legitimate' queerness" (ibid.) as
"out and proud politics", for example (p. 119).

Conclusion

First, a caveat: the aim of the study out of which these stories emerged was not
the excavation and interrogation of gay and transgender identifications. This
chapter is therefore an incomplete account of the participants' lives and subjectivities. Nevertheless, it has provided at least a glimpse into the lives of some
gay and transgender Jamaicans and produced some useful insights.

There is a great deal of work to be done to fully understand the complexity
of identifications and how LGBTQ Jamaicans navigate their lives in an often
hostile environment. More ethnographic work on the contexts in which
different identities are engaged and performed – the play of (strategic) essentialism and constructivism; the meaning of claims to authenticity; the pecu-
liar dynamics of the various LGBTQ identities and strategic responses to
homophobia, for example – would provide a rich understanding of the diversity of ways of being LGBTQ[9] in Jamaica, and ample material for comparison
with LGBTQ people in other parts of the Caribbean and the world. So far,
research has (understandably) focused on homophobia; in so doing, it has
perhaps unwittingly placed the LGBTQ Jamaican in the position of victim.
This chapter suggests that there is insight to be gained both at the micro and
macro levels by putting the individual or group, rather than the structure,
at the centre of the research. This is not to negate the powerful influence of
homophobia in Jamaican society, but to acknowledge that "over-generalising
statements [about homophobia] . . . silence and flatten out the complex ways
in which bodies and their desires are organized and evaluated in everyday life"
(Murray 2009a, p. 17).

Goffman's theorization has proven a useful starting point for understanding stigmatized people's attempts to manage the impressions of others. However, it has ultimately proven insufficient: corrections, complications and extensions of his theorization have been necessary to allow for a nuanced account of the strategies of these gay and transgender Jamaicans. As Renfrow (2004) says, passing is a complex phenomenon, not just a "one-to-one handoff of identities" (p. 499). This research suggests that passing techniques involve multifarious negotiations of identity, not only determined in conversation with social norms (Renfrow, 2004), but with the actors' own level of desire to completely obliterate the "spoiled" identity and/or their inclination to subversion. Passing should be considered a phenomenon occurring under a system of domination rather than simply for fun or convenience (Renfrow, 2004), and its potential effects on that system must be examined. Importantly, the research has also shown that some people are not willing to pass, whether out of fatigue, resignation or defiance. As a result, they make important ontological and political statements, and even potentially reshape Jamaican heterosexual masculinity.

A key theme running through many of these participants' responses is the rejection of binaries. This is one of the central pillars of queer theory: that LGBTQ identity destabilizes the categories of homosexual and heterosexual, male and female (Irvine, 1994). Murray (2009a) agrees with this eschewal of either/or: for him, gay Barbadians' identifications are "pieced together in myriad, contextually shifting ways . . . resulting in contextually produced, potentially multiple subject positions" (p. 5).

There is emancipatory potential in these participants' behaviours. They are not necessarily hapless victims of structure, but agents with potentially subversive agendas within it. For Moore (2014), the presence of MSM in the dancehall shows the "radical potential . . . that allows the queer to stay at home and change the meaning and possibility of the place" (p. 127). In the de- and reconstruction that Butler (1990) says inevitably happens through performance, there is the chance to – knowingly or unknowingly – produce identities that challenge the status quo. Hutton (2007, quoted in Moore [2014, p. 75]) stated that performativity has long been a survival strategy for African descendants in the Caribbean. Creating an identity palatable to the power structure functioned as misdirection then, and it can be argued, serves a similar purpose now (Moore, 2014).

The participants engage with fixity and authenticity and slide along the scale of identifications in their performances. Crespo Kebler's (2003) prescription for lesbians in Puerto Rico could apply to this Jamaican example: that identities be "contingent, rather than fixed . . . sites of revisions and contestations of normative categories [and] rallying points for a resistance to classifications"

(p. 191). This is a flexibility that can only be useful in the tricky navigation of the Jamaican environment.

And beyond, perhaps. The participants in this study would give Walcott (2009) added justification for his belief that Euro-American LGBTQ could learn from their counterparts in the developing world. He says that, "queers of the global south . . . continue to keep sexuality in flux, often offering some of the most provocative ways of re-imagining what sexual minority practices might look like and what kinds of politics might be required to secure those practices" (p. 14). For Moore (2014), an important lesson to be learned is that "queer liberations [sic] may be sought outside of a Human Rights framework" (p. 128). The examples here certainly suggest that the unsettling achieved at the micro level has a range of macro-level implications. What is to be made of them – by LGBTQ and heterosexual, by Jamaican and non-Jamaican – remains to be seen.

Notes

1. The respondents were participating in a study exploring HIV-related stigma and discrimination and HIV risk among men who have sex with men. To understand the context of HIV risk, we asked participants to talk about their lives in Jamaica. They ranged in socio-economic status from homeless sex workers to professionals, and in age from late teens to their fifties.

2. Politicians have refused to include the rights of sexual minorities in the Charter of Fundamental Rights and Freedoms or to strike off the Victorian-era anti-buggery law.

3. For confidentiality reasons the actual code word is not presented here.

4. Marcus Garvey and Nanny of the Maroons were declared Jamaican National Heroes for their acts of resistance to authority.

5. Homophobia is being "complicated" in other contexts as well. See Murray (2009b) and Weiss & Bosia (2013) for examples.

6. "Mati-work" is an African-derived practice engaged in by Surinamese working-class women. These women have relationships with men and women and do not claim a distinct sexual or gender identity (Wekker, 2006).

7. Ballroom culture is an underground community of LGBT and straight blacks and Latinxs who "use[s] performance to create an alternative discursive terrain and . . . kinship structure" (Bailey, 2011, p. 367). "Balls" are opportunities for their participants to engage with and perform a variety of gender and sexual identities.

8. This is not to deny the complexity of the project of performance of "realness" in ballroom culture, which has been explored by Bailey (2011) and Caldwell (2009) *inter alia*, but simply to point out what appears to be a clear distinguishing feature of the two understandings of "real". A comparison based on a fuller understanding of realness in Jamaica is necessary, but beyond the scope of this chapter.

9. The "L" in "LGBTQ" has been virtually ignored: research on lesbians in Jamaica is well overdue.

References

Alexander, B. (2004). Passing, cultural performance and individual agency: Performative reflections on black masculinity. *Cultural Studies: Critical Methodologies 4*(3), 377–404.

Anderson, P. (2009). *The changing roles of fathers in Jamaican family life (Working Paper No. 10).* Kingston, Jamaica: Planning Institute of Jamaica.

Bailey, M. (2011). Gender/racial realness: Theorising the gender system in ballroom culture. *Feminist Studies, 37*(2), 365–386.

Bristow, J. (1989). Being gay: Politics, identity, pleasure. *New Formations, 9,* 61–81.

Butler, J. (1990). *Gender trouble: Feminism and the subversion of identity.* New York, NY: Routledge.

Caldwell, R. (2009). Gender queer productions and the bridge of cultural legitimacy: "Realness" and "identity" in *Paris Is Burning.* In B.G. Harden & R. Carley (Eds.), *Co-opting culture: Culture and power in sociology and cultural studies* (pp. 77–90). Lanham, MD: Lexington Books.

Carr, R. (2003). On "judgements": Poverty, sexuality-based violence and human rights in 21st century Jamaica. *Caribbean Journal of Social Work, 2,* 71–87.

Chevannes, B. (1993). Sexual behaviour of Jamaicans: A literature review. *Social and Economic Studies, 42*(1), 1–45.

Cowell, N. (2011). Public discourse, popular culture and attitudes towards homosexuals in Jamaica. *Social and Economic Studies, 60*(1), 31–60.

Crespo Kebler, E. (2003). "The infamous crime against nature": Constructions of heterosexuality and lesbian subversions in Puerto Rico. In L. Lewis (Ed.), *The culture of gender and sexuality in the Caribbean* (pp. 190–212). Gainesville: University Press of Florida.

Crichlow, W. (2008). History, (re)memory, testimony and biomythography. In T. Glave (Ed.), *Our Caribbean: A gathering of lesbian and gay writing in from the Antilles* (pp. 101–131). Durham, NC: Duke University Press.

Ellis, N. (2011). Out and bad: Toward a queer performance hermeneutic in Jamaican dancehall. *Small Axe, 15*(2), 7–23.

Epstein, S. (1996). A queer encounter: Sociology and the study of sexuality. In S. Seidman (Ed.), *Queer theory/sociology* (pp. 145–167). Malden, MA: Blackwell.

Figueroa, M. (2004). Male privileging and male "academic underperformance" in Jamaica. In R.E. Reddock (Ed.), *Interrogating Caribbean masculinities: Theoretical and empirical analyses* (pp. 137–166). Kingston, Jamaica: University of the West Indies Press.

Gamson, J., & Moon, D. (2004). The sociology of sexualities: Queer and beyond. *Annual Review of Sociology, 30,* 47–64.

Glave, T. (2008). *Our Caribbean: A gathering of lesbian and gay writings from the Antilles.* Durham, NC: Duke University Press.

Goffman, E. (1959). *The presentation of self in everyday life.* New York, NY: Anchor.

Goffman. E. (1963). *Stigma: Notes on the management of spoiled identity.* New York, NY: Simon & Schuster.

Gutzmore, C. (2004). Casting the first stone! Policing of homo/sexuality in Jamaican popular culture. *Interventions, 6*(1), 118–134.

Hines H. (2012, July 8). Cross-dressers held at St Ann fete. *Sunday Observer*, p. 3.

Hope, D. (2006). *Inna di dancehall: Popular culture and the politics of identity in Jamaica.* Kingston, Jamaica: University of the West Indies Press.

Hope, D. (2010). *Man vibes: Masculinities in the Jamaican dancehall.* Kingston, Jamaica: Ian Randle.

Hutton, C. (2007). The creative ethos of the African diaspora: Performance aesthetics and the fight for freedom and identity. *Caribbean Quarterly, 53*(1/2), 127–149.

Inness, S. A. (1997). *The lesbian menace: Ideology, identity and the representation of lesbian life.* Amherst: University of Massachusetts Press.

Irvine, J. (1994). A place in the rainbow: Theorizing lesbian and gay culture. *Sociological Theory, 12*(2), 232–248.

Johnson, C. (2002). Heteronormative citizenship and the politics of passing. *Sexualities, 5*(3), 317–336.

Kimmel, M. (2002). Masculinity as homophobia. In E. Disch (Ed.), *Reconstructing gender: A multicultural anthology* (3rd ed.) (pp. 103–109). Boston, MA: McGraw-Hill.

King, R. (2014). *Island bodies: Transgressive sexualities in the Caribbean imagination.* Gainesville: University Press of Florida.

La Fountain-Stokes, L. (2009). *Queer Ricans: Cultures and sexualities in the diaspora.* Minneapolis: University of Minnesota Press.

Lafont, S. (2009). Not quite redemption song: LGBT-hate in Jamaica. In D. Murray (Ed.), *Homophobias: Lust and loathing across time and space* (pp. 105–122). Durham, NC: Duke University Press.

Lewis, L. (Ed) (2003). *The culture of gender and sexuality in the Caribbean.* Gainesville: University Press of Florida.

Lewis, R.A., & Carr, R. (2009, November). Gender, sexuality and exclusion: Sketching the outlines of the Jamaican popular nationalist project. *Caribbean Review of Gender Studies, 3.*

Moore, C. (2014). *Wah eye nuh see, heart nuh leap: Queer marronage in the Jamaican dancehall.* MA thesis. Queen's University, Kingston, Canada.

Murray, D. (2002). *Opacity: Gender, sexuality, race, and the "problem" of identity in Martinique.* New York, NY: Peter Lang.

Murray, D. (2009a, November). Bajan queens, nebulous scenes: Sexual diversity in Barbados. *Caribbean Review of Gender Studies, 3.*

Murray, D. (Ed.). (2009b). *Homophobias: Lust and loathing across time and space.* Durham, NC: Duke University Press.

Padgett, T. (2006). The most homophobic place on Earth? *Time* [online]. http://www.time.com/time/world/article/0,8599,1182991,00.html

Powell, P. (2008). Dale and Ian. In T. Glave (Ed.), *Our Caribbean: A gathering of lesbian and gay writing from the Antilles* (pp. 296–303). Durham, NC: Duke University Press.

Prosser, J. (1998). *Second skins: The body narratives of transsexuality.* New York, NY: Columbia University Press.

Renfrow, D. (2004). A cartography of passing in everyday life. *Symbolic Interaction,* *27*(4), 485–506.

Rich, A. (1994). Compulsory heterosexuality and lesbian existence. In A. Rich, *Blood,* *bread, and poetry. Selected prose 1979–1985.* New York, NY: W. W. Norton.

Schleifer, R. (2004). *Hated to death: Homophobia, violence and Jamaica's HIV/AIDS* *epidemic.* New York, NY: Human Rights Watch.

Seidman, S., Meeks, C., & Traschen, F. (1999). Beyond the closet? The changing social meaning of homosexuality in the United States. *Sexualities, 2*(1), 9–34.

Shakhsari, S. (2012). From homoerotics of exile to homopolitics of diaspora: Cyberspace, the war on terror, and the hypervisible queer. *Journal of Middle Eastern* *Women's Studies, 8*(3), 14–40.

Spivak, G.C. (1988). Subaltern studies: Deconstructing historiography. In R. Guha & G. C. Spivak (Eds.), *Selected subaltern studies* (pp. 3–34). New York, NY: Oxford University Press.

Virtue, E. (2018, April 17). "No problem with gays in my Cabinet" – Holness. *The* *Gleaner.* https://jamaica-gleaner.com/article/lead-stories/20180417/no-problem -gays-my-cabinet-holness

Walcott, R. (2009, November). Queer returns: Human rights, the Anglo-Caribbean and diaspora politics. *Caribbean Review of Gender Studies, 3.*

Walker K. (2013, June 3). Unruly gays back with a vengeance. *Jamaica Observer,* p. 1.

Weiss, M., & Bosia, M. (Eds.). (2013). Global homophobia: States, movements, and the politics of oppression. Chicago: University of Illinois Press.

Wekker, G. (2006). *The politics of passion: Women's sexual culture in the Afro-Surinamese* *diaspora.* New York, NY: Columbia University Press.

West, K., & Hewstone, M. (2012). Culture and contact in the promotion and reduction of anti-gay prejudice: Evidence from Jamaica and Britain. *Journal of Homosexuality,* *59*(1), 44–66.

White, R.C., & Carr, R. (2005). Homosexuality and HIV/AIDS stigma in Jamaica. *Culture, Health and Sexuality, 7*(4), 347–359.

Williams, L. (2000). Homophobia and gay rights activism in Jamaica. *Small Axe, 7,* 106–111.

7.

The Myth of the "Free Pass" in Jamaica

An Assessment of the Representation
of Women Who Love Women in the Media

"GEMMA D."

Haiku on being the only lesbian from Jamaica
Wonder whose pussy
I was eatin' when I had
a P.O. Box there?
—Staceyann Chin

In conversations with my gay male friends, I have often heard them claim lesbians get a "free pass" in Jamaican society. The invisibility of lesbians and bisexual women in public discourse is too often considered a signal of our liberation in Jamaica. Whereas the nation's colonial-era buggery laws have legislatively placed gay men in the crosshairs of state-sanctioned homophobia, they have simultaneously alienated lesbian and bisexual subjects through the erasure and occlusion of female same-gender eroticism. The queer female subject is an unimaginable figure or an anomaly in Jamaica's national imaginary. Her invisibility forecloses a much-needed dialogue about the abuse, rejection and harassment that so often shape her experiences. Put differently, the "buggery law" has engendered a public understanding of homophobia as a phenomenon lived only by gay men, with little acknowledgement of how it has produced a larger environment of stigma that impacts the lives of female queer subjects. Implicit in claims that lesbians get a "free pass" is the notion that women who love women are subject to less harassment, are fully integrated and accepted into Jamaican society, and that their relationships are socially acknowledged as valid.

This chapter seeks to contest this notion by investigating public narratives about lesbianism and queer female eroticism represented in the media. Jamaica's local newspapers offer a considerable, albeit superficial, archive of public narratives of and local engagement with lesbianism.[1] While news coverage is not an adequate social barometer for local attitudes towards homosexuality, it does offer considerable insight as to what the media and the gatekeepers of information would have the public believe about queer women. So I use this chapter to uncover the circumstances under which women who love women appear in public discourse and to ultimately decipher what are the terms of their representation on the national stage. Since there is no legislation criminalizing lesbian sex, we often do not question the ways queer women are portrayed when they do appear in public discourse, and this chapter is an attempt to change that. I offer a counterpoint to these representations by using memoirs of and/or interviews with Jamaican lesbian activists in order to also make room for their stories. Their voices are particularly valuable because while more same-gender-loving women are becoming increasingly visible, few speak publicly about navigating heterosexism in Jamaica. Undoubtedly what follows is coloured by my own experience as a Jamaican queer activist and academic; many of the claims I advance are based on personal experience.

The representations of women who love women in the media are salient because they exist within a context where the vast majority of the Jamaican public find homosexuality to be morally reprehensible. In a study measuring local attitudes and perceptions towards sexual minorities in Jamaica (Boxill et al., 2011), 72.2 per cent deemed homosexuality in women, and 82.2 per cent homosexuality in men, to be morally wrong. That small statistical disparity indicates that all homosexuality is subject to moral condemnation and that by extension, same-gender relationships are not generally recognized as valid or socially acceptable regardless of the gender of the sexual minorities. Yet of those surveyed 67.1 per cent believed society to be more accepting of female homosexuality and thought it to be the case because "women can do things men cannot do whilst suffering few negative consequences" (Boxill et al., 2011, p. 3). The authors of the study did not explicate what those "things" may be, but the statistic does affirm that it is generally perceived that women who love women experience less stigma or alienation in Jamaica. I can only speculate that this perception is due to the difference in how masculinity and femininity are policed – particularly the level of physical affection allowed among women but prohibited among men in public. It also has to do with the virtual absence of media reports chronicling violence against women who love women in contrast to the prevalence of reports of mob violence against gay men. It is easy to interpret this absence as a signal that violence against queer women does not or rarely occurs. In her brilliant study of lesbophobia, theorist Charmaine Crawford argues that whereas extreme expressions of homophobia against gay men take the form of mob violence or public shaming, women who love women often experience intense homophobia through sexual violence or "corrective rape" that takes place in the private sphere (2012). In this chapter, I expound on this nuance by assessing the public and private configuration of homophobia in Jamaica.[2]

I seek to counter the notion of the "free pass" by making three central claims: The first is that women who love women appear in a discourse of pathology and deviance. For lesbians are summoned into public discourse only to be portrayed as predators on high school girls, as born-again Christian ex-gays[3] or as exotic objects of entertainment in media reports. The second is an assessment of exotification and voyeurism of lesbianism inherent to invasive coverage of same-sex marriages among women in the media. The invasion of privacy that takes place on the national stage is an extension of practices of voyeurism and objectification of women generally. I assess both aspects of voyeurism taking place in the media and in one's daily life. The third is an assessment of the private versus public configuration of homophobia in Jamaica mentioned earlier.

I employ the terms lesbian, bisexual and women who love women interchangeably to give credence to the diversity of labels and categories to which women in Jamaica subscribe. I do recognize, however, that women involved in same-gender relationships often do not identify with any of these terms. In fact, the refusal of Jamaica's sexual minorities to embrace labels or to name their desire is typical if not central to the Caribbean context. The rejection of the verbal appellation for one's desire fits a larger Caribbean script where visibility and queerness as identity are decentred as ideals of sexual liberation in local advocacy platforms. This is a notable contrast to imperial celebrations of an "out" gay identity in the North tied to neoliberal ideals of consumerism and globalization. The indifference towards naming in the Caribbean has enabled women to more freely pursue their relationships with other women while avoiding the stigma of imposed Western, colonialist labels like "lesbian" (see Calixte, 2005; Wekker, 2006). I privilege the term "same-gender" instead of "same-sex" in this chapter to make room for women whose gender identities do not align with their assigned biological categories. In doing so, I seek to denaturalize gender as the presumed marker of and "natural" extension of sex as a biological class. Too often theorizations of womanhood exclude transgender people, and consequently I find the term "same-gender" to be more inclusive of the variations of gender identities and loving relationships that exist across the region.

I concede that my usage of the term "queer" in this chapter unavoidably enacts a type of imperialism on the subject of discussion. First, the term queer simply has no currency in Jamaica or in the wider anglophone Caribbean context. Second, it is often used by Eurocentric queer theorists to fashion same-sex eroticism of brown people living in the Global South as a new, postmodern invention without historical antecedent. Indeed, many scholars have noted that queer theory itself has often framed sex-gender love through an unmarked whiteness and inevitably reiterates whiteness as universal to queerness (Hames-García, 2011; Tinsley, 2008). In their estimation, while queer theory has inaugurated groundbreaking critique of the assumed stability of hetero- and homonormative terms, it has often failed to assess how sexuality and gender identity are mediated or complicated by constructs of race.

This critique notwithstanding, I choose to use the term "queer" as other Caribbean scholars have done to signify a refusal to conform to normative structures. For example, theorist Tinsley (2008) uses queer "in the sense of marking disruption to the violence of normative order and powerfully so" (p. 199) in her recuperation of an archive of homoeroticism in her article "Black Atlantic, Queer Atlantic". Similarly, Ellis (2011), in her brilliant study of a queer performance hermeneutic in dancehall entitled "Out and Bad", reclaims the term "queer" to make room for nations of the Global South. She claims: "If queer began as a critical term within a European American-oriented academic sphere, it has since expanded its limits, staying true to its roots as a term of unstable and shifting signification, and has been deployed by scholars of various backgrounds, theoretical orientations and fields" (11).

Like Ellis, I too seek to expand the limits of the term by applying central aspects of its meaning to the Jamaican context. Like so many other theorists, I claim the word "queer" in order to name a vast array of practices, relationships and gender performances that include but are not limited to same-gender desire. Thus, for my purposes here, I use "queer" as an inclusive, umbrella term that acknowledges behaviour and identities that do not conform to hegemonic structures and cultural norms.

Theoretical Work on Women Who Love Women in the Anglophone Caribbean

There is a paucity of theoretical work on lesbianism in Jamaica specifically, but there is a growing body of research on lesbianism in the anglophone Caribbean in general. Theorists M. Silvera (1991), Alexander (1991, 2006), Wekker (2006), Crawford (2012), Elwin (1997) and Tinsley (2008) all affirm in some way that heterosexuality is paramount in regional constructs of sexuality and is accompanied by naturalizing discourses of gender. There is a deep-seated intolerance of same-gender practices and desires that pervades the region, but the increasing visibility of gay rights activists and more vocal calls for "tolerance" in the face of violence against sexual minorities suggest that attitudes may be changing. Religious ideology is often used as justification for intolerance, but negative attitudes and perceptions towards sexual minorities are due in part to our colonial legacy that imposed Eurocentric concepts of respectability, sexuality and gender in the region. Heterosexuality is central to local constructs of masculinity and femininity (Lewis, 2003; Chevannes, 2001; Alexander, 1991, 2006), so a "real" man and a "respectable" woman are heterosexual. In Jamaica, like the rest of the region, heterosexuality relies on patriarchal constructs of gender that require the subordination of women and the veneration of men as wielders of power and is justified through biological determinism. This chapter takes as its theoretical foundation the view that lesbians occupy a particular position in what Alexander and Crawford refer to as a heteropatriarchal structure. Heteropatriarchy refers to the intersection of patriarchy and heterosexism – a system where heterosexuality is adjudicated as "natural" and the only legitimate form of sexuality. This is true for places like Jamaica whose national identity is defined as staunchly heterosexist and whose homophobia has been the subject of particular international scrutiny. Women who love women therefore defy patriarchal constructs of womanhood that stipulate motherhood, subordination to men and heterosexuality as defining characteristics of femininity and national identity. Hence representations of them in the media reveal how public discourse frames subjects who refuse to comply to prescribed norms.

Discourse on Pathology and Deviance

When the queer female subject enters the public discourse, she is often portrayed as a sexual deviant or predator. On 6 March 2006, the *Gleaner* ran the headline "High School Girls Gone Gay", decrying the "presumptuous" advances of lesbian girls on unassuming young women ("High School Girls Gay", 2006). In the article, a past student from a local school in Kingston recounts a solicitation by a young woman who said "I like you" and who persisted in her pursuit of the other student despite being rebuffed. The writer describes the events of the night as a series of "sickening" episodes in which the young lady is so "numb with disbelief" that she leaves. The student proclaims: "I felt like I was raped." The article also catalogues stories from students across all-girls high schools who have witnessed affection, flirting, kissing or "fondling" among their peers. It postulates that the administrations of the schools and even the Ministry of Education itself were concerned and outraged at these reports. Other administrators claimed ignorance or denied the reports. It recounts the story of a fifth-former who claimed that some girls were "pretending to be the males in the relationship" and would "wear their skirts on their hips instead of their waist, male shoes and carry wallets". The article concludes that "lesbianism is rampant" and that all all-girls schools are "being affected".

This report is salient for the following reasons: First, the claim in the headline that high school students had "gone gay" affirms heterosexuality as the natural, default state and connotes same-gender desire as an unnatural deviation from that state. Lesbianism appears as an exposé on sexual deviance. Second, sexuality is described through a binary of health and disease in which lesbianism is the illness and heterosexuality the healthy state of being. In the language of interviewees in the article, same-gender eroticism and desire among women is seen as a contagious illness and labelled a "malignant practice". One anonymous senior official even states that "homosexual behaviour among the girls is spreading like a fungus" ("High School Girls Gay", 2006). Fungus is a metaphor that names sexual difference as debased, putrid, rot. Moreover, "fungus" encapsulates the fear of contagion of homosexuality and on some levels its inherent contradiction. For if same-gender desire is contagious, then heterosexuality cannot be the "natural" default state for everyone. Third, the panic over the prevalence of same-gender desire and eroticism among the youth is undoubtedly a fear of the "contamination" of the future generation and perhaps impending ruin of the natural (heterosexual) order. More significantly, throughout the article lesbianism is coded not as a natural variation of human sexuality but as "behaviour" or simply a series of actions that contaminates the well-being of a healthy (read: heterosexual) student body. Language steeped in a dichotomy of health and illness and descriptions of same-gender love and expressions as "practices" or "behaviours" reduces lesbianism to simply the realm of the carnal and physical. It overlooks the emotional connection and natural affinities that occur among women in their relationships with other women.

Additionally, the disbelief highlighted in the article at the presumptuousness of the queer female subject's decision to openly express her interest in another woman is also about the threat that the visibility of same-gender love poses to Jamaica's cultural mores. Heterosexist order and social purity are maintained through the policing of public space and the prohibition of expression that show otherwise. As such, same-gender desire is to remain hidden, and queer women, like all queer subjects, are to be invisible and to police ourselves by keeping our desires a secret. My critique of the woman's disbelief is not intended as a defence of the queer woman's continued pursuit of the young lady with no regard for her wishes. Nor is it even to accept that dynamics of domination and exploitation expressed in the article are inherent to same-gender relationships among women. Rather it is an assessment of the implications of reporting this encounter in the media. For the crux of the story is the fact that the lesbian has transgressed the norms of a public space that is defined as staunchly heterosexist. Throughout the article, the queer female subject is fundamentally guilty of not "knowing her place" and of daring to openly expose that those who occupy public spaces are not all heterosexual. The expression of same-gender desire is an intervention that counters the homogenization of public space and citizens in a nationalist discourse that defines Jamaican national identity as resolutely heterosexist. As such, in an attempt to compensate for the intervention, the article's final paragraph discounts the possibility of a credible relationship between two women by ascribing a "male" and "female" role to the parties involved. In doing so, same-gender relationships among women are portrayed as mere failed copies of heterosexual partnerships. Thus, a relationship between two women cannot be a threat because no woman can really take the place of a man in a relationship. Perhaps what is most egregious of the representation of the queer female subject in this article is its conflation of lesbianism with sexual abuse. School officials explain lesbianism as a process whereby older students recruit younger ones: "The Queens High School official pointed out that the lesbians in the upper school usually endeavour to recruit the young girls from the first and second forms." Here lesbianism is defined as a relationship of predator and prey, victimizer and victim. The conflation of lesbianism with sexual abuse justified outright discrimination against students as officials claimed at one school that they would not accept "professing lesbians" into sixth form to curb the recruitment of younger students.

The representation of the lesbian as aggressive, sexual predator preying on young high school girls is a trope that continues to be deployed in media reports after 2010. At the time of writing, new reports of alleged "recruitments" of younger students at high schools in Kingston resurfaced in the media. The headlines and stories egregiously stereotyped lesbians as either delinquents – "Lesbian Gangs Terrorise Schools: Students, Parents Complain about Sexual Advances" (Budd, 2011) – or as sexual predators: "Lesbians and Learning – Younger Students under Siege at Corporate Area All-Girls Schools" described lesbianism as a problem in need of rectification: "Lesbian Issue Tops Agenda – Principals to Address Matter at Next Meeting" (Hunter, 2012). In fact, in the latter article, the head of JAPSS (Jamaica's Association for Principals of Secondary Schools), Mrs. Sharon Reid, claimed that the alleged increase in lesbianism was due to a paradigm shift whereby young women have begun to see certain "practices" as normal and acceptable. The conflation of sexual abuse with lesbianism and the editorializing of it in the press totally ignore the fact that sexual exploitation and harassment are problems that exist across categories of sexual orientation. Moreover, it is improbable that if the students involved were of the opposite sex, the media would label their activities as "heterosexual practices". Nor would there be any headlines proclaiming "heterosexual gangs terrorise schools" in coverage of unwarranted sexual advances by older male students on younger female students at local high schools. These reckless, stereotypical portrayals only ultimately sustain and create an environment of stigma for queer youth and particularly queer women who are the main subjects of these reports. For they use the offence of abuse as an excuse to portray the behaviour as inherent to homosexuality itself. Furthermore, the sensationalism of the coverage foreclosed what had the potential to be a constructive public conversation about the presence of queer students as a sector of youth in high schools who need guidance and affirmation. The emphasis on lesbianism as "practice" or "behaviour" prohibits its conceptualization in public discourse as an aspect of the identities of young people who, like all youth, need tools and outlets to express their sexuality in healthy ways. These representations in the media complicate the notion that the invisibility of lesbians in discussions of homophobia signals an environment of acceptance. Instead, the coverage reveals that queer female subjects are presented in discourses of pathology, deviance, delinquency, contamination and sexual exploitation. These discourses ultimately deny queer women our humanity.

Voyeurism and the Objectification of Women Who Love Women

Deviance and pathology, however, work alongside the media's penchant for voyeurism in its coverage of lesbian weddings. The media attention given to marriages and same-gender relationships among queer women when taken at face value may be perceived as a form of public acceptance of gay women. In my conversations with those who claim lesbians get a "free pass", the media coverage of marriages between women who love women is often cited as a form of visibility that is not equally afforded to relationships among gay men. There is a very real absence of representation of relationships among gay Jamaicans in the media in general, and typically the only visible gay relationships (outside of the ones people may know of in their local communities) are those featured in North American television shows. Thus, media coverage of lesbian weddings is perhaps one of the few moments in which gay relationships become visible on the national stage and offers an opportunity, though limited, for the public to interface with a representation of a queer relationship involving Jamaican citizens. The fact that these visible relationships featured in the public sphere are among queer women and not gay men is typically used as an affirmation of the free pass or to shore up the perception that lesbianism is "less threatening" to a heterosexist society. Another observation that props up the myth of the free pass is the fact that there is seemingly less public repudiation of physical affection among queer women. In fact, many reference, without query, the desire of many men to "watch" intimacy between two women and once again take it as a sign of acceptance or "freedom" for queer women. Indeed, this phenomenon is also cited as an explanation for why there seems to be no media attention to violence against queer women. I will address the invisibility of violence later in my discussion of the private and public configuration of homophobia.

Both arguments cloud critical engagement of the terms of our visibility in the media. I argue that both our visibility in the media and the excitement of eroticism among women operate under the rubric of voyeurism, which is ultimately disempowering. Voyeurism in the media and the desire to "watch" are fundamentally about the co-optation of queer eroticism and a fascination with difference. This co-optation, whether for the purposes of newspaper sales or for male entertainment in local social circles, is about the power of looking and the capacity to look-in at will. Here, making us visible or making our intimacy the subject of scrutiny is an exercise of power, not a signal of our freedom. Hence, what follows are two sections in which I assess voyeurism in the public and private sphere in an attempt to debunk the myth of the free pass. I offer a brief theoretical discussion of voyeurism, followed by an assessment of the coverage of lesbian weddings in the media as well as an analysis of the desire of men to "watch" lesbian eroticism. In doing so I ask us to consider: what are the terms of our visibility in the media, and is visibility itself synonymous with freedom or acceptance of women who love women?

Voyeurism and the Pleasures of Watching

Voyeurism is an instrument of scopophilia (pleasure in looking). In her brilliant study *Visual and Other Pleasures*, Mulvey uses psychoanalysis to establish how patriarchy has structured film form and offers an analysis of the gendered nature of looking and representation in film. While the medium and context in her theory differ from the subject of this chapter, her analysis of scopophilia is still apt for our understanding of voyeurism. She postulates that pleasure is derived from reducing the on-screen person to a passive object that is visually consumed by an active spectator. This spectator lives out a voyeuristic fantasy through the illusion of looking in on the private world on screen. The voyeurism that I refer to here is not about partaking in private fantasy worlds on screen, but it is about pleasure in looking at the Other. It is about using a gaze to objectify, reduce and consume that which is different for one's own pleasure.

Voyeurism of Lesbianism and Same-Sex Marriage in the Media

The media has frequently featured queer women as objects of wonder or as subjects of gossip particularly in reports of marriages among Jamaican female couples. If the state uses the buggery law to police intimate activities of consenting adults, then media reportage on lesbian weddings enacts a type of voyeurism through coverage of marriages among queer citizens. In June 2012, the *Gleaner* ran a headline "Lesbian Nuptials at Silver Sands" (Frater, 2012), chronicling the responses of members of the community to the wedding ceremony of same-sex couple Nicole Dennis-Benn and Emma Benn that took place in the parish of Trelawny. In the story, local religious figures decried the illegitimacy of the union by emphasizing that Jamaican law does not recognize same-sex marriages. Dennis-Benn, a Jamaican citizen, was unaware as to how news of her wedding reached the press and the coverage of her ceremony, intended as an intimate, private ceremony with family and close friends, became a scandalous, gossipy tidbit. The newspaper's decision to report the wedding of a private citizen without her or her partner's consent is an outright invasion of privacy. In reports such as this one, same-gender love among women functions as the object of a heterosexist gaze on the national stage, where an otherwise invisible group of people are made visible only so their "difference" as non-heterosexuals can be put on display. Looking in at same-gender weddings is about wondering at our "strangeness". Same-gender relationships between women are odd, bizarre objects of fascination, and women who love women are mere subjects of curiosity.

This voyeurism typifies coverage of the weddings of many sexual minorities in Jamaica: lesbians, bisexuals and gay men alike. But lesbians and bisexual women have more frequently been subjected to this in the media than gay men. On 25 June 2012, Jamaican Nadine Derby's marriage to her partner Heather Thomas was reported in the *Jamaica Observer* ("Jamaican Lesbian Weds", 2012) simply to inform the public that pictures of their wedding were posted on her Facebook page and that she had gone to her first gay pride parade. Neither Derby nor Thomas is a public figure in Jamaica, and so the coverage begs the question as to the relevance of reporting the weddings of private citizens in national media. Similarly, Jamaican human rights advocate Maurice Tomlinson's wedding to his partner in Canada was featured in the *Jamaica Observer* ("Jamaican Gay Activist Marries Man", 2012) and in the *Gleaner* (J. Silvera, 2012). In the *Gleaner*'s story, Tomlinson reported receiving several death threats following the news report and was ultimately forced to flee the country. The fact that Tomlinson, the only one of the subjects mentioned above who actually resided in Jamaica at the time of the report, was forced to flee the country points to the very real dangers of being visible and openly gay in Jamaica. When sexual minorities in Jamaica decide to be visible, they do so at considerable risk to themselves and to their loved ones. News coverage that thrusts them into the limelight not only scandalizes and exploits sexual minorities through titillating media reports, but it takes away from these citizens their agency in determining when and to whom they disclose their sexuality. While visibility is essential to changing public perception of a stigmatized community, when members of marginalized groups are made visible without their consent and in ways that endanger them, then visibility undermines the potential progress that can be made. Those who use our representation in the media as proof of the free pass overlook the fact that visibility that bypasses our right to consent works counter to respecting our privacy and the legitimacy of our relationships as deeply personal aspects of our lives that ought not to be the subject of public speculation. In these media reports, the representation of queer women is about the spectacle and consumption of difference on the national stage.

It is worth noting, however, that even in the face of sensationalist media coverage, queer citizens have sought to recuperate their agency by using the unwanted attention to engage the public. Following the initial report and after reading senseless comments to the online article calling for the hotel to be fined and for her and her spouse to be charged, Dennis-Benn decided to speak publicly (Dennis-Benn, 2012). She contacted the *Gleaner* to share the story of her marriage on her own terms and to reclaim this aspect of her life as her own. While on 4 June 2012 the *Gleaner* ran a sensationalist, misleading headline, "Lesbians Legally Wed", the details of the story itself were groundbreaking in some ways. It was perhaps one of the few instances in which a queer woman was able to share her own experiences and her own story on the national stage. Dennis-Benn explained that she returned to Jamaica to re-enact her wedding to her African American partner, Dr Emma Benn, in Brooklyn in order to share with family and friends from home. She also outlined her own struggles with coming to terms with her sexuality in the latter years of her high school education. Dennis-Benn described feeling alone, as if she were the "only lesbian in Jamaica" (*Gleaner*, 2012). As underscored in Staceyann Chin's haiku at the beginning of this chapter, invisibility inscribes lesbianism as a singular anomaly, and so loneliness and enforced hiding or silence are central aspects of the marginalization of queer female subject. Countering the typical narrative that sexual minorities flee to the North due to Jamaica's homophobia, she explained that her decision to leave the country was as a result of classism and not merely hostile attitudes towards gays and lesbians – often portrayed as a function of Jamaica's presumed backwardness. The capacity to speak for herself and to share her story was particularly powerful because of the general absence of the narratives of queer subjects on the national stage. In recounting her personal journey, Dennis-Benn enabled other young queer subjects to identify themselves in her, to hear their stories told and consequently to imagine themselves as members of a national imaginary that includes them. I relate her story to underscore that for visibility to be empowering, it must be done on our own terms. Women who love women should be able to decide when to make our relationships visible and when to critically engage the public. Dennis-Benn's capacity to transform the invasion of privacy into an opportunity for critical engagement with the public does not excuse the insidious nature of the initial coverage. Instead, it only emphasizes the power and importance of enabling queer subjects to be willing participants in public dialogue about sexual diversity.

Voyeurism in the Daily Life: "Can I Watch?"

The myth of the free pass often confuses male fascination with intimacy between two women as a sign of acceptance. The failure of local media to report violence against queer women is explained as a result of male fascination with intimacy between two women, which is in stark contrast to public repulsion at intimacy between two men. I argue that the allure of lesbian eroticism is merely an extension of voyeurism and affirmation of heteropatriarchal constructs of sexuality. I unpack the requests "Can I watch?" or "Can I join?" in order to make two central claims: First, lesbianism and bisexuality can pose no danger to a heterosexist normative order if same-gender eroticism among women is a mere object of pornographic entertainment and queer women are agents working to fulfil a heterosexual, male fantasy. Second, since queer women defy prescribed norms of femininity, voyeurism is a technology of reappropriation that seeks to reinscribe men's claims to women's bodies in a patriarchal society.

"Can I watch?" is an (in)famous request or demand made by men to which many same-gender female couples have had to respond. It is typically followed by or alternated with "Can I join?" Women whose gender presentations conform to normative expectations of performances of femininity are more likely to be subject to this than masculine-identified, or masculine-presenting, women. Instead, in online forums and communities of lesbian and bisexual women, masculine women often report being subject to verbal abuse by men who perceive them as "threats" or "competition" in their pursuits of women. In the context of an underground, though increasingly visible, LGBT population, the most accessible avenues for same-sex eroticism among women are porn industries and North American television programmes. The popularity of threesomes, "girl-on-girl action", in these markets sutured to male voyeurism has undoubtedly informed how the public relate to women who love women. The pornography industry is not solely responsible for male voyeurism because it operates in relationship to already pervasive heterosexist constructs of gender and sexuality. It does, however, shape how same-gender eroticism is perceived and certainly offers a context for the popularity of the request. "Can I watch?" co-opts and delegitimizes female same-sex eroticism by making it an object of the male gaze. "Can I watch?" is not a request for permission;

rather it is a notification to the subjects that they are already being watched and that their expression of intimacy is not private. The request transforms the unwitting female couple into performers for a male spectator, and in this instance, their intimacy is no longer their own. The demand is therefore an affirmation of lesbian eroticism as spectacle or taboo, a reminder that it exists outside of the realm of the "norm". It is an act of co-optation reducing intimacy to the realm of the pornographic. Here their intimacy is only desirable and nonthreatening because it has been domesticated as a mere spectacle of difference or pornography.

The fact that same-gender female couples are most commonly subject to the request is unquestionably part of a larger cultural practice of objectifying women's bodies. For watching also affirms a heteropatriarchal notion of female sexuality, pleasure and desire. Enlightenment constructs of gender and sexuality were transplanted from Europe and imposed upon the Caribbean. They stipulate that masculine sexuality be aggressive, forceful, and female sexuality be passive (Lewis, 2003). Within this binary, sex is about procreation, enforcement of male dominance with female as submissive receptor. Crawford (2012) writes: "[W]omen's sexuality is restricted through men's claims over their bodies for sex and reproduction. . . . While men have been granted sexual autonomy through codes of hegemonic masculinity, women have been seen as relying on men for sex, and only receiving it through them." Same-gender eroticism between women disrupts men's claims to women's bodies as they are suddenly forced to confront the possibility of female pleasure and female sexuality outside of the masculine counterpart. As such, the requests "Can I watch" or "Can I join" reinscribe men's claims to women's bodies through the act of looking. Voyeurism is a tool of compensation in the face of heteropatriarchal panic, a type of policing of that which disrupts heteropatriarchal norms.

It is easy to misinterpret this request as a form of acceptance of the female queer subject as it exists in stark contrast to copious policing of expressions of affection among men and particularly gay and bisexual men. Due to the naturalization of gender dynamics endemic to constructs of heterosexual sex, anal sex between men inevitably involves a supposed feminization of homosexual men. For within heterosexual constructs, only women are penetrated (dominated) and "real men" are the penetrators. The request "Can I join" is easily construed as approval because it implies that the spectator considers same-sex eroticism among women as less threatening, whereas affection among gay and bisexual men is greeted with outright hostility, public shaming and mob violence. The reality that lesbianism or bisexuality among women is less "threatening" is not a function of acceptance as a legitimate or equal relationship; rather it is a signal that they are not taken seriously. It is not socially acceptable for a man to approach a heterosexual couple with a similar request because traditional constructs of masculinity and heterosexuality view women as property of their male partners, and the solicitation would be considered an insult to the male ego. Yet for lesbian couples, the solicitation is commonplace. This is so partly because a lesbian relationship is not recognized as legitimate for there is no man to claim either woman as "his" and to be afforded the social recognition and respect that accompanies his claim. Moreover, "Can I join?" reaffirms a heterosexist logic that does not recognize lesbian sex as "real" sex due to the absence of the phallus. For sex can only happen through sexual intercourse or the penetration by the penis. So sexual activity that occurs before the male "joins" is mere foreplay. The request is not a signal that same-sex relationships are equal to those among heterosexuals; rather it is an affirmation and reminder that the relationship and the intimacy are not credible. Thus, when "watching" is an act of domestication and lesbian eroticism is appropriated as spectacle, it is neither likely nor even necessary for the media to report public outrage over queer eroticism among women. For voyeurism already stymies any threat that eroticism could pose on the national stage.

Private versus Public Configuration of Homophobia

Voyeurism as a local technology of control does not preclude women who love women from being subject to acts of violence. The absence of media reports of violence against queer women has led many to believe that we are never subject to physical abuse or assault. The myth of the free pass relies on the invisibility of violence perpetrated against queer women, and the dearth of media reports obscures the victimization that many queer women experience. In this section, I first use the reports of women who love women to debunk the claim that queer women do not experience violence. This is in stark contrast to the virtual nonexistence of reports of violence against queer women in the local media. I then explicate that homophobia operates in public and private spheres by comparing violence against queer women and queer men. I postulate that violence in public and private spheres has a specific type of cultural meaning that corresponds to a heteropatriarchal logic. Within this logic, the invisibility of violence is crucial to keeping queer women and their contestation of prescribed norms invisible.

When lesbians and bisexual women refuse to "perform" for spectators, they are often subject to violence. The most common form of violence against them is sexual violence and verbal abuse. Unfortunately, there is very little official statistical evidence about sexual violence against queer women, but in public accounts from those who have dared to speak and write publicly about their experiences, sexual violence is a regular feature. Local activist Angeline

Jackson explains that when she and other women were sexually assaulted some years ago, they all understood that their sexual orientation was the motive ("Jamaican Case of Women", 2015). In Staceyann Chin's memoir *The Other Side of Paradise*, she recounts being held in the bathroom by a group of men threatening to sexually assault her at a university campus. Much of the verbal abuse and threats referred to her sexual orientation. Similarly, JFLAG has archived reports from lesbian and bisexual women whose family members collaborated with their attackers in attempts to change their sexual orientation (personal communication, 2013). Some women have reported being raped by members of the judicial system. Sexual violence perpetrated against queer women, otherwise known (problematically) as "corrective rape", is an instrument of homohatred. The term "corrective rape" is problematic because it privileges the perspective and purported intention of the perpetrator, as well as his underlying assumption that lesbianism is a pathology or illness needing to be "corrected". Rape is always about power and abject abuse. For lesbians, rape is a form of punishment for daring to contest the social order, a horrendous attempt to reclaim a female body that does not belong or acquiesce to heterosexual male desire. Like other victims of sexual violence, many queer women participate in a culture of silence and often do not come forward for fear of reprisal. The prevalence of sexual assault against women is also underreported and rarely acknowledged in public platforms advocating gay rights in Jamaica. The lack of media reports or public discussion about violence against women who love women often bolsters the claim that we get a free pass. That claim overlooks the fact that violence is not always visible in the public sphere, and the narratives of these queer women prove that, like gay men, abject abuse is a typical feature of their experiences as sexual minorities.

Due to the sexual nature of violence against queer women, their humiliation operates in a private sphere, and is not publicly seen or acknowledged. In stark contrast to the invisibility of violence against queer women, violence against gay men is not only commonplace, it is often more public. In November 2012, a YouTube video (M1pq1m, 2012) showcased a violent attack on a young gay male student alleged to have been in a compromising position with another male student in the bathroom at the University of Technology, Jamaica. While there was no evidence affirming whether the allegations were true or not, the accusations themselves were enough to draw a bloodthirsty mob threatening to assault the students. One successfully escaped, while the other sought refuge in the outpost of campus security. The video captured the security guards beating the young man while other guards stood by watching. The video also captured the cheers and jeering of the students outside. Some onlookers requested that the victim be released so they too could "have their fun". This episode sent shockwaves throughout local media and prompted the university to dismiss the security guards and to implement a programme calling for tolerance and respect for diversity. I recount this incident to highlight that violence against gay men is primarily about public shaming and exposure. Whereas beating gay men is a ritual performance reinforcing the heterosexuality of public space and affirming heterosexual identity, sexual violence against queer women in the private sphere is about silencing and dominating them. It ultimately makes them less likely to flaunt their sexual identity in public. In both instances, fear of punishment and repudiation whether in a private or public sphere for sexual "deviancy" keeps the queer population under control.

Thus, it is not that women who love women do not experience violence in Jamaica, as do their male counterparts; it is that public violence against gay men has a specific type of cultural meaning. In the context of a Jamaican culture where homophobia is seen as a badge of honour and heterosexuality is celebrated as a central aspect of national identity and hegemonic masculinity, violence against gay men is an expression of loyalty to a heterosexist national imaginary, an affirmation of normative gender and sexual paradigms and a ritual reinforcement of the boundaries of citizenship. Public violence against them is a type of communal expulsion and rejection, an act of discipline of the social outsider in attempts to ultimately affirm the self. Public violence against women who love women is unnecessary because we are already controlled through the dis-acknowledgement of our very existence. The enforced invisibility of the queer female subject necessitates that punishments for her "transgressions" be meted out privately so that the violence itself does not disturb her designated role in society as invisible deviant. For public recognition of her would signal that she – a woman no less – wields enough power to pose a threat. Thus, homophobic violence enacted in the public and private sphere has strategic meanings that ensure gay men and women who love women continue to occupy their designated place within the social body.

Conclusion

In June 2012, Jamaican singer Diana King came out as a lesbian on her Facebook page. The reaction of her fans was overwhelmingly positive. It was an incredible and empowering moment for so many young queer women and men because King is a distinguished artist who is adored both nationally and abroad. The narratives of pathology and deviancy, as well as the practices of exotification and objectification so endemic to media representations of women who love women in Jamaica, become less powerful when we and the public at large can identify this aspect of our identities in a person we all love and celebrate.

Diana King's status as a Jamaican icon and her coming-out perhaps enable us to envision a brighter future of how queer women will be represented on the national stage. The newspaper articles featured in this study not only do not tell the full story of who we are and our experiences; they are also stereotypical, prejudicial distortions that deny us our humanity. We may not be imagined as criminals in the way our gay brothers have been, but these types of representations tell us that women who love women in Jamaica are not free. When gay men embrace the myth of the free pass, they overlook the ways in which queer women share their struggle for acceptance and equality in Jamaica. We cannot act in solidarity with each other until we unlearn the myths about each other's experiences and realize that we are mutually imbricated in each other's struggles. In debunking the myth of the free pass, I have sought to demonstrate that the buggery law is but one facet of a larger system of heterosexism at work in Jamaica. Perhaps if we develop a more integrated vision of the complex ways in which that system operates, we will be better equipped to change it.

Notes

1. This study is limited to focusing primarily on media coverage of queer women. An ethnographic study on how gay men view women who love women in Jamaica is beyond the scope of this study, but it remains an area open for further research.

2. Crawford's essay offers the best analysis of the private and public configuration of homophobia and its impact on queer women in the Caribbean. The arguments advanced here seek to situate Jamaica within larger theoretical work about the experiences of queer women in the region.

3. The most notable ex-lesbian is Sister Michelle, who has appeared in television interviews and been featured in newspaper articles. She claims her story confirms the notion that gayness is a result of sexual violence and that homosexuality can be cured. See http://jamaica-gleaner.com/gleaner/20110828/lead/lead3.html

References

Alexander, M. (1991). Redrafting morality: The postcolonial state and the sexual offences bill of Trinidad and Tobago. In C.T. Mohanty, A. Russo, & L. Torres (Eds.), *Third world women and the politics of feminism* (pp. 133–152). Bloomington: Indiana University Press.

Alexander, M.J. (2006). *Pedagogies of crossing: Meditations on feminism, sexual politics, memory, and the sacred.* Durham, NC: Duke University Press.

Boxill, I., Martin, J., Russell, R., Waller, L., Meikle, T., & Mitchell, R. (2011). *National survey of attitudes and perceptions of Jamaicans towards same sex relationships.* Kingston, Jamaica: Department of Sociology, Psychology and Social Work, University of the West Indies.

Budd, J. (2011, June 12). Lesbian gangs terrorise schools. Students, parents complain about sexual advances. *Jamaica Observer*. http://www.jamaicaobserver.com

Calixte, S.L. (2005). Things which aren't to be given names: Afro-Caribbean and diasporic negotiations of same gender desire and sexual relations. *Canadian Women Studies, 24*(2/3), 128–137.

Chevannes, B. (2001). *Learning to be a man: Culture, socialization, and gender identity in five Caribbean communities.* Kingston, Jamaica: University of the West Indies Press.

Chin, S. (2005, April 28). *Haiku on being the only lesbian from Jamaica* [Web log post]. http://insmallpieces.blogspot.com/2005_04_01_archive.html

Chin, S. (2009). *The other side of paradise: A memoir.* New York, NY: Scribner.

Crawford, C. (2012). "It's a girl thing": Problematizing female sexuality, gender and lesbophobia in Caribbean culture-critical essay (Barbados). *Theorizing homophobias in the Caribbean – Complexities of place, desire and belonging.* http://www .caribbeanhomophobias.org/node/22

Dennis-Benn, N. (2012, June 2). Revolutionary love [Web log post]. http://ruminations -of-a-brooklyn-soul.blogspot.com/2012/06/revolutionary-love-by-nicole-y-dennis .html

Ellis, N. (2011). Out and bad: Toward a queer performance hermeneutic in Jamaican dancehall. *Small Axe, 15*(2), 7–23. http://muse.jhu.edu/journals/smx/summary /vo15/15.2.ellis.html

Elwin, R. (1997). *Tongues on fire: Caribbean lesbian lives and stories.* Toronto, Canada: Women's Press.

Frater, A. (2012, June 1). Lesbian nuptials at Silver Sands. *The Gleaner.* http://jamaica -gleaner.com

Hames-Garcia, M.R., & Martínez, E.J. (2011). *Gay Latino studies: A critical reader.* Durham, NC: Duke University Press.

High school girls gone gay! (2006, March 12). *The Gleaner.* http://jamaica-gleaner.com

Hunter, N. (2012, March 12). Lesbian issue tops agenda – Principals to address matter at next meeting. *The Gleaner.* http://jamaica-gleaner.com

Jamaican case of woman lured by rapists posing as lesbians in online chatroom gains international attention. (2015, April 28). *CBS SF Bay Area.* sanfrancisco.cbslocal .com/2015/04/28/jamaican-rape-case-of-woman-lured-into-online-chatroom-by -attackers-posing-as-lesbians-gains-international-attention/

Jamaican gay activist marries man in Canada. (2012, January 7). *Jamaica Observer.* http://www.jamaicaobserver.com

Jamaican lesbian weds. (2012, June 25). *Jamaica Observer.* http://www.jamaicaobserver .com

Lesbians and learning: Younger students under siege at corporate all-girls high schools. (2012, March 9). *The Gleaner.* http://jamaica-gleaner.com

Lesbians legally wed. (2012, June 4). *The Gleaner.* http://jamaica-gleaner.com

Lewis, L. (2003). *The culture of gender and sexuality in the Caribbean.* Gainesville: University Press of Florida.

Mıpqım (Producer). (2012, November 2). Beat di fish 2 youtube [Video file]. http://www.youtube.com/watch?v=sQiSjzYhrSo

Mulvey, L. (1989). *Visual and other pleasures*. Bloomington: Indiana University Press.

Reid, T. (2012, January 30). Threats force gay lecturer to flee. *The Gleaner* Lead Stories RSS. http://jamaica-gleaner.com/gleaner/20120130/lead/lead8.html

Silvera, J. (2012, January 8). Jamaican gay activist marries "soulmate". *The Gleaner.* http://jamaica-gleaner.com

Silvera, M. (1991). *Piece of my heart: A lesbian of colour anthology*. Toronto, Canada: Sister Vision.

Tinsley, O. N. (2008). Black Atlantic, queer Atlantic: Queer imaginings of the Middle Passage. *GLQ: A Journal of Lesbian and Gay Studies, 14*(2–3), 191–215. doi:10.1215/10642684-2007-030

Tinsley, O. N. (2010). *Thiefing sugar: Eroticism between women in Caribbean literature.* Durham, NC: Duke University Press.

Wekker, G. (2006). *The politics of passion: Women's sexual culture in the Afro-Surinamese diaspora*. New York, NY: Columbia University Press.

Yes I am a lesbian – Diana King. (2012, June 28). *Gleaner Power 106*. http://jamaica-gleaner.com

8.

The Impact of Jamaican Popular Culture in Shaping Normative Conceptions of Gender and Sexuality

DONNA P. HOPE

This chapter builds on my earlier work on gender and sexuality in Jamaican popular culture to explore the manifestations of normative and nonnormative formations of gender and sexuality in Jamaica. It attempts to map a thematic structure of popular cultural output, and its construction and dissemination of normalizing cues that impact on the conceptions of gender and sexuality. In so doing, this work uses themes from popular cultural formations, in particular Jamaican dancehall culture and roots theatre, to identify and explore the movement of patriarchal mores across the body politic of Jamaica's gender/sexuality structures. Here, the masculine formations that flit across these stages are explored and discussed. In addition, dancehall's popular slang and its graphic depictions are briefly examined. In order to craft a clear picture of the foregoing themes and structures, a brief examination of the underlying historical foundations is essential at the outset.

First, the gender debates that are evident in Jamaican popular culture operate within the wider context of Jamaica's social and cultural history. From the country's fundamentalist religious traditions, particularly the Christian and the Rastafarian, to its colonial legislative framework, notably the Offences Against the Person Act of 1864, which made certain sexual acts illegal, and which has long been used to prosecute homosexuals, there is a long history of conservative attitudes towards gender and sexuality in Jamaica. Notions of citizenship and nationhood are seen through the lens of creolization, and heterosexual bodies are promoted as the ultimate forms of nationhood. In concert, these factors have resulted in a reification of Jamaica's rigid class, gender and sexual hierarchies that privilege certain categories of people above others. In the context of this work on gender and sexuality, Jamaica's rigid patriarchal culture is enforced through strict policing of masculine boundaries and a simultaneous playing with and against these boundaries. Consequently, the rich and colourful terrain of Jamaican popular culture mirrors and refracts the country's gendered and classed structures, encoding multiple themes in the guise of entertainment and fun. Two very visible and very popular forms are dancehall culture and roots theatre.

Gender/Sexuality in Jamaican Popular Culture: Thematic Trends

Dancehall

At the time of dancehall culture's evolution in the 1980s, Jamaica's masculine ideal was an extremely conservative one, with hegemonic masculinity defined as wealthy, educated, employed and definitely heterosexual. Expensive cars, liaisons with multiple attractive women and absolute control over domestic arrangements were among the appurtenances and traits of idealized Jamaican manhood during and after the 1980s. As I noted in *Man Vibes: Masculinities in the Jamaican Dancehall* (Hope, 2010), dancehall culture's visions/fantasies of masculinity have been solidified and are interwoven with multiple identity debates. These visions/fantasies of masculinity flit across the stages of dancehall culture, and are often reflected in its highly sexualized and graphic lyrics. Known for its fashionable and flamboyant displays, dancehall culture's ritual performances of heterosexual masculinity are prominent. These masculine performances often feature graphic and explicit lyrics, and extreme role-playing. For example, in *Man Vibes*, I highlight five masculine debates in dancehall culture – a hyper-heterosexuality that stresses promiscuity and sexual prowess ("Ole Dawg"), which is also evidenced in the aggression articulated through gun talk/lyrics as exemplified in the Badman or "Shotta" representations of gun/violence (Bad Man), and via the vigorous policing of the hegemonic heterosexual consensus in Jamaica, which condemns male homosexuality through an extreme, graphic and violence-laden discourse (Chi Chi Man). Conspicuous consumption and excessive male posing are another site of dancehall's male identity (Bling Bling), as well as the softened and feminized masculinity evident in the growing, post-millennial, refined aesthetic physicality and the choreographic impulses and colourful and flamboyant styles exhibited by some male artistes and dancers in the dancehall (Fashion Ova Style). These five masculine exemplars are riven through with the key themes and debates that undergird dancehall's gender and identity debates. These thematic strands provide the foundation for dancehall's often problematic lyrical discourses, its graphic performances and its multiple contestations with male and female identity. If one examines these debates on a continuum, the figure of the polygamous, heterosexual and violent Badman is polarized against its antithesis, the feminized, passive, homosexual male.

Indeed, since the early 1990s, dancehall's sexualized male-on-male contests have historically displayed a marked hostility towards the figure representing male homosexuality, even while female homosexuality is often a non-issue. Within the dancehall, male homosexuality is ridiculed, chastised, rejected, purified by fire and fatally sanctioned. For example, Buju Banton's "Boom Bye Bye" in 1993 was an early and particularly direct response to the emergence of male homosexual identity into Jamaican public spaces from which it had previously been excluded. Dancehall's absolute lyrical rejection of male homosexuality represents a denial and refutation of any kind of feminization (Hope, 2006).[1]

As such, moving from Buju Banton's inflammatory "Boom Bye Bye" through the 1990s and into the twenty-first century, dancehall culture's lyrical debates insisted that, by their very definition, "real men" are expected to police the boundaries of heterosexual masculinity and, where necessary, expose another man's feminine traits or homosexual leanings. These lyrical debates run the gamut from naming, calling forth or "outing" of compromised masculinity, such as Alozade's, treatise "Chi Chi Crew", which also suggests that the conscious fraternizing with known or reputedly gay men (and women) is taboo.[2] Other songs in this vein include TOK's "Chi Chi Man" (2000), which suggests that guilt by association is a valid and viable option that merits the same sanctions as those reserved for male homosexuals – burning by fire or purification. The "fire burn" or "bun dem" ethos that signifies Rastafari's religious fundamentalism and Victorian notions of sexual conservatism are often conflated with the patriarchal impulses of dancehall/Rastafari in rendering of male homosexuality as an aberration of male heterosexuality that demands urgent attention – for example in Capleton's "Bun out di Chi Chi".

Elephant Man and Ward 21's turn-of-the-millennium treatise "Chi-Chi Man fi Get Sladi" suggested extreme and final sanctions for male homosexuals thus:

Chi-chi man fi get sladi
Di whole a dem a fi go tell di whole world ba-bye
Mi nuh wann nuh chi-chi frien man so nuh frien I
Run pass Olive an gawn wine pon Popeye

(Male homosexuals should be slain
All of them will have to tell the world goodbye
I do not want any male homosexual friends so do not try to befriend me
[You] run past Olive and are wining up on Popeye)

Here, male homosexuality is strongly denounced and fatal sanctions are proposed because "men have run past Olive and are wining up on Popeye". The symbols Popeye and Olive from the fictionalized world of popular cartoons suggest the "natural heterosexual" male/female couplet revered in dancehall culture. Those who have "run past" (that is, renounced) the "natural heterosexual" couplet corrupt the "natural" ordering of heterosexual relationships and deserve fatal sanctions.

Yet even with dancehall culture's extreme anti-male-homosexual debates and lyrical posturing, the creeping manifestation of what I label as the Fashion Ova Style masculine performance that has exploded in the postmillennial era[3] raises multiple questions as to the range of sexualities that are privileged in the spaces of dancehall culture. Harry Toddler's "Badman nuh Dress Like Girl" of the late 1990s sets the trend for a growing body of popular dancehall songs that directly identify, question and chastise a range of female aesthetics, including skin bleaching, increasingly appropriated by Jamaican men in the dancehall and beyond. Others include Bounty Killer's "Caan Believe Mi Eyes", Mavado's "Nuh Bleach wid Cream" and Cecile's "Woman Tings".

Within the context of this work, the fashioned and styled bodies of dancing men in tight pants in the centre of dancehall was backed by the rise of controversial, and highly popular, dancehall artiste Vybz Kartel. Kartel's body (which he has referred to as his "colouring book") is marked by multiple and competing gendered discourses that raised questions about the range of sexualities that are truly privileged in the dancehall. This includes the consternation around Kartel's obvious dalliance with skin lightening or skin bleaching. In Jamaica, this practice is identified by many as a social and cultural taboo, and often perceived as a feminized aesthetic practice. Since Kartel explicitly transgresses into what has been historically identified in Jamaica as feminine aesthetic territory, his song "Cake Soap"[4] encodes necessary refutations of his perceived slide into femininity – which in Jamaica is often conflated with a slide towards homosexuality. This song, therefore, contains multiple references to his desirability to the female as well as his virility as a man, including the statement that he does not depend on sexual enhancements or aphrodisiacs like "Viagra and horse tonic".[5] In addition, he explicitly rejects male homosexuality with the statement "Mi nuh love man so tek you yeye offa mi" (I am not attracted to men so take your eyes off me) among several others in the song. In so doing, Kartel makes significant attempts to ensure that his identity as a virile, sexually potent, heterosexual and non-feminized male is intact, even with his incursions into feminized skin bleaching/cake soap territory. As noted in the foregoing, many of these practices often depend heavily on the use of specific language codes or slang for their strength.

Slang

The framework of Jamaican language is also a rich and often extreme cultural space that is interconnected with popular cultural forms such as dancehall and roots theatre. As noted by Fancy Cat in one episode of the popular television comedy series the *Ity and Fancy Cat Show*, aired on TVJ in Jamaica, "Jamaicans have three language, English, Patwa and dancehall." This rather comical statement highlights the notion that Jamaican dancehall culture contributes to the development of Jamaican language through its pervasive and dynamic slang words and phrases, which are often transmitted into Jamaican Patwa or Creole.

The development of language in the region has been dominated by the structure of the society that developed under plantation slavery and colonialism, and this is reflected in Jamaica's sociolinguistic structure. The social stratification of the plantation system created a spectrum of language varieties in each territory where the European language was the target language and acquisition and mastery of this target language was in direct relation to social position and the degree of social contact with speakers of the target language. This resulted in the pyramid structure of the society being the same as the linguistic structure of the society, with those at the top socially speaking the European language, those at the bottom furthest away from it, and those in between gradually approximating it. In Jamaica, the pyramid structure of the society is oriented around standard English at the top and Patwa (also referred to as Creole or dialect) at the bottom (Barrett, 1997; Cassidy, 1971; Pollard, 2000; Pryce, 1997; Roberts, 1988).

"Patois", or "patwa", is a French term that is also used in English. It usually refers to a geographical dialect that is different from the standard language. In this regard, it denotes a lack of prestige that the association with a standard language creates. In Jamaica, the term is used interchangeably to refer to the Creole spoken by Jamaicans.

The term "slang" as used in this paper refers to only a segment of the language characteristic of a group, particularly restricted phrases, words or expressions that are usually novel, dramatic and contemporary. As such, slang can be ordinary English words that become imbued with unusual meaning, or it can be where new, concocted words are used to capture normal everyday meanings. This is very popular in Jamaican Creole or Patwa and also in the language of Jamaican dancehall. Additionally, slang is often associated with teenagers and youths. Jamaican dancehall culture, which is also a very popular form of youth culture, often throws up multiple variations of slang, many of which emanate from Kingston's inner cities and some of which are eventually often absorbed into ordinary Jamaican language. Rastafari language has also been a useful site of slang-making (cf. Pollard, 2000). In the context of this work, linguistic renditions that emanate from Patwa and slang that tackle, question, ridicule and negate male homosexuality have been an important part of the Jamaican language context for decades. As a child growing up in Jamaica, I learned early that "some man ah Maama Man" because they exhibited what were considered to be feminine tendencies. And a man was considered to be "lean" or "not straight" if he seemed to be moving towards homosexual tendencies. On the contrary, a "straight" man exhibited the approved heterosexual behaviours that are privileged in Jamaican culture. Indeed, many young men whose physiological and psychological makeup made them poor candidates for engagement in the hypermasculine activities at school (e.g., sports, chasing girls, brawls), or who simply preferred to engage in serious pursuit of an education, were labelled, ostracized and sometimes severely punished by their counterparts with statements such as "dah bwoy deh ah fish. Him fi stay wid di girls dem" (That boy is a homosexual. He should remain among the girls) being levelled against them.

Where this movement into the linguistic framework is concerned, some men utilize language codes to selectively identify themselves as a true heterosexual male. For example, during one period of my research, one male university student stated that the residents of the famous, all-male Chancellor Hall of residence at the University of the West Indies, Mona, refer to themselves as a plural group of "mans", as in "Mans of Chancellor" or "Chancellor Mans" and not by the grammatically correct term "men". According to this respondent, this was inspired by a line in a song by dancehall artiste Tiger, whose song "Yuh Dead Now" rescripted the meaning of the word "men" in popular Jamaican culture thus: "Two man a love up love up, Dem a men ." ([If] two men are engaged in romantic/intimate relations, they are homosexual.)

In this culturally coded framework of language, Jamaican Creole, slang and dancehall lyrics variously label and stereotype a homosexual man as pungai man, battyman,[6] batty bwoy, bugger man, funny man, poop man, Chi-Chi man, gay guy, faggot, Mr Faggoty, Anti-Man, Mr She and fish. These pejorative labels generally construct a gay male as someone involved in anal sex. Other terms such as Maama Man, Mr She, gay guy or funny man identify a man who wilfully renounces the accepted behaviours, aesthetics and practices that denote "true" (read as heterosexual) masculinity. These forms of gender policing through slang work to modify the behaviours of those who claim true heterosexuality. For example, another related label that imputes anal sex is the dreaded "number 2" which is immortalized in Jamaican Creole, popular slang and dancehall lyrics as in "him a play number 2" (he is engaging in anal sex or he is a homosexual). Based on this association, the number 2 is so dreaded by some men that they refuse to use the word "two", substituting "twice" instead, while others refuse to don the number on their jerseys in football games.

The foregoing labels are also used in ordinary dialogue or verbal confrontations as verbal missiles against male homosexuals, men suspected of having homosexual leanings, or generally against any male rival. In addition, the propensity to avoid overutilization of terms that may suggest or impute "too many many men" has resulted in sometimes humorous linguistic contortions. For example, Montego Bay is rendered in slang as GyalTego Bay and Mandeville is rendered as Gyaldeville in an effort to avoid the prefix Mon ("Man") and substitute the term Gyal (Girl) that denotes the feminine. In concert with this, dancehall lyrics and culture have developed and continue to use particular terms and phrases such as "dem switch" (they have switched from heterosexuality to homosexuality), "dem ah go di wrong way" (they are going in the wrong direction sexually), "man to man" (man in conjunction with another man) and "dem ah men" (they are homosexuals), to add to the growing range of slanguage that is used to construct heterosexuality as normative while simultaneously rejecting homosexuality or any other form of sexual being as deviant. Jamaican roots theatre has also utilized related mechanisms to question and engage with gender identity.

Roots Theatre

Ellis (2010) notes: "In a climate of violent – chiefly male targeted – homophobia, and in a society that valorizes machismo, comedy is undoubtedly and surprisingly, an empowering and powerful performative space."[7] Comedy is an important component of entertainment in Jamaican popular culture, as well as in the way of life of Jamaicans, and the recognition that humour has power cuts across multiple frames. Humour can deflect animosity, tension or anger; it can reflect ideas, feelings, and opinions; it can perpetuate prejudices and stereotypes; and it can also serve to confront oppressive systems and structures. This is reflected in the popular Jamaican phrase made famous by the late Miss Lou:[8] "tek kin teet an kibba heart bun" ("use smiles to cover heartache") where multiple personal and social issues are tackled, challenged, ridiculed and caricatured in different stages of undress in playhouses across the country.

This has proven true, particularly within the frame of Jamaican roots theatre with its offerings of roots plays that developed in the 1970s. Cited in a 2006 *Gleaner* article by Asher, Balfour Anderson described a roots play as "one that reflects the concerns of the people at the bottom of the society". According to Anderson (Asher, 2006), "it also utilises their language, which sometimes includes expletives, as it is a part of their vernacular. It is usually of a hilarious nature and the tempo is high, lots of energy. These plays usually evoke sharp responses from the audience, to which the characters counteract. Its style is comedy or farce." A subsequent *Gleaner* article (Jebbinson, 2007) provided us with the then existing definition of roots plays by the Actor Boy Awards Committee to wit: "A particular type of Jamaican theatre employing predominantly Jamaican Creole and social stereotypes with somewhat rudimentary set and lighting and expressing exaggerated character-type in ludicrous, even improbable situations. The emphasis is on the belly laugh in productions marked by much physical energy and boisterous vocal expression." Here, roots plays are comedies associated with the local vernacular, the ordinary and sometimes exaggerated portrayals of particular situations in Jamaica. The foregoing definitions impute the particularities of Jamaican life and its rigid classism, where roots plays are associated with ordinary and often poor people, who are members of Jamaica's marginalized groups. As such, its primary target audience share similar demographics with dancehall culture's main creators and adherents.

Gender identity, particularly masculinity, remains a crucial point of departure in Jamaica, and the portrayal of men in various guises is a popular component of the ongoing engagement with this issue onstage and via comedic activity. In this vein, Jamaican roots theatre has had a long dalliance with what I like to label as comedic portrayals of men in drag – men dressed as women. This propensity has resulted in success for many actors as one of the most common tools for guaranteeing onstage success in theatrical and stand-up comedy in Jamaica (and the wider Caribbean) is the employment of cross-dressing men and/or the portrayal of gay or effeminate characters.[9] Some popular characters where men played women in Jamaican roots plays include Maxwell "Maama Man" Grant of the *Maama Man* series, Nicholas Hemmings as Sister Betsy in the play *Brother Desmond* and Keith "Shebada" Ramsay, as Shebada in several Stages Productions including *Bashment Granny 1* and *Bashment Granny 2* (which also featured Maxwell Grant of Maama Man fame) and *Shebada Comes to Town*.[10]

Yet the theatrical ploy of men costumed as women and presenting farcical spoofs of this obviously male body in female costume in Jamaican roots plays like *Maama Man* and *Brother Desmond,* transitioned at the turn of the millennium from the reliance on clothing and garish makeup to an embodied performance of sexual identity with the entrance of Keith "Shebada" Ramsay. In the 2007 and 2008 *Bashment Granny* productions, Keith Ramsay the actor becomes more than the sum total of fabricated costuming and clever lines in his role as the ever-present next-door neighbour, who appears male yet seems to personify the stereotype that is "ghetto-female", or what some Jamaicans/dancehall fans refer to as the "skettel" – a loose and vulgar woman, usually dressed in erotic, revealing clothes. These performance styles continue into 2010 and beyond, for example in another popular Stages Production, *GhettOut,* starring Shebada and Delcita.

What is important is that Shebada's uncanny ability to perform a transgendered identity, both onstage and offstage, effectively ruptured the comfortable notions of essentialized gender identities that had been preserved in the preceding era, with the use of obviously male bodies in ill-fitting costumes and garish makeup, plodding through comedic portrayals of masculinized femininity that maintained the conservative, patriarchal mores of Jamaican society. After all, these were "real men" whose attempts at performing femininity fell prey to the expected bloops and blunders that allowed their true gender identity – that is, heterosexual masculinity – to constantly be on display. Not so with Keith "Shebada" Ramsay.

The question of his sexuality is perhaps answered best by Shebada himself when he says "mi deh pon di border line" ("I am on the borderline"). In his debut *Bashment Granny* plays, Shebada's massive success at portraying "borderline" sexuality as a gendered performance is played against the perpetual, tried-and-true role of a man costumed as a female in the persona of Bashment Granny played by Maxwell "Maama Man" Grant. Shebada performs this borderline sexuality onstage (and offstage) without the aid of flamboyant costuming or overdone cosmetic artifice. Responses to Shebada's flamboyant gender-bending antics onstage, and his questionable sexuality offstage, include adulation from his primarily female fans; denunciations and hostile confrontations, primarily from males; and ambivalent tolerance from many other individuals. Signature phrases like "yuh luddy" and the affectionate diminutive "Shibby" are favourites of his female fans. Here, Shebada's incarnation both on and off the comedy stage, and his ambivalent renderings of gender and sexuality, tampers with the clearly demarcated notions of masculinity and the rigid definitions of gender and sexuality that have been historically inscribed in Jamaican society.

Converging Stages? Jamaican Popular Culture and Normative Conceptions of Gender and Sexuality

While it is indeed difficult to pinpoint impact without conducting scientific, longitudinal studies, one can make inferences based on ongoing research and the themes that continue to arise from the terrain of Jamaican popular culture, social activity and, in this instance, gendered cues. As such, the foregoing discussions from three interrelated components of Jamaican popular culture, dancehall, popular language and roots theatre are best highlighted in the two related events and their surrounding narratives that coalesce around all three areas and converge more particularly around Jamaica's theatre of life, dancehall culture.

As mentioned before, in 2007, Shebada's explosive "mi deh pon di borderline" sparked intense discussions in traditional and social media (Facebook, blogs). Questions about his sexual orientation, and the apparent opening up of alternative spaces of sexual engagement in the public sphere, were fuelled by Shebada's posturing and posing within the public space of the roots theatre stage, accompanied by his even more public offstage activities. In the wake of Shebada's growing popularity, the organic link between dancehall, slang and roots theatre was energized, as Annie Paul (2009) succinctly notes:

> The induction of the name "Gaza" into the Jamaican firmament came about because in the very first insanely popular Stages Production, Bashment Granny, there is a scene where a policeman confronts the sinuous Shebada asking "Yu a man or yu a woman?" "Mi deh pon di borderline," declares Shebada unabashedly, emphasizing his retort with an exaggerated wag of his hips. The phrase became so popular in the context of discussions about sexuality that Vybz Kartel decided that the name of his community "Borderline" in Waterford, Portmore, St Catherine, had been irrevocably contaminated by association. He therefore adopted the name of the most violent place he could think of at the time – Gaza in Palestine. (para 6)

The subsequent dancehall competition and feud between Vybz Kartel's Gaza Empire and Mavado's Gully made significant headlines and sparked intense controversy within the dancehall throughout 2008 and 2009. What is important in this discussion, however, are the social and gendered impulses that cut across the popular cultural spheres of dancehall and roots theatre that prompted Vybz Kartel, the self-proclaimed Emperor of the Portmore Empire, to hastily distance his fiefdom from any linguistic association with the term. This move by Kartel cut all ties, inferred or otherwise, with the highly popular roots theatre star, Shebada, and dampened the obvious heterosexual transgressions and anxieties that Shebada's borderline identity invoked in social, gendered and popular cultural frameworks. Yet this renaming occurred simultaneously with Vybz Kartel's own progressive gendered transgressions that led many to question his heterosexual impulses and his right to the title of hardcore Emperor of the Portmore Empire – one associated with dancehall dominance, high levels of violence and unquestioned heterosexuality. Kartel's dalliance with once-taboo and highly feminized aesthetic practices, including skin bleaching (or lightening), use of hair extensions, and multiple body tattoos, backed by his self-declaration "mi pretty like a colouring book", created a controversial image. This image, which simultaneously challenged and upheld hardcore heterosexuality, attracted multiple questions about his masculinity that he continues to refute.

Kartel's borderline forays may also be compared and simultaneously contrasted with a second series of events oriented around the tango between Keith "Shebada" Ramsay and dancehall artiste Beenie Man in 2011. As noted in the foregoing discussion, Shebada's controversial, postmillennial entry into the spaces of Jamaican popular culture created waves across the social, gendered and cultural spaces of Jamaica, including popular dancehall culture, with the term "Shebada" and "borderline" subsequently used in slang, dancehall lyrics and clashes to impute questionable or homosexual identity. Dancehall's deeply patriarchal mores and its idealized continuum of masculinity project the Badman, a hardcore and violent heterosexual male, as the antithesis of the Chi Chi Man – an effeminate homosexual male. Since Buju Banton's release of the controversial song, "Boom Bye Bye" in the early 1990s, dancehall culture has consistently expressed its disavowal of any challenges to hardcore male heterosexual in humorous, negating and sometimes hostile terms.

However, as Jamaica's postmillennial mores continue to shift, dancehall culture has become a site for the signalling of incremental transformations in the terrain of gender and sexuality, particularly male identity. For example, at the end of July 2011, reports surfaced that Shebada was in studio laying down tracks for a new and controversial album. A video and photographs of Shebada recording in studio wearing long, French tips and sporting a pink Mohawk surfaced on the Internet and on various social networking sites. The resulting contentious discussions surrounded his usual female attire, but more so Shebada's provocative lyrical jabs that "a bear fish een yah", and his lyrical challenges to Beenie Man, which exploded on social media sites and in talkback sessions on several websites that hosted the footage. In a subsequent interview on the television show *E-Mix* then aired on TVJ in Jamaica, Shebada outlined his plans for a career in music to complement his successful career in popular roots theatre and delivered a challenge to Beenie Man, who was booked to appear with Shebada, Delcita and his then wife, D'Angel, on the Stages Production 2 for 1 performance show during the upcoming weekend, when Jamaica would be celebrating its independence day. This show, while ostensibly a showcase of roots theatre comedy, became increasingly billed as a clash between Beenie Man and Shebada. The clash motif, which is popularized and celebrated in the Jamaican dancehall, included Shebada's comments during the video advertisement for the show where he disparagingly referred to Beenie Man as "Betweenieman, the one with the Sisterlocks inna him hair". Both references imputed questionable masculine identity to Beenie Man, suggesting a flirtation with homosexuality on the one hand (that is, between men) and a preference for female hair aesthetics on the other (that is, the locks of sisters, or a hairstyle for women), which could also be imputed as homosexual within the Jamaican cultural context. The ad also cemented the ongoing suggestion of a lyrical clash between Beenie Man and Shebada at the upcoming comedy show. Beenie Man's apparent contribution to the growing controversy was sparked in a television promo, subsequently hosted on YouTube when he indicated that he would be appearing on the 2 for 1 show with D'Angel, Delcita and "the other one". Shebada's acerbic response to Beenie Man's attempt at lyrical othering was revealed in a YouTube video that surfaced on Wednesday, 3 August 2011 (no longer available) in which Shebada made negative, disparaging comments about Beenie Man, and issued an insulting "pork trotter" comment that was viewed as particularly touchy, according to Beenie Man's management, in light of Beenie Man's Rastafarian religion, which explicitly renounces any contact with the contaminating effects of pork in any form.

The saga continued to unfold when, in another interview, pre-empting the upcoming 2 for 1 stage show, on Friday, 5 August 2011, on *CVM at Sunrise* (a morning television show hosted on CVM Television), Shebada declared, "mi ago dun Beenie Man a 2 for 1 . . . mi ago finish Beenie . . . mi ago empty Beenie Man like a wata bottle and clean him like a fridge".[11] Here, Shebada was predicting that he would lyrically clash with Beenie Man in true dancehall style, and come out the victor. As a clash is considered to be the crowning glory of lyrical performance within the dancehall and is used as a competitive arena where equally matched lyrical gladiators, usually male, can challenge each other and showcase their lyrical prowess. After a few minutes of lyrically sparring onstage, monitored and assessed by the cheers, boos or silence of the dancehall audience, one person is eventually crowned the victor over the symbolically dead (lyrical) body of his opponent. However, since Shebada is not a dancehall artiste, his attempts were ignored. In addition, Shebada's gender-bending antics and borderline pose put him outside of the accepted persona of a dancehall artiste, who is always imaged as a hardcore heterosexual.

Thus, for Shebada and the Stages Production management to even suggest the notion of an upcoming clash with top dancehall artiste Beenie Man was to immediately promote or elevate Shebada to the status of dancehall royalty and impute notions of comparative male identity between both individuals. Indeed, the parallel positioning of Beenie Man's and Shebada's image on the poster for the upcoming 2 for 1 stage show imputed a level of comparative heterogeneity in both their identities that many dancehall fans staunchly disavowed. On the other hand, the primarily female fans of Shebada found the proposed lyrical clash a worthy matchup and a welcome move away from what many viewed as dancehall's nastiness and violent machismo Badmanism into a more socially acceptable comedic portrayal.

Consequently, Beenie Man's last-minute rejection of Shebada's offer to clash and cancellation of his performance at the 2 for 1 stage show was, in the words of his management, based on the fact that "it appears that the producers of the show are building up Beenie Man's performance as a clash with Shebada and we won't have Beenie Man be a part of something like that. Beenie Man is not a circus act . . . and an international artiste of his calibre simply cannot be pulled into this situation, we are not being paid for a clash so their deposit will be returned, we will not be doing the show." Even while Beenie Man's (estranged) wife D'Angel did participate on the show, no attempt was made to clash with her as there would be no crown, lyrical or otherwise, to be gained from such a match-up. What is more critical to this discussion, however, was the understanding that this related series of events suggested critical moves within the framework of popular culture and the mores that govern ideas about gender and sexual identity in Jamaica – in short, a crossing of borders between roots plays and dancehall culture and a mixing of male sexual identities that had not been permissible prior to this.

Subsequent responses from within Jamaican popular culture included two episodes on the popular *Ity and Fancy Cat Show* television series (aired on TVJ). The first, titled "Beany and di Odda One", first aired in August 2011, presented a comedic caricature of a quarrel between Beenie Man and Shebada, with Shebada taking Beenie Man to task for daring to call him "the odda one" and suggesting that Beenie Man's estranged wife D'Angel loved him and "wanted his body", that is, she was romantically interested in Shebada (no longer available). The second, titled "Beany vs di One and di Odda One", first aired in September 2011, presented a comedic caricature of Beenie Man and D'Angel's divorce saga where Shebada is humorously introduced as the new man in D'Angel's life and thus the new stepfather for Beenieman and D'Angel's son (see http://www.youtube.com/watch?v=pQHwPv4D6s8). In addition, during his explosive closing performance at Sting 2011, in December, Bounti Killa, one of dancehall's hardcore heterosexual lyrical gladiators and the former arch-rival of Beenie Man, chastised an absent Beenie Man for his involvement with Shebada, caricaturing his absent rival as "Betweenieman" (that is, Beenie Man between men or sliding into homosexuality) and "Fisheenieman" (Beenie Man the fish[12] or Beenie Man the homosexual). Both terms imputed a slide into questionable sexuality or outright homosexuality. Bounti Killa also expressed his ire and disbelief at the extremes to which Shebada had aspired in the dancehall, a space reserved for true hardcore, heterosexual activity.

Conclusion

The foregoing discussion highlights several mixed and competing messages from the frame of Jamaican popular culture. Jamaican roots plays and other comedic forms of popular culture (e.g., the *Ity and Fancy Cat Show*) continue their relationship with comedic portrayals of alternative male sexuality; however, in the postmillennial forms the onstage and offstage borders have proven more fluid, with the capacity to signal new possibilities. Here, the moniker Shebada has been absorbed into dancehall slang and Jamaican language, where a "Shebada" is another term used for a man whose sexuality is suspect or, alternatively, for a woman who behaves "like a skettel". This also reverses the trend where the term "Maama Man" first developed in language and was then absorbed into popular roots theatre. This suggests the continuing impact of these multiple stages on language codes and approaches to gender and sexuality. Here, Shebada may be an unwitting Jamaican pioneer in the use of comedy/humour to disrupt social norms and challenge the status quo.

Where dancehall culture is concerned, its ambivalent readings project incursions across borders while simultaneously holding onto normative conceptions of a hardcore, violent, heterosexual masculinity as idolized and idealized. At the same time, the Patwa-infused slang that emanates from the belly of the society continues to reflect on the social movements and utilize terminologies that account for new ways of being (Shebada, borderline) even while attempting to subsume same into old mores (Fish, funny).

Yet even with the simultaneous existence of competing and ambivalent discourses, dancehall's dancing men in tight pants, controversial artiste Vybz Kartel's gendered transgressions, and roots theatre's borderline Shebada exemplify Jamaican popular culture's newly validated and refashioned performances of Jamaican masculinity that traffic in postmillennial, borderline masculinities. One can be funny but not really gay, and a freaky freaky badman can wear tight pants and braids, imputing feminized masculinity through the use of feminine aesthetics and formerly taboo styles of dress. For researchers with antennae honed to the minute, almost imperceptible movements of social and cultural transformations, these culturally bound performances of gender and sexuality and the cultural responses to them signal transitions in the state of Jamaica's hegemonic gender debates and hopefully indicate the incremental opening up of sites of engagement with alternative sexualities.

Notes

1. I have argued elsewhere that this perhaps reflects a particular form of anxiety about male disempowerment that resonates strongly with Jamaica's disempowered lower classes – femmephobia – which could be related to the "Delilah complex" and other female taboos, where the female and the feminine are often perceived as a danger to the masculine, a force that can weaken a man's dominance and strength or contaminate his masculine ethos (Hope, 2006).

2. From dem a par inna chi-man crew
Dem a Chi-chi man too Chi-chi man too
From a gyal a par inna Chi-chi gyal crew
Dem a Chi-chi gyal too Chi-chi gyal too.

[Once they are socializing with gay men,
Then they are also gay men (rept.)
Once they are socializing with lesbians
Then they are also lesbians (rept.)]

3. See chapter 6, "'Fashion Ova Style': Dancehall's Masculine Display" in Hope (2010).

4. The term "cake soap" has become synonymous with the most recent wave of skin bleaching/lightening by many Jamaicans, particularly fans and not-so-fans of dancehall. In the current era, this was engineered particularly by Vybz Kartel's public referencing to cake soap as a part of his theatrics onstage and in his music videos. However, as I note in other work (see Hope, 2011b), despite Kartel's apparent ownership of the cake soap debate, the use and value of cake soap as a component of Jamaican cultural and aesthetic practice predated Kartel's superstar status, his entry to dancehall and even his year of birth. I was introduced to the apparent dermatological wonders of cake soap as a teenager at high school in the late 1970s/early 1980s. For many working-class and inner-city individuals, the cheap and easily accessible cake soap was more than just a cheaper version of laundry soap that many preferred to use because it made your clothes cleaner and your whites whiter, but also a dermatological wonder. If one's face was washed with cake soap only, it had the capacity to reduce the dreaded "shine and greasy" look, leaving your face "cool" and free of pimples – or so the story goes. Assertions by Kartel that the blue version of "cake soap" (often referred to by the name of the popular Blue Bomber brand) is his cosmetic of choice, backed by the appropriate dancehall lyrics, was brokered on this culturally approved and decades-old relationship with cake soap by ordinary Jamaicans.

5. Jamaican folklore identifies "horse tonic" as a viable aphrodisiac that enhances male sexual stamina and sexual performance. The term usually refers to a popular plant, medina, which is also known as "horse tonic". The leaves of this plant are often boiled as a tea. The leaves may also be boiled along with those of several other plants, and mixed with other condiments to produce a "tonic". According to Jamaican folklore, the term also refers to a special concoction that is prepared and fed to horses, and which have similar positive value for men as outlined above.

6. *Batty* is the Jamaican Creole term for the buttocks or "bottom".

7. Owen "Blakka" Ellis is a renowned Jamaican comedian and one of the principals of Ellis International, an entity that showcases Jamaican comedy, for example through the popular *Ity and Fancy Cat Show*, a comedic series aired on TVJ in Jamaica.

8. The late Miss Lou – the Honourable Louise Bennett-Coverley, is Jamaica's First Lady of Comedy, who pioneered the use of Jamaican Creole in poetry, song and comedy. The term "tek kin teet an kibba heart bun" means "use laughter to cover heartache".

9. During the Renaissance era, women were banned from theatre, and all female parts were played by men dressed as women. These ranged from young boys whose voices

had not yet broken to more obviously masculine men, who would play the less feminine female roles.

10. This propensity to utilize men dressed as women in theatre is a historical fact, which has also become common fare in Hollywood cinematography (e.g., Marlon and Shawn Wayans in *White Chicks*, 2004; Robin Williams in *Mrs Doubtfire*, 1993; and Dustin Hoffman in *Tootsie*, 1982).

11. "I will be finishing off Beenie Man at the 2 for 1 Stage Show. I am going to finish off Beenie. I am going to empty him out just as how you empty the water out of a water bottle, and I am going to clean him out just as how you clean a refrigerator." This type of lyrical throwing of words is common buildup to an onstage clash in the dancehall; however, since Shebada is not a dancehall artiste, the attempt to engage Beenie Man in this engagement was ignored.

12. *Fish* is another term used in Jamaican Creole to stand in for male homosexuality.

References

Asher, K. (2006, January 22). Roots plays tone down. *The Gleaner*.

Atluri, T.L. (2001). *When the closet is a region: Homophobia, heterosexism and nationalism in the Commonwealth Caribbean. Working Paper No. 5*. Kingston, Jamaica: University of the West Indies Press/Centre for Gender and Development Studies.

Barrett, L.E. (1997). *The Rastafarians*. Boston, MA: Beacon Press.

Batson, T. (2002, February 17). Costume dressing, not a drag. *The Gleaner*.

Beenie Man cancels two for one performance with Shebada. (2011, August). http://www.one876entertainment.com/news/beenie-man-cancels-two-for-one-performance-with-shebada.html

Brathwaite, E. (1971). *The development of creole society in Jamaica 1770–1820*. Oxford, UK: Clarendon Press.

Cassidy, F. (1971). *Jamaica Talk: Three hundred years of English Language in Jamaica*. London, UK: Macmillan Caribbean.

Chevannes, B. (2001). *Learning to be a man: Culture, socialization and gender identity in five Caribbean communities*. Kingston, Jamaica: University of the West Indies Press.

Cooke, M. (2004, September 30). And now "homofibia" (Part 1). *The Gleaner*.

Cooper, C. (2004). *Sound clash: Jamaican dancehall culture at large*. New York, NY: Palgrave Macmillan.

Drama, Shebada and Beenie Man beefing "What you hiding". Aired on the *EMix*. YouTube Video. http://www.youtube.com/watch?v=CAFMBXXHTyY

Ellis, N. (2011, July). Out and bad: Toward a queer performance hermeneutic in Jamaican dancehall. *Small Axe*, 35, 7–23.

Ellis, O.B. (2010). *Why are "funny" men so funny? Questioning masculinity and sexuality in the Caribbean comic space: A call to conversation*. Paper presented at the 35th annual Caribbean Studies Association Conference, Barbados, May 24 to 28, 2010.

Hope, D.P. (2009). From *Boom Bye Bye* to *Chi Chi Man*: Exploring homophobia in Jamaican dancehall culture. *Journal of the University College of the Cayman Islands (JUCCI)*, (3)3, 99–121.

Hope, D.P. (2010). *Man vibes: Masculinities in the Jamaican dancehall.* Kingston, Jamaica: Ian Randle.

Hope, D.P. (2011a). The dancehall story: Exploring male homosexuality. *Rockstone and Bootheel Catalog.* Connecticut: Real Artways, 38–43.

Hope, D.P. (2011b). From *Browning* to *Cake Soap*: Popular debates on skin bleaching in the Jamaican dancehall. *Journal of Pan African Studies, 4*(4), 164–193.

Ity and Fancy Beany vs di Odda One. (2011, August). http://www.youtube.com /watch?v=yVgmvlQ5vKo

Ity and Fancy Beany vs di One and di Odda One. (2011, September). http://www.youtube.com/watch?v=pQHwPv4D6s8

Jebbinson, A. (2007, April 1). Roots too shallow to hold. *The Gleaner.*

Paul, A. (2009, September 27). Eyeless in Gaza (and Gully): Mi deh pon di borderline. http://anniepaulactivevoice.blogspot.com/2009/09/eyeless-in-gaza-mi-deh-pon-di .html

Playwright, actor, reject roots label. (2009, April 5). *The Gleaner.*

Pollard, V. (2000). *Dread talk: The language of Rastafari.* Kingston, Jamaica: Canoe Press.

Pryce, Jean T. (1997). Similarities between the debates on Ebonics and Jamaican. *Journal of Black Psychology, 23*(August), 238–241.

Roberts, P. A. (1988). *West Indians and their language.* Cambridge, UK: Cambridge University Press.

Roots theatre declared "dead": Now under the "mainstream theatre" umbrella. (2009, April 5). *The Gleaner.*

Shebada and Delcita 2 for 1 ad. YouTube Video. (2011, August 5). http://www.youtube .com/watch?v=pFoD5Y_W1nw

Shebada gets hype with long nails, records music in studio. http://thehypelifemag .com/2011/07/31/video-shebada-gets-hype-with-long-nails-records-music-in-studio

Shebada on *Entertainment Report.* YouTube Video. http://www.youtube.com /watch?v=qwn68nwGKv8

Shebada interview about dancehall artist (Beenie Man diss). YouTube Video. http://www.youtube.com/watch?v=nkaNUUJX4Nw

Shebada vs Beenieman on *CVM at Sunrise.* (2011, August 3). YouTube Video. http://www.youtube.com/watch?feature=endscreen&v=ffcq__dwo_Y&NR=1

9.

Dem Bow
Translation, Globalization and Dancehall's Recalibrated Anti-Gay Discourse

R. ANTHONY LEWIS

For the better part of four decades now, Jamaica's popular culture has been defined predominantly by dancehall or ragga. At its core, dancehall is a set of visual and performance art forms characterized by an edgy blend of toasting[1] over heavy bass sounds accompanied by fast-evolving seasonal dance idioms and outrageously loud fashion. As "the latest manifestation on a continuum of New World performance cultures" (Stanley-Niaah, 2004, p. 104), dancehall serves as "a memory bank of the old, new, and dynamic bodily movements, spaces, performers, and performance aesthetic of the New World and Jamaica in particular" (pp. 104–105). It is possible, then, to conceptualize dancehall as "a system that can be disaggregated into the particularity of its space, music, song, dance, fashion, language, art, embodied meanings, performance practice, attitude, politics, economy/industry, and style" (p. 105).

As an expressive form, dancehall emerges from the Afro-Jamaican masses, who use it to "create their own stage, write their own scripts and perform their own social commentary dramas, through rapidly enunciated and cleverly concocted lyrics". The progeny of socially conscious "roots reggae", which critiqued the sociopolitical context that disempowered Jamaica's poor, early dancehall featured lyrical content that "reflected the cultural consciousness of the times . . . with generally positive sociopolitical messages" (Tafari-Ama, 2006, p. 165). However, the high sociopolitical stakes of the Cold War context into which the art form was born triggered important changes in its lyrical content. In the 1970s, Jamaica, because of its espousal of socialism, its relationship with communist Cuba and the strongly anti-American rhetoric of the Michael Manley regime, became the object of political pressure from the United States. Cautious to avoid the scrutiny of the spotlight that the United States shone on the country, artists began to shy away from political critique and social commentary – fearing real or imagined victimization from agents of the US government – and turned their attention instead to the more mundane issues of violence and sex (Manuel, Bilby & Largey, 2006; Tafari-Ama, 2006). Performers such as Winston "Yellowman" Foster pioneered a brand of music thematically dominated by what Hope (2006) called "the conquest of the punaany".[2] Others such as Shabba Ranks (Rexton Gordon) later built on this heritage and helped to define a tradition that praised and encouraged male sexual exploitation and/or control of the female body. This control has often been depicted in violent terms, such as those of a man ploughing (into) (*dig out di red*), stabbing (into) (*stab out di miit*), or slamming into a vagina (*wikidis "slam"*), or using a grinding implement on his penis to do damage to it (*Stuon de pahn mi bodi ed/If a gyal waahn ded tel ar kom ina mi bed* [There is a stone on the head of my penis/If a girl wants to die (of pleasure?), tell her to get into my bed]). Nelson (2008), in a pointed critique, described this strain of dancehall as "blatantly heteronormative, revealing a hypermasculinist posture of sexual defiance" that is presented as "the only legitimate version of Jamaican manhood". Hypermasculine lyrics, she contended, revealed "an attempt to gain respect in the contested space . . . [of] the dancehall", which was "a zone for the cultural creation of Jamaican masculinity, replacing the church, the political sphere, and traditional systems of education in the framing of what it mean[t] to be a man in Jamaica and a Jamaican man in the world" (p. 239).

Linked to hypermasculinity and the hypersexual conquest of the female body was what Tafari-Ama (2006) referred to as an "inordinate anxiety to prescribe 'normal' and 'taboo' sexual practices of the body" aimed at rein- forcing "heterosexuality while outlawing 'other' practices of embodied pleasure which [did] not conform to this norm" (p. 166). Among such "other" practices figures sexual activity between members of the same sex, but more particularly between men. In this way, what in prior decades were humorous barbs directed at the "curiosity" of homosexuality in Jamaican popular culture soon trans- formed into proscriptions in the lyrics of emerging stars and cultural icons such as Buju Banton and Capleton. This condemnation, Hope (2006) wrote, was typically violent, with anti-gay works being "rife with narratives in which male homosexuals [were] stereotyped, labelled, nicknamed, disrespected, burnt, stabbed, beaten, run out of town, shot and killed in a variety of creative [*sic*] and excruciating fashions" (pp. 83–84). The discourse of violence, Hope claimed, was deployed as a strategy to consolidate heterosexual masculinity and to highlight the "paranoia and unease about male homosexuality that, as a general rule, underpins Jamaican masculinity" (2010, p. 69).

Because of the violence emblematic of anti-gay dancehall, Marshall (2008) has pointed to the fact that, in recent times, "Jamaican society, politicians, and especially reggae [dancehall] performers have come under fire from interna- tional groups advocating for gay rights and human rights" (p. 136). As a result, a number of campaigns were launched to rebuff this trend in the music. Using the framework of creole nationalism, this chapter seeks to problematize both the Jamaican and international reactions to the deployment of anti-gay lyrics in dancehall. First, it examines how campaigns against anti-gay dancehall, through a reliance on translation, made the undervalued Jamaican language (cf. Christie, 2003) in which dancehall is produced central to a global debate. The chapter also traces the contours of the clash of values in a rights discourse between global LGBT activists and purveyors of anti-gay dancehall, and explores how, within the Jamaican Creole nationalist project, conflicting and contradictory cultural analyses came to frame concerns about the rights of both gays and deejays. Finally, the chapter assesses how political and economic responses to the critique of anti-gay dancehall reflected not only opposition and resistance to both global capitalism (cf. De Certeau, 1984) and the amorphous West (Babylon) but also an eventual accommodation of them.

"Murder Music"

Beginning almost thirty years ago, a number of international campaigns of varying sizes and intensity attempted to counter the discourse of violence against gays in Jamaican dancehall music. One of the most recent was the 2013 move by the Canadian-based Jamaica Association of Gays and Lesbians Abroad (JAGLA). The organization sought to sanction dancehall artiste Queen Ifrica (Ventrice Morgan) for her performance as headline act at Jamaica's fifty-first National Independence Grand Gala celebration at the National Stadium on 6 August of that year. In her performance, Ifrica paused to render homage to straight people for their relationships and issued a denunciation of gays, stating her opposition to homosexuality by declaring to her audience, "no gays roun' here". She further cautioned the government against bowing to international pressure to repeal the country's colonial-era law against anal sex. JAGLA's protest, which followed expressions of disappointment by J-FLAG,[3] Jamaica's foremost LGBT rights organization, at Ifrica's performance ("Queen Ifrica's", 7 August 2013), called for Canadian government intervention to block her participation in a reggae festival in Toronto (Houston, 21 August 2013).

The controversy over Ifrica's performance followed another, more sustained, international effort against anti-gay dancehall. In July 2004, a campaign dubbed "Stop Murder Music Campaign", initiated by J-FLAG but fronted internationally primarily by the UK-based rights organizations Outrage! and the Black Gay Men's Advisory Group, was launched against homophobic music in general and anti-gay dancehall in particular. Organizations such as Lesben-und Schwulenverband in Deutschland [the Lesbian and Gay Federation of

Germany] (LSVD), Italy's Arcigay and France's Inter-LGBT and Tjenbé Rèd, among others, were members of the coalition. The campaign targeted the most popular proponents of anti-gay lyrics: seven individual artists, Beenie Man (Anthony Moses Davis), Bounty Killer (Rodney Price), Buju Banton (Mark Myrie), Capleton (Clifton George), Elephant Man (O'Neil Bryan), Sizzla (Miguel Orlando Collins), Vybz Kartel (Adidja Palmer) and one group, Touch of Klass (TOK) (Alistaire McCalla, Roshaun Clarke, Craig Patrick, Anthony Thompson and Xavier Davidson) (Hope, 2006; Marshall, 2008).

This campaign mirrored two others, dating to 1992, when dancehall performers Shabba Ranks and Buju Banton were sanctioned for their anti-gay expressions on the global stage. Marshall (2008) pointed to how Ranks, a two-time Grammy winner, saw his attempt to cross over into North American pop music cut short because of publicly expressed anti-gay sentiments on a Channel 4 interview in 1992. This was the genesis of a downward spiral for his music career, as he became the target of the Gay and Lesbian Alliance Against Defamation (GLAAD). At about the same time, GLAAD launched a campaign targeting Buju Banton's "Boom Bye Bye", a song Farquharson (2006) described as epoch-defining given its propulsion of Jamaican antipathy towards homosexuality onto the global stage. Robinson (Larcher & Robinson, 2009) characterized GLAAD as then being "a newly emergent advocacy nonprofit in the US powered by gays and lesbians in the entertainment industry". He noted that the organization, though initially focusing on negative television representations of gays and lesbians, had begun "to take on the popular music industry". Robinson, who lived in the United States during that period, wrote that his Jamaican roommate, Fabian Thomas, had provided GLAAD with a standard English "rendering" of Banton's lyrics, which had then been "enjoying a second wind in the North American music market". According to Robinson, GLAAD's media advocacy, which "produced a slew of coverage in mainstream newspapers and broadcast television" was based on the simple approach that "prejudicial representations of GLBT people in popular culture could be fought through bad publicity, which meant not only shame, but also economic consequences". Robinson identified this campaign, which was not "targeted specifically at Jamaica or at dancehall" as the "birth of the international 'murder music' protest movement" (p. 4).

Against the backdrop of the discourse on LGBT rights that was emerging from the shadows of the HIV and AIDS panic in the United States, Jamaican entertainers soon learned that their knee-jerk support of the anti-gay "communitarian ethos" that was "embedded in the very forms of a great many songs" (Marshall, 2008, p. 138) would become the subject of trenchant critique from LGBT activists and rights advocates who had begun to find their voice. Further, within a context of a more sensitive and responsive First World entertainment consumer market, the translation from Jamaican Creole of lyrics recommending the killing of gays disrupted the sympathies that liberals had towards Jamaican popular music as a form of social protest. In short, the violence in the lyrics made it difficult for foreign consumers of dancehall in the Global North to simply romanticize its songs as "progressive" music arising from a response to social injustice (Manuel et al., 2006). With the translation of anti-gay dancehall lyrics, Jamaican artists such as Shabba and Buju, whose market was global, had become unwitting frontline soldiers in a culture war for which they were ill-prepared. Their unpreparedness was compounded by the fact that "built into the cultural products which circulate more widely, reggae's [dancehall's] homophobia finds itself replicated in other reggae scenes, where similar aesthetics and performance practice styles are maintained, perhaps as much as reggae's other central themes" (Marshall, 2008, p. 138). Thus, the export of popular dancehall was, in the terms of the war and the battle, the export of Jamaican homophobia. Shabba, who depended heavily on the US market, soon learned that both dancehall lyrics and craft had become elements of global ideological narratives over which Jamaican artists had only apparent control.

Being the first major casualty of what will be characterized, following Nelson (2012), as a war between hyper-heteromasculine creole nationalists[4] and presumed neocolonial oppressive forces, Shabba emblematizes well the paradoxes and sociocultural stakes of anti-gay dancehall. Marshall (2008) contends that in his iconic track "Dem Bow", Shabba admonishes his audience not to bow to oppression, "in particular the (implicitly foreign) pressures toward such 'deviant' sexual practices as oral sex (both fellatio and cunnilingus) and homosexuality". Marshall draws parallels between the anti-gay discourse in dancehall and that which comes from some Jamaican churches, noting that "it is a longstanding charge in Jamaican public discourse – particularly from fundamentalist Christian quarters and certain sects of Rastafari – that oral and anal sex and same sex relationships are not only taboo and proscribed by the Bible but are 'decadent' products of the West, of Babylon, and are thus to be resisted alongside other forms of colonization, cultural or political" (p. 136).

An assessment of the campaigns against anti-gay dancehall reveals that a constellation of specific local and global dynamics fuelled the battle between artists and LGBT activists. The 2013 campaign against Ifrica and the earlier ones against Shabba and Buju reflected a clash of values between Jamaican popular culture and the West (broadly understood) in relation to homosexuality. Yet as historically significant as these campaigns were, the one that J-FLAG started and then abandoned, and that Outrage! et al. continued for many years after, made the clash of values a central concern in the international discourse on

Jamaican music and popular culture. Locals framed the question of anti-gay dancehall as one of deejays' right to express disapproval of homosexuality. Such was the character of the national paranoia regarding the perceived normalization of homosexuality that "appealing to what are assumed to be a set of shared morals, to a fear of double exile – not only in Jamaica rather than Africa, or Babylon rather than Zion, but pariah in Jamaican society itself – reggae artists and audiences embrace[d] homophobia as a uniting cause" (Marshall, 2008, p. 137). By contrast, gay activists construed it as an invitation to violence, which placed it under the rubric of hate speech. Defenders of dancehall defined this characterization as a cultural imposition by powerful foreign interests aligned against purveyors of Jamaican popular culture for nefarious reasons. In their conception, international gay rights activists were the social and cultural heirs of Jamaica's colonial overlords. For their part, gay rights activists felt that Jamaicans, because of their history of violent subjugation, should more readily understand the plight of the LGBT community. With this framing of dancehall's "dis" of gays and lesbians as a human rights issue, LGBT organizations repositioned and complexified the dominant discourses in Jamaica on both homosexuality and oppression.

Dancehall, Language and Popular Jamaican Identity

The differences between dancehall and its predecessor, "roots" reggae, are so stark, Manuel et al. (2006) question whether the two types of music should be treated as the same genre. Stylistically, reggae uses "a 'song' format, with original compositions with flowing melodies, changing chord progressions, and verses and refrains". Dancehall, on the other hand, "typically features the deejay intoning verses in what is often a short, repetitive tune . . . superimposed over a 'riddim' (rhythmic accompaniment)" (pp. 200–201). The differences between the two forms of Jamaican popular music derive from a complex mix of factors that Hope (2006) located in the sociopolitical and economic environment of the late twentieth century from which dancehall emerged. This environment, she noted, was marked by the "fallout of [sic] Jamaica's experiment with structural adjustment; the rise of free market capitalism; increasing urbanization; rising political violence; a growing ideological convergence between the People's National Party (PNP) and the Jamaica Labour Party (JLP); the explosion of Jamaica's informal economy and ongoing transformations in the class/status hierarchy" (p. 1).

Hope's analysis is consistent with that of Manuel et al. (2006), who argued that, for reasons noted earlier, in the 1980s, emphasis in the musical culture moved from a vision associated with Rastafari ideology of "overthrowing imperialism, casting down Babylon, or returning to Africa" towards "the politically safe topics of sex and boasting" (p. 199). Additionally, the death of icons Bob Marley in 1981 and Peter Tosh in 1987, and the temporary disappearance from the music scene of producer Lee "Scratch" Perry contributed to the shift in format and focus. As a result of these changes, dancehall became, according to Hope, "critically exiled from all preceding genres of Jamaican music culture" (2006, p. 27). One of the most striking features of this exile was the choice of the deprecated but widely spoken Jamaican Creole over English as the genre's medium of lyrical expression.

Given the nature of the technology through which Jamaican popular music was transmitted, and Jamaica's sociolinguistic reality, it was a matter of time before English would cede ground to Jamaican Creole. This happened gradually, Cooper and Devonish (2004) remarked. Initially the lyrics of popular Jamaican music (circa 1960s) "were predominantly in English or a close approximation thereof", but the choruses of these songs "would often be in some variety of Jamaican" (p. 296). There soon emerged an alternative trend, characterized by "songs with predominantly Jamaican Creole lyrics" (p. 297). This shift in language use is a phenomenon that Cooper and Devonish have attributed to the change in attitudes that accompanied the increased use of sound recording technology. The "talking improvisations against the background of recorded music" (p. 297), for instance, gave oral – and by extension common – language space to become a more important vehicle in musical expression and production. This use of the vernacular had the impact of massifying aspects of Jamaican folk (becoming popular) culture, with the consequent marginalization of elite culture and some of the values associated with it. With massification came not only the diffusion of the language but also its consequent commercialization (Abrahams, 2005), all of which helped to consolidate a form of popular Jamaican nationalism based tenuously on language.

Today, the ubiquity of dancehall performed in the technologized Jamaican language serves as a reminder that the denigrated identity of the Afro-Jamaican has been definitively patriated. Prior to the emergence of dancehall, repatriation to Africa loomed large as a theme in Jamaican popular music due to the sense of dispossession and social alienation that many purveyors of popular music felt in their native land. The discourse on return to African roots thus became part of a quest for psychic redress (Giovannetti, 2005). Importantly, this alienation from national identity was made even starker by the dominance of English, standard and nonstandard, as the mode of expression of early Jamaican popular music (Cooper and Devonish, 2004). This fact was attributable to the significant impact of American forms and technology on early Jamaican popular music, with mimicry, imitation and innovation being key features in its development (Manuel et al., 2006). The shift from English to Jamaican Creole thus signalled an important break in this creative tradition, and represented a deepening and broadening of the local audience base of the music. Furthermore, the social location of dancehall at the heart of inner-city Jamaica meant that for authentic communication to take place between artists and their community of listeners, particularly in the context of live perfor-mances, Jamaican Creole – the language of the vast majority of Jamaicans – had to be the language of choice. In this way, Jamaican popular music came not only to include but to depend on Creole-dominant speakers as its lifeblood. Over time, this in turn excluded non-Creole speakers, which meant that access to the content of the music was reduced for non-Creole-speaking audiences. Revelling in their greater capacity for expression in Jamaican Creole, deejays delivered lyrics "at high speed" with little regard for foreigners or the local middle classes. In effect, their attitude was that if "Yankees or local uptown elites had trouble following [the music], then too bad for them" (Manuel et al., p. 200).

It was this reliance on Jamaican Creole that gave confidence to the Jamaican underclass that began communicating vernacular values through vernacular music. One such value was extreme antipathy towards gays and homosexuality. Hope (2010) remarked that in Jamaica, "any form of sexual contact between two men is deemed homosexual and deviant . . . and is routinely condemned in dancehall culture" (p. 68). Many male dancehall performers paved their way to fame by including in their repertoire at least one work ridiculing or calling for the death of gays. Expressed in Jamaican Creole, these sentiments were effec-tively masked from much of the outside world, unless the lyrics were translated and disseminated. In both the campaign against Buju in 1992 and the "Stop Murder Music Campaign", translation served a key role in providing outsiders access and thereby scrutiny of the lyrical content of anti-gay dancehall music.

Cooper (2004) remarked that the challenges posed by anti-gay dancehall lyrics derived from the genre's entry onto the international stage, "where highly politicized groups of male and female homosexuals wield[ed] substantial power", placing squarely on the table "the issue of language in DJ culture, and the separation of aesthetic and ideological issues that can arise in the exporting of Jamaican music" (p. 170). Just like Manuel et al., she argued that the threat to dancehall emerged when non-Jamaicans who appreciated the beat of the music without understanding its lyrics came to understand but not accept its cultural content. J-FLAG and its North American and European collaborators sought to capitalize on that fact, and by so doing placed Jamaican Creole firmly in the cross-hairs of the debate about cultural and personal rights, and freedom of expression.

Hegemony and Hierarchies

Although the use of Jamaican Creole for purposes of excluding foreigners might be seen as counterhegemonic, it also served as a vehicle of hegemony on the part of the disempowered. In the practice of their craft, purveyors of dancehall, while seeking through language to undo the damage of years of linguistic and cultural domination under colonial and colonial-type sociopolitical structures, themselves unleashed and reified already existent forms of tyranny in vernacular culture, viz. misogyny and homophobia. The aggressive sexuality of the dancehall depicted an essentially hyper-heterosexual/heterosexist space in which men and women played out "eroticized gender roles in ritual dramas" that could become violent (Cooper, 2004, p. 17).

The hypermasculine language deployed to convey ideals of male sexual dominance over females during heterosexual encounters, as well as the hostility towards same-sex practices referred to earlier in the chapter, are examples of how this kind of violence manifested itself. These foregrounded the extent to which violence had become embedded in vernacular conceptions of gender and sexuality, as well as how it had been normalized in social interactions. Further, in a broader context of social disempowerment, when lyricized by Afro-Jamaican males born into conditions of privation – the main purveyors of dancehall – misogynistic and anti-gay violence became a way of exercising gendered power. The projection onto others of marginal status by these already marginalized men, themselves seeking pathways to social status and economic power, illustrated what Figueroa (1998) described as the underprivileged inevitably carving out for themselves "spaces which they hegemonise" (p. 114). In other words, dancehall, as a creole phenomenon, creates its own peripheral and suppressed phenomenon – male homosexuality – which becomes a force to be resisted because it threatens the survival of an established gendered order.

Hope (2006) captures the paradoxical dynamics operating in dancehall by reference to the term "dis/place", which plays on Jamaican Creole and English usages. In its English rendition, "dis/place" ("this/place") situates dancehall in "this" place, a site where dominant values of subjugation are displaced and contested but where "dissing" also occurs and is permitted, and people fight to have their rights or sense of identity recognized.

In the dancehall dis/place, dissing is deployed primarily against persons perceived as having transgressed a set of vernacular norms. Behaviours deemed undesirable are proscribed; those who choose to act them out, typically the "bowcats", "informers" and members of the compact of "funnyman/freakyman/batiman/chichiman" – persons whose actions disrupt the political and gender hierarchies of the ghetto, where a creole subaltern state within the national state is maintained by force of arm (Carr, 2007) – are censured. It is not surprising, therefore, that from Buju Banton's 1992 "Boom Bye Bye" anthem to T.O.K.'s appeal in 2000 for the burning of those who par with "chi-chi man" or Dwayno's (Dwayne Forrester) 2013 "Mr Faggoty" denouncing fellow deejay Alkaline's (Earlan Bartley) praise of a woman performing anilingus on him, dancehall has displayed an intense preoccupation with denouncing homosexuality in general and gay men in particular. As has been established before, this preoccupation has come to define not only the music and the artists who perform it but also the culture of those who listen to and participate in it, with listeners of mostly reggae and dancehall being "more likely to hold stronger negative views about homosexuality than those who say they mostly listen to other types of music" (Boxill, Martin, Russell, Waller, Meikle and Mitchell, 2011, p. 36). In this regard, antipathy towards homosexuality can be linked through Jamaican popular culture to Jamaican popular nationalism. When twinned with the antipathy derived from forms of religious nationalism, it becomes clear that antipathy towards homosexuality is viewed as a necessary mark of Jamaicanness.

An Alienated Voice

After years of attempting without success to make a case regarding the danger anti-gay dancehall lyrics posed to members of the Jamaican LGBT community, J-FLAG's appeal to the outside world was a move designed to draw attention to what it perceived as its just cause. The aim was to bring to the fore questions relating to hate speech and freedom of expression that could not be engaged locally because members of the LGBT community were targets not only of denunciations by the dominant vernacular nationalist discourse but also of silencing. The "Stop Murder Music Campaign" became a vehicle that allowed J-FLAG as part of a global coalition to unveil and elucidate critical elements of dancehall's reputation for discursive violence against sexual minorities. As the campaign gathered momentum, the coalition was able to depict anti-gay lyrics as contributing to an atmosphere of violence that threatened the fundamental human right to life of gays and lesbians in Jamaica.

The collaboration between J-FLAG and overseas gay rights organizations was badly perceived at home and by many in the wider Caribbean and African community. The fact that the campaign had a distinctively First World – some say "white" First World – character made it difficult for many commentators to associate it with the efforts of a struggling Caribbean activist organization to contest a nationalist discourse that placed gays and lesbians at the margins of society. One example of how this erasure of J-FLAG from the campaign operated was evident in a call for papers for a November 2011 conference dubbed

"Emerging Sexualities and Race: Responses to Sexuality in Jamaica and the English-Speaking Caribbean and Caribbean Diaspora" at Warwick University. In framing the call, the organizers of the conference noted that the 2002–2004 "acrimonious international 'debate' about purported homophobia in Jamaica that initially focused on a group of reggae artists" was marked by "the relative exclusion of Jamaicans and other black people from [the] discussion, which for the most part, was carried out in the western mainstream press" (Emerging Sexualities, 2011). The drafters of this call for papers seemed unaware that the campaign had been launched as a strategy by Jamaican LGBT activists living in Jamaica.

Other commentators cared little for the "gay rights" dimension of the debate and framed the campaign as a clash on the global stage between white imperialists and struggling black entertainers, the former seen as having a vested interest in depriving the latter of opportunities to make a living. Given the nature of the alliance in the "Stop Murder Music Campaign", Cooper's (2004) reading of the GLAAD campaign against Banton in 1992 as an attempt by powerful gay groups to play "the role of imperial overlords in the cultural arena" (p. 177) still resonated with Jamaicans and other Caribbean people at home and abroad. Marshall (2008) identified the "anti-colonial, anti-establishment cultural politics" of Jamaican popular music as well as its reputation as "rebel music" as one of the factors driving local opposition to critique of the music and its primary purveyors. Noting that even if this critique was "focused on such a seemingly narrow dimension as anti-gay bias [it] more often than not resulted in redoubled public support", particularly if the critique came from outside Jamaica. This heightened support, Marshall claimed, could be viewed as part of a national discourse against the decadent and oppressive West, such that "foreign pressures to cease and desist gay bashing tend[ed] to make the issue a real rallying point on the island" (p. 137).

The struggle between Jamaican popular culture, viz. dancehall, and global LGBT organizations may be read through the lenses of critical theory and cultural theory. According to Morrell (2004), critical and cultural theory treat popular culture not as an imposed mass culture or the people's [folk] culture but rather as "a site of struggle between the forces of resistance of subordinate groups in society and the forces of incorporation of dominant groups in society". Invoking neo-Gramscians, Morrell points to popular culture as "a terrain of ideological struggle between dominant and subordinate classes, or dominant and subordinate cultures, expressed through music, film, mass media artifacts, language, customs and values" (pp. 7–8).

J-FLAG seemed to have made a deliberate decision to locate the fight against anti-gay dancehall within a context that could easily be labelled "imperialist" or "alien". This could be seen as constituting a clear strategy to force engagement from the dancehall community using the creole logic, where the forces of contestation, resistance and accommodation are usually directed at those perceived to be further up on the sociocultural hierarchy. The international LGBT community, because of its location in the Global North, was perceived as being higher up in that hierarchy. In this regard, while the debate did get the attention of the Jamaican dancehall community, the character of J-FLAG's alliance with First World LGBT groups proved especially problematic, as activists on the international scene sometimes had expectations that were divorced from the lived realities of members of the local LGBT community. A key test of the strength of the alliance came in early 2008, when "Stop Murder Music Canada" called for a tourist boycott of Jamaica. On 2 March, J-FLAG issued a press statement appealing to "Stop Murder Music Canada", then headed by St Lucian-born Akim Adé Larcher, to call off its campaign.[5] In its release, J-FLAG noted that while it shared the concern its international partners had with the "slow progress towards transforming the social climate that makes it difficult for gays and lesbians in Jamaica to lead lives free from homophobic violence", it was more concerned about the impact such a boycott could have on Jamaica and members of the LGBT community. The statement continued:

> Because of the possible repercussions of increased homophobic violence against our already besieged community, we feel that a tourist boycott is not the most appropriate response at this time. . . .
>
> In our battle to win hearts and minds, we do not wish to be perceived as taking food off the plate of those who are already impoverished. In fact, members of our own community could be disproportionately affected by a worsened economic situation brought about by a tourist ban. (Rau, 2008)

Further complicating matters for the organization was the support lent to the call by its former programmes manager, Gareth Henry, who by then had fled to Canada. Henry insisted that because of the precarious nature of its situation in Jamaica, J-FLAG could not call for a boycott but that a Canadian organization could and should.

In reflecting on his work with "Stop Murder Music Canada", Larcher remarked that he was motivated by concern about the damage that anti-gay lyrics were doing to the African and African diaspora communities in Canada. He thus "formed a coalition of supporters" – twenty-five organizations, including Egale Canada, Canada's foremost LGBT rights organization – "both to bring attention to the violent homophobic lyrics available in Canada and to bring support to queers in Jamaica" (Larcher & Robinson, 2009, p. 2).

With the establishment of "Stop Murder Music Canada", a formidable international network of partners against anti-gay music, particularly anti-gay dancehall, had been formed. More significantly, and as Larcher pointed out, this network aimed strategically to economically damage dancehall acts that sought access to Northern markets even as they continued to perform homophobic music. With their most lucrative markets – those of western Europe, the United States and Canada – locked off to them, the purveyors of anti-gay dancehall were up against a significant obstacle.

Dancehall Music and Global Cultural Imperatives

The "Stop Murder Music Campaign" initially met with significant vocal opposition from the dancehall fraternity and its supporters in the media and the academy. Soon, however, the campaign was able "to discourage promoters in London, New York, Los Angeles, and other large cities from booking reggae artists for shows", and "succeeded in getting concerts cancelled, and in some cases . . . elicited apologies from artists interested in exerting damage control over their international reputations" (Marshall, 2008, p. 136). Eventually engagements between dancehall artists and key international players in the LGBT rights movement brokered agreements that resulted in a general decline in the output of explicitly violent anti-gay lyrics. A number of critical points need to be raised regarding these engagements to illustrate the strategic and tactical failures of the local LGBT rights lobby and the dancehall community.

First, at the local level, the power differential between a small organization without a street address that lobbied for the rights of a socially outcast group and internationally known and locally revered artistes was significant. Put otherwise, the gap was between a group representing men discoursed as "feminized and powerless", and men whose "masculinized dancehall [bodies were] incarnated and elevated on the cadaver of the powerless, feminized male homosexual" bodies (Hope, 2010, pp. 87–88). Such a scenario raised the spectre of an improbable or even impossible engagement between the local LGBT rights lobby and the dancehall fraternity. Not only did this cast members of the local LGBT community as silent interlocutors in a conversation about violence against them, it also favoured local hegemonic values that insisted on depriving LGBT Jamaicans of voice. Given this understanding, gay and lesbian Jamaicans continued to be silenced, with the only fit place generally accorded them being that of social outcasts. In this way, they remained objects of discursive if not actual violence, and were doubly silenced through the lack of contestation of the cultural order that demanded their death, as well as by the rebuff they received when seeking to interrogate their culture's tolerance of the violence directed at them.

Jamaica's creole history may provide an important prism through which to analyse the response by defenders of anti-gay dancehall. As a (post)colonial society, the country's system of values is the product of oppositional tensions initiated when the first Europeans set foot on the island at the end of the fifteenth century. From the early stories of autochthonal and African marronage, and African and Afro-Creole revolt to Bedwardian messianism and the Rastafari quest for a "return" to Africa, the Jamaican national psyche has been marked by a desire and need to escape or oppose European or Western impositions – even as it accommodates and accepts, without a sense of contradiction, a sociocultural hierarchy in which the Western is valorized and privileged. The paradoxical imprint of processes of accommodation to social imposition are visible in, for instance, Jamaica's tribalized politics, which has been grafted onto the British-imposed Westminster parliamentary model (cf. Robotham, 2009); its Afro-Judaeo-Christian syncretistic religious compact of Myal-Revivalism-Rastafari-Christianity (cf. Besson, 2009); its coveting of the title "English-speaking", even if many nationals do not speak English and most refuse to (cf. Boufoy-Bastick, 2009); and its decisive rejection of socialism in favour of American-style capitalism. All these suggest that the Jamaican society, despite its antagonism to the West, derives much of its social meaning from being embedded in global/Western sociopolitical and socio-economic structures. Indeed, the attempts by dancehall purveyors to market their performances in western Europe, the United States and Canada show the depth of the symbiosis between the Jamaican socio-economic culture and the West, and at the same time its vulnerability to dominant Western discourse.

In the contest between dancehall and the global LGBT rights community, Cooper (2004) suggested a form of accommodation in which the foreign is accorded different standards and values from the local. In the question, "Should the artist do one kind of song for the local market and another for export?" (p. 170), she implied that conciliation between international LGBT rights activists and the "Jamaican community" might be achieved by appeasing foreign audiences but with no concern for how this might have an impact on the local gay and lesbian community, the group primarily affected by anti-gay lyrics. In Cooper's formulation, there was no questioning of the standards of the intimate "yaad", which were constructed as including antipathy towards homosexuals. The "yaad" accepting dancehall culture would, in some miraculous way it seemed, be devoid of the contestation of anti-gay lyrics that characterized the "foreign". On the other hand, "foreign", treated as a metaphor for the West (essentially, western Europe and anglophone North America), was constructed, inadvertently perhaps, as a monolith, a place that offered blanket acceptance to gays and lesbians. Consequently, for peace to reign in dancehall, and for the artists to continue making money, the foreign should be treated as such with the music destined for it reflecting its "foreign" values of tolerance towards gays and lesbians. By contrast, the local space should guarantee "authenticity" to the artist, whose anti-gay rhetoric was an essential mark of legitimacy, especially in the face of an aggressive form of globalization seen as displacing or weakening local culture (cf. Cooper, 2004). That this kind of erasure of an oppositional voice within the local context was the reason that J-FLAG engaged international LGBT activists in the first place was lost in the debate.

Conclusion

Popular Jamaican antipathy towards homosexuality may be explained from the viewpoint of an insecure but increasingly assertive postcolonial nationalism seeking to consolidate itself. Through vernacular language, this nationalism presents itself unvarnished as the authentic face of Jamaica, with no concern to respond to alternative subordinated discourses within the native space. Yet with its energy and vibrancy, which have taken it onto the global stage, it comes face-to-face with the oppositional discourses it refuses to contend with locally. Treachery through translation, an act that domesticates the foreign, makes this discourse accessible to others, and converts it from an exotic, romanticized narrative of the oppressed into one forced to account for the marginalization it perpetuates. Furthermore, as the formation of JAGLA has shown, alternative voices writing a nationalism that seeks to be inclusive, and that embodies the cry for liberation of all Jamaicans, continues to be deployed by multiple actors in multiple locales: from the now-out LGBT rights activists at J-FLAG and their heterosexual allies who host events at public locations, to the homeless transgender youth in Kingston, or the gay scammer from Montego Bay. This nationalist cause reflects the longings not only of a marginalized minority but of a transnational collective that is empowered through networks made possible by new communication technologies and global identity-based discourses to which they now have easy access. Notwithstanding, this face of the nationalist quest, based primarily on a reading of civil and political rights, bears its own mark of irony, as it too is largely borrowed from North America and is unable to remove itself from the culture war that is funded through aid money and the goodwill of foreigners.

For its part, dancehall is caught in a similar trap. Manuel et al. (2006) have argued that under pressure from globalization, Jamaican dancehall culture is beginning to modulate its anti-gay discourse. They claim that increasingly

deejays are being forced to make choices about what they sing based on prag-
matic market concerns but also based on demands from gays and lesbians and
"open-minded people who care about things like human rights" (p. 210). It is
not surprising that economic pressures from foreigners have forced all but the
most recalcitrant members of the dancehall fraternity to take a fresh look at
the cost of singing anti-gay lyrics. They seem to have made the calculus that
this cost, in monetary terms, is hardly worth bearing in a materialist-capitalist
economy, not when "values" and "authenticity" do not help to create the image
of prosperity and upward mobility that those in the dancehall crave. As Robotham (2009) avers, Jamaica or the entire Caribbean "is too weak to shape the
international environment – whether this environment is moving to the Right
or to the Left politically. Because of size, openness and history, [Caribbean
nations] are environment takers, not environment makers" (p. 232). In this
regard, even the values and authenticity that ostensibly accompany violently
homophobic dancehall seem constrained to be shunted aside in favour of the
almighty dollar.

Notes

1. This is usually defined as the practice of overlaying musical tracks with rhythmic
talking or chanting.

2. Jamaican slang of the 1980s for vagina.

3. The organization, which was formerly known as the Jamaica Forum for Lesbians,
All-sexuals and Gays, now simply goes by the acronym J-FLAG.

4. Nelson (2012) argues that both politicians and dancehall artists who inveigh against
homosexuality share a common purpose, that despite their "differences in class, color
and politics, they are bound by their adherence to a nationalist project that is hyper-
heteromasculine" (p. 265). This nationalist project is imbued with irony because it is
bolstered by an imported colonialist legal framework, an imported American culture
war, its alignment with anti-gay religious discourse and the funding it receives from
overseas.

5. The author of this chapter was involved with the negotiations between J-FLAG and
Egale to rescind the call for a boycott.

References

Abrahams, R.D. (2005). *Everyday life: A poetics of vernacular practices*. Philadelphia:
University of Pennsylvania Press.

Besson, J. (2009). Myal, Revival and Rastafari in the making of western Jamaica:
Dialogues with Chevannes. In H. Levy (Ed.), *The African-Caribbean worldview and
the making of Caribbean society* (pp. 26–45). Kingston, Jamaica: University of the
West Indies Press.

Boufoy-Bastick, B. (2009). Creoles as linguistic markers of national identity: Examples from Jamaica and Guyana. In H. Levy (Ed.), *The African-Caribbean worldview and the making of Caribbean society* (pp. 203–210). Kingston, Jamaica: University of the West Indies Press.

Boxill, I., Martin, J., Russell, R., Waller, L., Meikle, T., & Mitchell, R. (2011). *National survey of attitudes and perceptions of Jamaicans towards same sex relationships.* Kingston, Jamaica: Department of Sociology, Psychology and Social Work, UWI, Mona.

Carr, R. (2007). Citizenship and subalternity of the voice within globalization: Dilemmas of the public sphere, civil society and human rights in the periphery. In A. Paul (Ed.), with Y. D. Addoun. *Creole concerns: Essays in honour of Kamau Brathwaite* (pp. 403–421). Kingston, Jamaica: University of the West Indies Press.

Christie, P. (2003). *Language in Jamaica.* Kingston, Jamaica: Arawak.

Cooper, C. (2004). *Sound clash: Jamaican dancehall culture at large.* New York, NY: Palgrave Macmillan.

Cooper, C., & Devonish, H. (2004). The dancehall transnation. In C. Cooper. *Sound clash: Jamaican dancehall culture at large* (pp. 279–301). New York, NY: Palgrave Macmillan.

De Certeau, M. (1984). *The practice of everyday life*, trans. Steven Rendall. Berkeley: University of California Press.

Emerging sexualities and race: Responses to sexuality in Jamaica and the English speaking Caribbean and Caribbean diaspora conference at University of Warwick on 21–22 October 2011. Call for Papers: http://peoplewithvoices.com/2011/04/23 /conference-aims-to-facilitate-informed-opinion-on-sexuality-in-jamaica-and-the -caribbean/

Farquharson, J. (2006). Faiya-bon: The socio-pragmatics of homophobia in Jamaican (dancehall) culture. In S. Mühleisen & B. Migge (Eds.), *Politeness and face in Caribbean creoles* (pp. 101–118). Philadelphia, PA: John Benjamins.

Figueroa, M. (1998). Gender privileging and socio-economic outcomes: The case of health and education in Jamaica. In W. Bailey (Ed.), *Gender and the family in the Caribbean. Proceedings of the Workshop "Family and the Sexuality of Gender Relations", 5–6 March, 1997* (pp. 112–127). Kingston, Jamaica: Institute of Social and Economic Research.

Giovannetti, J. (2005). Jamaican reggae and the articulation of social and historical consciousness in musical discourse. In F.W. Knight & T. Martínez-Vergne (Eds.), *Contemporary Caribbean cultures and societies in a global context* (pp. 211–232). Kingston, Jamaica: University of the West Indies Press.

Houston, A. (2013, August 21). Toronto music festival to feature homophobic Jamaican headliner. *Daily Extra.* http://www.dailyxtra.com/toronto/news-and -ideas/news/toronto-music-festival-feature-homophobic-jamaican-headliner -67719?market=207

Hope, D. (2006). *Inna di dancehall: Popular culture and the politics of identity in Jamaica.* Kingston, Jamaica: University of the West Indies Press.

Hope, D. (2010). *Man vibes: Masculinities in the Jamaican dancehall.* Kingston, Jamaica, and Miami, FL: Ian Randle.

Larcher, A., & Robinson, C. (2009). Fighting "murder music": Activist reflections. *Caribbean Review of Gender Studies, 3*. http://sta.uwi.edu/crgs/november2009/journals/akimadelarcher.pdf

Lewis, R.A., & Carr, R. (2009). Gender, sexuality and exclusion: Sketching the outlines of the Jamaican popular nationalist project. *Caribbean Review of Gender Studies, 3*. http://sta.uwi.edu/crgs/november2009/journals/Lewis_Carr.pdf

Manuel, P., Bilby K., & Largey, M. (2006). *Caribbean currents: Caribbean music from rumba to reggae* (Rev. ed.). Kingston, Jamaica: Ian Randle.

Marshall, W. (2008). Dem bow, dembow, dembo: Translation and transnation in Reggaeton. *Lied und Populäre Kultur/Song and Popular Culture, 53*, 131–151. doi:10.2307/20685604.

Morrell, E. (2004). *Becoming critical researchers: Literacy and empowerment for urban youth*. New York, NY: Peter Lang.

Nelson, C. (2008). Lyrical assault: Dancehall versus the cultural imperialism of the north-west. *Southern California Interdisciplinary Law Journal, 17*, 231–278.

Nelson, C. (2012). Sexuality without borders: Exploring the paradoxical connection between dancehall and colonial law in Jamaica. In F. Cooper & A. McGinley (Eds.), *Masculinities and the law: A Multidimensional approach* (pp. 252–269). New York, NY: New York University Press.

Queen Ifrica's. (2013, August 7). Queen Ifrica's Grand Gala performance disappoints. *The Gleaner*. http://jamaica-gleaner.com/power/47022

Rau, K. (2008, May 6). Murder music and boycotts: Is attacking musicians or boycotting the country the best way to stop homophobic violence in Jamaica? *Daily Xtra*. https://www.dailyxtra.com/murder-music-and-boycotts-15891

Robotham, D. (2009). The third crisis: Jamaica in the neoliberal era. In H. Levy (Ed.), *The African-Caribbean worldview and the making of Caribbean society* (pp. 223–240). Kingston, Jamaica: University of the West Indies Press.

Stanley-Niaah, S. (2004). Kingston's dancehall. *Space & Culture 7*(1), 102–118.

Tafari-Ama, I. (2006). *Blood, bullets and bodies: Sexual politics below Jamaica's poverty line*. Kingston, Jamaica: Multi Media Communications.

Washabaugh, W., & Greenfield, S.M. (1983). The development of Atlantic Creole languages. In E. Woolford & W. Washabaugh (Eds.), *The social context of creolization* (pp. 106–119). Ann Arbor: Karoma Press.

Contributors

Marjan de Bruin is Chair of the Principal's Technical Working Group on the Equity, Diversity and Inclusion Policy, the University of the West Indies, Mona, Jamaica.

R. Anthony Lewis is Associate Professor, Language Teaching and Research Centre, the University of Technology, Jamaica.

Moji Anderson is Senior Lecturer, Department of Sociology, Psychology and Social Work, the University of the West Indies, Mona, Jamaica.

"Gemma D." is a Jamaican scholar who works on gender and sexuality and culture studies at a university in North America.

Donna P. Hope is Professor of Culture, Gender and Society, the Institute of Caribbean Studies, the University of the West Indies, Mona, Jamaica.

Anna Kasafi Perkins is Senior Programme Officer, Quality Assurance Unit, the University of the West Indies, Mona, Jamaica, and an adjunct lecturer at St Michael's Theological College and Seminary, Kingston, Jamaica.

David Plummer is Adjunct Professor of Public Health, James Cook University, Queensland, Australia. He is also an international development consultant.

Rhoda Reddock is Professor Emerita of Gender, Social Change and Development, the University of the West Indies, St Augustine, Trinidad and Tobago.

Ronald E. Young is Emeritus Professor of Human and Comparative Physiology, the University of the West Indies, Mona, Jamaica.

www.ingramcontent.com/pod-product-compliance
Lightning Source LLC
Chambersburg PA
CBHW020705270326
41928CB00005B/282